BELIEFS THAT CHANGED THE WORLD

The History and Ideas of the Great Religions

John Bowker

NEW AND UPDATED EDITION

First published in hardback 2007 by Quercus Editions Ltd

This paperback edition published in 2015 by

Quercus Publishing Ltd
Carmelite House
50 Victoria Embankment
London EC4Y 0DZ

An Hachette UK company

A CIP catalogue record for this book is available
from the British Library

PB ISBN 978 1 84866 900 0
Ebook ISBN 978 1 78429 213 3

10 9 8 7 6 5 4 3 2 1

Text designed and typeset by Hewer Text Ltd, Edinburgh

Printed and bound in Great Britain by Clays Ltd. St Ives plc

Contents

ISLAM

INDIA

BUDDHISM

CHINA

JAPAN

Introduction

Systems of belief can be extremely powerful and dangerous. Living at the beginning of the twenty-first century, with the realities of terrorism all around us, it is not difficult to see how true that is. Some of those systems are secular and are often fairly recent ideologies – like Marxism or Maoism. Others are religious and are the latest moment in what may be extremely long and ancient histories.

Religions, or perhaps more accurately religious believers, are involved in many of the fierce and seemingly insoluble conflicts in the world. Think only of the most obvious in recent years: Afghanistan, Bosnia, CAR (Central African Republic), Chechnya and Dagestan, Cyprus, Egypt, Iran, Iraq, Kashmir, Lebanon, Mali, Myanmar/Burma, Nigeria, Northern Ireland, Pakistan and India, Palestine/Israel, Punjab, Somalia and Eritrea, Sri Lanka, Sudan and Darfur, Syria, Ukraine, Xinjiang Uighur, Xizang/Tibet.

We are all affected by these conflicts in different ways. We cannot hope to bring any kind of resolution to them unless we (and politicians in particular) understand why such extreme and often violent actions are rooted in religious beliefs and histories. It is certainly not the case that religions alone are the cause of those conflicts. Each of them is different and each of them has been brought into being by many interacting causes and constraints. Nevertheless, religious beliefs are deeply involved in all of them.

The almost complete failure to take the beliefs seriously, let alone to understand them, is one reason for the writing of this book. That failure has made a mockery of diplomatic or political or military efforts to respond to the conflicts involved. It has led to shallow and naive analyses that misunderstand and therefore all too often misrepresent the beliefs and feelings of those involved. To take an obvious example, that can be seen with particular and tragic clarity in the conflict between Palestinians and Israelis, not least in the violence between Israel and Gaza.

Each side has an entirely different perspective on the conflict. On the one side, Israelis and their supporters isolate Hamas as terrorists who fire rockets indiscriminately at civilians; the Israelis insist on their right to defend a sovereign state which they declared to be independent in 1948 on the basis of 'the natural and historic right of the Jewish people and in accordance with the Resolution [181, 27 November 1947], of the United Nations General Assembly.' On the other side the Palestinians see the Israelis as invaders who have been imposed on their own land. The invaders have seized their homes and farms, and they now extend their aggression into the colonization of the West Bank: far from being 'terrorists', many Palestinians see themselves as 'resistance fighters'.

The choice of those contrasting words is a value judgement, exactly as it was in occupied France during the Second World War: the Maquisards who called themselves *la Résistance* were called by the Germans *Terroristen*. But even more critically, the choice of words is a historical judgement. The words chosen belong to very different understandings of what has happened in

the past. For the Israelis, the claim to Israel as their own home-
land goes back 3,000 years to God's command to Abram, לֶךְ לְךָ,
'Take yourself to the land which I will show you' (*Genesis* 12:1).
The descendants of Abraham then obeyed the further command
of God to drive out and destroy the existing inhabitants of the
Promised Land (see, for example, *Deuteronomy* ch.7).

The Palestinians, however, regard themselves as descendants
of the original inhabitants of that land which was thus being
seized from them by force all those years ago. The intervening
millennia are filled with events and memories (sometimes of
savage conflict but sometimes also of peaceful coexistence)
which the two sides bring to present-day issues. For them, history does not begin in 1948.

Religious beliefs of this kind are extremely deep-rooted, going
back not just for centuries, but for thousands of years. They give
an entirely different and distinctive character to the lives, families and societies of the people who treasure them and hold
them dear. They lie embedded in memories that have been
passed on from one generation to another, and they have pene-
trated every aspect of life from birth to death – and even beyond
that, from *before* birth to *after* death.

It is emphatically not the case that all Jews share identical beliefs
and practices, nor do all Muslims. Far from it. It is true that in the
case of each religion the basic and fundamental beliefs have great
authority because they are believed ultimately to come from
God. They confer identity and they may well be regarded as non-
negotiable not least because they have been tested through time.

But what do those beliefs mean and how are they to be understood and applied? It has never been the case, either among Jews
or among Muslims, that there is complete and universal agreement about the nature and application of their beliefs, or about

what they should mean in practice. In fact exactly the opposite is the case. There have been many different ways of being Jewish and many different ways of being Muslim. That can be seen, in each case, in the separate movements and sects which are independently organized and often polemically, sometimes violently, opposed to each other. That is why it is usually misleading to talk in a generalized way about conflicts between 'Jews' and 'Muslims'.

It is not the case, for example, that all Jews believe that it was right to establish a Jewish state in Palestine in 1948: some Jews believe that God alone can re-establish Zion as the Holy City when the time has come to send the Messiah, and many believe that that cannot happen until all Jews follow the commands of the Torah entrusted by God to Moses. What is now known as Zionism is actually a complicated and contested belief. The modern search by Jews for a homeland began in the fierce and brutal persecution of Jews at the end of the nineteenth century, particularly in the pogroms (persecutions directed against a particular group) in Russia and Poland. The first suggestions were that Jews should find a safe homeland in Uganda (in what is now Kenya), or in Arish in Egypt, or in Argentina (where a settlement was indeed established). Theodor Herzl, one of the important founders of modern Zionism, published in 1896 a brief essay, *Der Judenstaat*, which has been regarded as the beginning of modern political Zionism. In that essay he left it open whether that Jewish settlement should be in Palestine or Argentina, writing, 'Shall we choose Palestine or Argentina? We shall take what is given us, and what is selected by Jewish public opinion.'

In the interwar years (1918–39) there were successive attempts to persuade Jewish opinion at large that there should be a return to Jerusalem and the surrounding territory, but it was only after the Holocaust that international opinion, and not just *Jewish* public opinion, felt that Jews must be given their homeland in the area of the biblical promise to Abraham. Even then, an attempt was made in the United Nations to create an independent Arab state based on enclaves within the scattered territories of the newly formed Israel.

That, however, was profoundly unsatisfactory for many Arabs because it gave away their homeland and rode roughshod over their own memories and beliefs. Even so, there were Arabs who believed that there could be coexistence. After the Oslo Accords in 1993, the Palestinian Authority was set up to take over gradually the administration and security of the Occupied Territories (divided initially into two different areas). That was immediately denounced by Hamas and other like-minded groups who rejected any cooperation with Israel. Hamas opposed the Fatah party of Yasser Arafat and eventually (after an election) took control of Gaza and conducted hostilities against both Israelis and other Palestinians. When Palestine decided to join the International Criminal Court and was admitted in 2015 (allowing the possibility of war crime accusations against Israel), Israel withheld the £83 million in tax revenues collected on behalf of the Palestinian Authority. That and the continuing Israeli settlement in the West Bank led the Palestine Liberation Organization to recommend that the Palestinian Authority should stop all forms of security cooperation with Israel.

The point of that brief summary is to illustrate the fact that the conflicts *between* different religions cannot possibly be understood unless one realizes that there are also profound conflicts *within* each religion. There are contrasting interpretations of beliefs (often going back to distant centuries in the past), and these have produced within each religion tense and sometimes violent disagreements about how to act and what to do in the changing circumstances of the world. It is simply not possible for diplomats and politicians (or for that matter anybody else) to unravel the complexities of the conflicts listed at the beginning of this Introduction unless they understand the ways in which those conflicts are rooted, not only in religious beliefs, but also in different interpretations and applications of those beliefs.

Take as an obvious example the self-proclaimed 'Islamic State'. Some of the actions of Islamic State (the sadistic assassination of hostages, the massacre of women and children, the option offered of conversion or execution) are utterly repulsive and horrific, not just to outside observers, but to many Muslims as well who unequivocally reject Islamic State and disassociate themselves from it – 'not in my name'. Not surprisingly, therefore, we repeatedly hear distinctions being drawn by outsiders between those Muslims who are moderate and who represent 'the true face of Islam', and those Muslims who use violence and who are called 'extremists' or (bizarrely) 'Islamists'. On that basis the claim is often then made that those young Westerners who join Islamic State would never have done so if they had not been 'radicalized' and 'brainwashed'.

That division of Muslims into those on the one hand who are moderate and who are the truly faithful, and those on the other hand who are radicalized and extreme is now commonly made. But it is extremely misleading (and it has certainly misled many Western politicians) because it completely ignores the fact that Islamic State believes itself to be the true expression of the Islam that God intended and desires. It does so by drawing on arguments and interpretations of the Quran that go back to the earliest days of Islam and were already even then creating conflicts and divisions among Muslims. In other words, Islamic State arises from arguments *among Muslims themselves* about specific beliefs, deeply rooted in history, which create the immense complexity of the modern world.

Those contested beliefs arose in the first forty years after the death of Muhammad. They produced fundamental and divisive questions that continue to the present day (the details summarized here are discussed in more detail later on):

- Who has the right to succeed Muhammad as the leader or caliph of the Muslim community (the issue when Muhammad died between the followers of Abu Bakr and of Ali leading to the continuing division between Sunni and Shia Muslims)?
- If a leader seems to be acting in a non-Muslim way, is it a legitimate obligation to assassinate him or should the final judgement be left to God (the issue raised by the assassination of Uthman, the third Caliph, by other Muslims)?
- If a leader negotiates a settlement with an opponent, does that compromise the God-entrusted integrity of Islam and must it then be an obligation to secede from the existing community in order to follow 'the true Islam' (the issue raised when the Kharijites seceded after Ali negotiated a settlement with Muawiyya)?
- How should those who secede from Islam be treated given that a penalty for apostasy is execution?
- Since the Quran commands Muslims to create a single Umma or People throughout the world, preferably by conversion, how far and in what ways must those who refuse to convert to Islam be compelled to do so?
- Adult male Muslims are required to defend any other Muslims who are under attack from Kafirs (non-believers) in what is known as Jihad (the different meanings of Jihad are discussed later), but what actions belong legitimately to Jihad and are there any limits or restrictions on what may be done and who may be attacked?

Muslims through the centuries have been divided on those fundamental questions (as they still are), and those divisions run into many of the conflicts listed earlier, particularly and unmistakeably in Lebanon, Syria and Iraq. Where Islamic State is concerned, they are, in their own view, going back to particular answers derived from those early disputes: they are, in their view, the only truly faithful expression of Islam. They see themselves as implementing the command of God in the Quran to create a single worldwide community (Umma) under a caliph (the successor of Muhammad) whose responsibility it is to establish the Dīn, or life-way, that God desires. The Umma therefore transcends nation-state borders, many of which were imposed by colonial powers as recently as the twentieth century. Bringing the Umma into being clearly requires, in their view, the imposition of the Quranic death penalties on unbelievers, on apostates and on other 'Muslims' who do not agree with them and who have in effect seceded. It also requires the creation of Muslim families and communities exemplifying the fundamentals of Islam.

Those Muslims who oppose Islamic State reject emphatically what they consider to be the illegitimate ways in which Quran and history have been interpreted and applied. In their view the actions of Islamic State are in any case abhorrent, but they are also far outside the limits (*hudud*, a word to which we will return) of Islam.

But there are others who are attracted to that programme. The reasons and motives for joining Islamic State are extremely varied and may have little to do with Islam. On the other hand, the possibility of creating a worldwide Umma under a single Caliph is a dream that many Muslims articulated when I interviewed them for the BBC series *Voices of Islam*. As one Muslim put it: 'Muslims are feeling both spiritually and psychologically that they have to realize this Caliphate again, if they are to tackle the manifest problems which they and humanity face' (*What Muslims Believe*, 2004, p. 68).

Many Muslims share that dream, and it is unwise to neglect it when trying to understand why young people from many parts of the world join movements like Islamic State. It is a reminder, incidentally, of how extremely foolish it is to use the word 'brainwashing' as though it is a non-controversial way of referring to the coercion of young people into irrational commitment. The word was used in a similarly loose way of young people joining religious cults in the mid-twentieth century when what persuaded many turned out more accurately to be 'love bombing'. If anything like that is the case here, it is as much a comment on the families and societies in which the young people have grown up as it is on Islamic State.

The point of those controversial and oversimplified examples is not to take sides, still less to claim that religions are the sole cause of each conflict, but, rather, to show why contemporary conflicts cannot be understood, let alone resolved, without appreciating how deeply they are rooted in religious beliefs and history. Without that understanding, the recent failings of policy are inevitable, from the catastrophe of the Bush–Blair invasion of Iraq to the particular way in which the US followed by the UK are trying to implement a two-state solution to the Israel–Palestine conflict; even if that were the only possible solution, the way in which it is being pursued could only be imposed on, never agreed by, those concerned.

Not surprisingly Islamic State and the many other like-minded groups springing up around the world, both Sunni and Shia, have in effect declared war on the world since they follow a traditional division of the world into two domains, Dar al-Islam and Dar al-Harb, the domain of Islam and the domain of War. In that case it would seem to make sense to fight back, but it is a war that cannot be won in conventional ways: you can bomb bodies but beliefs survive. There are, however, other and entirely different ways to respond, as we will see later in this book. They are responses that arise from a better understanding of beliefs and of the histories in which they are embedded.

So far it must seem that religions are extremely bad news, and that we should all unite in a campaign (or should we call it a crusade?) to abolish religion. But that is to ignore the fact that religions are also extremely good news, and have been for several thousand years. Religions created such sufficiently secure and continuing contexts of family and society that at least some people were set free to explore what their own human nature is capable of being and of becoming, and also to explore the nature of the world around them.

Religions are thus the context in which people, through imagination and technique, have brought into being superb consequences of enduring worth in art, architecture, drama, poetry, music, dance, literature, education, agriculture – and even in the natural sciences in general which began as part of the religious exploration of the world and of human nature within it. The separate word 'scientist' was not even invented until 1834. The religious exploration of human nature led to even more stunning discoveries as our ancestors realized what we can become in our care for each other, in enlightenment, in our relatedness to God. Those are discoveries at least as exciting as those of science and technology, some would say even more so.

Equally important for human history and survival has been the part that religions have played in the creation of families and societies. Religions are the earliest social organizations of which we have surviving evidence that provided security for the birth and upbringing of children – in other words, for the next generation. In terms of evolution and natural selection, religions were brilliantly successful in securing gene replication and the nurture of children. Of course those distant ancestors of ours knew nothing about genes and natural selection, but that is beside the point: they were simply successful in securing and protecting the birth of children and their upbringing in worlds of such danger and threat that all too often they failed. But where they did succeed, they could only do so with the creation and testing of shared beliefs and practices, many of which survive and continue to the present day.

The survival of successful beliefs and practices is not accidental. They too need protection. They had to be transmitted from one life and from one generation to another. They therefore had to be coded as information, and that was achieved in many different ways – as sound, for example, as music, words, symbols, diagrams, gestures, stories, rituals and so on. All this in summary is communal information which, when it is internalized by individuals who belong to a particular group, helps to create coherent and successful communities.

In that sense, religions can be regarded as systems in which information is coded, protected, stored and transmitted. Information does not drift around the universe at random. It has to be channelled and protected in order to inform (form within) human lives: in that way beliefs change people who change the world.

So whatever else religions are (and they are much else), they are highly organized systems to protect the information that has been identified within the system as essential for successful outcomes in life – with success ranging from the care of an infant to the attainment of enlightenment or of God.

Protective systems require boundaries, and boundaries require maintenance. The boundaries may be metaphorical: they may, for example, be described as the Umma in Islam (as we have just seen) or the Body of Christ in Christianity. But they may also be literal, a Holy Land, for example, or a sacred space like a sanctuary or a temple; it is a critical reason why geography is so important in religious history. But whether literal or metaphorical, boundaries need protecting when they come under threat. Threats too may be literal or metaphorical: an army may attack and bombs may be dropped, but equally beliefs may be threatened by challenge, contradiction or even mockery. In either case, boundaries need protecting.

Here is a fundamental reason why religions are involved in so many seemingly intransigent conflicts. Beliefs matter. For many people their beliefs are so vital and life-giving that they will always be prepared to die and if necessary to kill in order to defend them and sometimes impose them on others. Religious beliefs are not here today and gone tomorrow, even though many of them have changed greatly through the course of time and have even disappeared. Far more seriously, religious beliefs have been tested and winnowed through time and have been found by countless people to be trustworthy and true. Of course there are others who believe them to be untrustworthy and false. But that too is a belief.

This book began life as part of a series on things or people that have changed the world – Speeches, for example, or Books, or Women 'that have changed the world'. Religious beliefs have certainly done that. But it needs to be remembered that 'the world' in religious belief is not a fixed item. It is not a planet, as we might say now, orbiting the sun. 'The world' in the perspective of belief systems is constantly changing. A look at any of the early maps of 'the world' will show how differently it has been imagined and understood at different times and in different civilizations. Sometimes it has been confined to a particular geographical area, as, for many centuries, in India or in China. At the opposite extreme it may be vastly greater than the earth, as in the cosmos of the Jains. I have simply taken the beliefs that made a difference in the immediate context ('world') in which they came into being. Often, of course, they have continued to make a difference long after they appeared, and still change the world as we now inhabit and understand it.

It needs also to be remembered that some particular beliefs have 'changed the world' in more religions than one. For example, few religions had in origin any belief that there will be a serious or worthwhile life after death. There is a widespread popular assumption that religions came into being in order to reassure people that death is not the end. That is historically wrong: when the major and continuing religions came into being there was no belief that there will be a worthwhile life after death. Nevertheless, a belief that there is, or is likely to be, a life after death did come into being in all religions, but it appeared for different reasons and in different forms. In a general way, a belief in life after death appears in more than one religion, and it is certainly a belief that has changed the world dramatically, but it is not the same in each religion.

Since that is true in general of most world-changing beliefs, it may be helpful to know that *The Oxford Dictionary of World Religions* includes entries on many beliefs which summarize the different ways in which they are understood in different religions. It also includes a Topic Index drawing together relevant entries.

That in itself is a reminder that some beliefs are so old and universal that they have many different meanings which are sometimes combined, sometimes held in isolation. Take, as an example, the beliefs and practices associated with sacrifice. The word 'sacrifice' comes from two Latin words meaning 'that which is made sacred' – 'sacred' being something set apart and offered to the gods. In a general way we might be able to define the word 'sacrifice' as 'the offering of something, animate or inanimate, in a ritual procedure which establishes, or mobilizes, a relationship of mutuality between the one who sacrifices (whether individual or group) and the recipient – who may be human but more often is of another order, e.g., God or spirit.'

But a brief definition of that kind is pointing to an immense variety of beliefs and practices entered into for many different reasons and purposes. When the sign in a shop window advertising a sale proclaimed, 'These trousers are being offered at a great sacrifice"', it clearly was not offering them to the local deities. 'Sacrifice' is found in virtually all religions and extensively outside them, but its meanings are extremely varied. It has been understood as a way

- of cleansing fault or sin;
- of dealing with misfortunes such as the illness of oneself or of another;
- of turning away the anger of a deity or of an enemy;
- of saying thank you;
- of offering to a deity or to another person a substitute for something that you owe them and is rightly theirs (for example, the life of an animal instead of the life of the first-born child);
- of establishing through a meal with recognized rituals a union with God or with others in a community;

- of giving something in order to receive something in return, often summarized as *do ut des*, 'I give in order that you may give';
- of maintaining and participating in the whole cosmic order;
- of celebration;
- of dealing with violence and anger through catharsis (defined, in part, by Aristotle in *Poetics* as leading through religious frenzy to healing and purgation);
- of accepting death in order to give life to others ('for your tomorrow we gave our today').

The beliefs and practices involved in sacrifice have completely changed the world by giving dramatic expression to the ways in which we have to interact with others and with the world around us. In other words, we have to live constantly in the way of exchange that lies at the heart of sacrifice. Of equal importance is the way in which sacrifice helps us to recognize and affirm that death is the necessary condition of life. That perception lies at the heart of the scientific understanding of the universe: from the death of stars to the succession of generations, death is not simply 'end' but also opportunity. As I put it in *The Meanings of Death*, 'It is not possible to have life on any other terms than those of death; but where you *do* have death, there immediately you have the possibility of life.'

Even in that one example alone, it can be seen that the understanding of beliefs, whether religious or scientific, is not simple. The philologist Max Müller famously said that those who understand one religion understand none. I would simply add that those who try to understand the world without understanding any religions understand nothing. That is extremely obvious among so many politicians. The purpose of this book, therefore, is to look at some particular beliefs that have changed the world, and at why they matter to those who believe them; I have also tried to give a glimpse at how they came into being historically. For that reason, the book is also a brief introduction to the history of religions.

Even then, it has not been possible to include all religions. Beliefs that changed the world (and continue to do so) are not confined to the religions whose histories we can trace. They belong also to religions which have not left the kind of records that enable history to be written. The religions of the Pacific Islands, of the Australian aborigines, of Africa, or of the First Nation Americans (to give only obvious examples) have accounts of their own past, but not of a kind that are extensively accessible to the historian.

Nevertheless, many of their beliefs have become so well known that they have changed our understanding of ourselves and of our world, so much so that some of the words describing them have passed into everyday language – as, for example:

Totem. In popular understanding, the totem has become something of singular importance especially to a group of people with a common interest, or for individuals almost a charm. In fact, a totem is something that helps people to organize themselves and to live with each other. The belief in totems is found all around the world, although the word itself comes from the Ojibwa, a tribe of the Algonquin. Their word *ototeman* means 'a close blood relative' (forbidden therefore in marriage), and thus a totem came to be regarded as the mark of the family to which a person belongs. In that way, the totem functions like the badge or favour of a football supporter: it indicates which team a person supports, or, in the case of a totem, to which family group or clan a person belongs. Often the clan will take the totem animal's name and will regard the totem animal as its ancestor. Usually, they will not eat or kill the animal. The words 'usually' or 'often' are necessary because the beliefs associated with totemism vary hugely around the world. But what is common to most of them is that the totem marks the boundaries of the group and shows what behaviour is allowed or forbidden. Totem came therefore to be closely linked with

Taboo (also spelled *tabu*, or *tapu*). Popularly, a taboo is something absolutely forbidden, a definite 'no-no'. The word itself is Polynesian, and it refers to a power in relation to particular people, places or objects. It may be positive, but if it is negative it marks them off as dangerous, so that the crossing of the boundary surrounding them will lead to a bad or even disastrous outcome. Sigmund Freud, whose views on religion have turned out to be almost entirely false, linked totem and taboo together in his book of that name (1913) by suggesting that they represent that which is much desired but totally forbidden – as, for example, incest.

Voodoo (also *vodou, voudou*) has come to mean any kind of dangerous black magic. It comes from the Fon language of Benin in Africa, *vodu*, 'deity', and is the name given to the folk religion of Haiti. Although it was suppressed when it was taken to the Caribbean and America by African slaves, it has become an indigenous religion in which elements of African religion and Roman Catholic Christianity have been merged. It includes beliefs in

Zombies. The word is now used of people half asleep when they ought to be alert and active, but a *zombi* is either a disembodied soul used in magic, or a corpse that has been raised from the grave in order to work as a labourer.

Those and other beliefs may appear in the religions dealt with in this book. Some, like belief in shamans and witches, are so extensive that they are in effect world religions. Space alone, quite apart from the relative absence of historical sources, means that their own histories cannot be included here.

For the same reasons of length, this book has not been able to look at all the many different ways in which religious beliefs have been expressed, as, for example, in art, architecture and systems of government – not because these things are unimportant, but because it is not possible to fit an ocean into a thimble!

The purpose of this book is not to make judgements about the truth or value of particular beliefs: there is an account of what those judgements are and of how they might be made in my recent book, *Why Religions Matter*. The purpose is to offer, much more simply, a first step towards understanding some of the most important of those beliefs and to indicate how they came into being and what changes they have made in their long histories.

This book was first suggested by Felicity Bryan and Wayne Davies, and I am grateful to them both – and to Richard Bauckham, David Bowker and Yao Xinzhong for their encouragement and suggestions. My thanks go to all those at Quercus and at Specialist Publishing Services (especially Nick Hutchins) who helped to bring it into being, and to Charlotte Fry for her meticulous and generously efficient work in producing this revised and updated edition. I am also grateful to John English, who copy-edited the revised text, to Kate Inskip, who did sterling work on the index, and to Mike Luxford, who helped me with IT issues. A special 'thank you' goes to Sarah Brunning for her unfailing support in so many ways. But above all, my thanks go to Margaret, my wife, who corrected (dates are not exactly my strongest suit) and wrote so much that she is in a real sense the co-author of the book. In the words of a Chinese proverb, 'When you drink from the stream, always remember the spring.' I do, with thanks and love.

Judaism

Overview

Jewish history begins in the Biblical period which lasted roughly from 2000 to 250 BCE. The Jews began as nomadic tribes, related to each other and therefore known technically as a kinship group. They were called originally, not Jews, but bene Israel (or bene Jacob): *bene* means 'sons', i.e., descendants of the ancestor Israel (also known as Jacob), hence Israelites.

The Bible is an anthology of very diverse writings from more than a thousand years. It is known by Jews by such names as Miqra ('reading' or 'recital'), ha-Sefarim ('the Books', or the Holy Books), or more often as Tanach, from the initial letters in Hebrew of its three component parts: **T**orah (the first five books of Moses, known in English as *Genesis*, *Exodus*, *Leviticus*, *Numbers* and *Deuteronomy*), **N**ebiim (the Prophets including the historical books), and **K**etubim (the Writings including such books as the *Psalms* and *Job*). The final agreement about which books should be included in Tanach was not made until about the middle of the second century CE, although most of the books were recognized much earlier as having authority because it was believed that they came, either directly or indirectly, from God.

The Bible tells the story of how the members of this kinship

group, under the guidance and direction of God, settled in territory on the eastern Mediterranean coast (known eventually as
Judaea, hence Judaeans and thus Jews). It tells also how they
came to believe that God is the Creator of all that is, in earth and
heaven, and that God alone is God. This extremely strong monotheism meant that all the many claimed deities in the ancient
world were false. God makes the unique and particular name of
God known only to this people as YHWH – it is too holy even to
be pronounced – and God calls them to specific work and
responsibilities in the world.

The Bible begins with a visionary account of the first humans,
Adam and Eve, who at the prompting of the serpent chose
knowledge rather than obedience. Further disobedience followed until Abraham obeyed the command of God to leave his
home in Ur (in Mesopotamia) and go to a new and promised
land in which he and his descendants first began to settle. It tells
how God rescued some of them from slavery in Egypt and led
them in a great rescue, or Exodus, through the wilderness where
Moses received the Law or Torah from God. After a time of loose
coalitions among themselves (known as the period of the Judges),
David introduced kingship in Jerusalem as a new way of uniting
the kinship group.

The following period under kings was ended by the capture of
Jerusalem by the Babylonians and the captivity or Exile in a foreign land. The Persian ruler Cyrus restored the Jews to Jerusalem,
and there then followed 400 years of reconstruction, leading to an
independent kingdom once more, under a family known as
Hasmoneans. Meanwhile, the Romans were beginning to build
their Empire, and they used Herod and his family as puppet rulers
in Judaea. A rebellion of the Jews against Rome resulted in defeat
and the destruction of the Temple in Jerusalem in the year 70 CE.

Such a massive defeat did not destroy Judaism. Under leaders and teachers known as Rabbis, the reconstruction of Judaism without the Temple in Jerusalem began. The Rabbis had long been teaching how Torah should be applied to new and changing circumstances of life, and the process now began of gathering these orally transmitted interpretations (known as 'oral Torah', *Torah shebe 'al peh*) into written collections. One such called the Mishnah became the basis for much larger collections known as Talmuds, of which one was made in Palestine and the other in Babylon: the Babylonian Talmud became the authoritative foundation of subsequent Judaism.

After the defeat in 70 and a second defeat after a further rebellion in 135, some Jews remained in Judaea, but the majority was scattered throughout the empire and beyond. This scattering of the Jews is known as the Diaspora (from the Greek meaning 'dispersion'). For the next nearly 2,000 years the history of the Jews is in the Diaspora – in Mediterranean lands, in Europe, especially in Eastern Europe and Russia (where Jews were frequently persecuted) and eventually in the United States. In the different places of Diaspora Jewish faith, worship and practice were developed in many different ways, as, for example, in Qabbalah and Hasidism.

Hostility and persecution continued wherever the Jews went, but gradually they came to be accepted in various places, and increasingly many were assimilated into European societies. That was divisive among Jews: some thought that the laws in Torah should be interpreted and applied to changing circumstances; others believed that written Torah is immutable, and that the laws should not be altered, still less ignored, beyond the obvious fact that the Temple no longer stands. The divisions led to the formation of different and organized movements. Prominent among them are those movements known as Orthodox, Reform (also Liberal and Progressive) and Conservative Judaism.

The Jews still remained vulnerable and were often the victims of persecution, especially in Russia and Eastern Europe. At the end of the nineteenth century, therefore, the first moves were made to find a safe homeland for the Jews. Eventually pressure developed to restore the Jews to the Promised Land and to Jerusalem, or to Zion, as Jerusalem is also known – hence the name Zionism. The destruction of European Judaism under Nazi policy in the Holocaust accelerated Zionism, and the State of Israel was established in 1948.

Foundations

Many Jewish beliefs were formed during the Biblical period. Far-reaching were two beliefs, that God alone is *God*, and that some writings have come from God as revelation.

These are the writings that eventually became the Jewish Bible (Tanach). It was believed that Torah came directly from God, that the Prophets (Nebiim) are the word of God mediated through inspired humans, and that the Writings (Ketubim) come from the less direct inspiration of the Holy Spirit.

So this belief in inspiration and revelation does not mean that God took over the hand of the writers and wrote the books of the Bible without their help, but rather that God brought them into being with the assistance of particular people, accepting the limitations in their knowledge of the world. God therefore wrote *with* the human author, an understanding of revelation and inspiration known technically as 'concursive' (Latin, 'writing with').

In some religions there may be stronger understandings of revelation, but in general the belief that God inspires some people to produce a revealed word has profoundly changed the world: at its most extreme, it allows the claim to be made that there are words which have absolute authority over human life.

Such people are fundamentalists because they insist on the fundamental and incontrovertible truth of what they believe to be revelation. Some, but not all, Jews regard Torah in that way. The consequence of this belief for world history is obvious in the conflicts which arise when two non-negotiable revelations, Tanach and the Quran, come into dispute, as in the conflict over Israel/Palestine.

Jewish history and its Bible begin with the words, 'In the beginning God created': only three words in Hebrew (*bereshith bara Elohim*), yet they contain a belief that completely changed the world. The words state that all creation comes from God: God is not contained within creation but remains apart from it, so that if this universe comes to an end, God does not.

That is very different from other creation stories in the ancient world in which gods and goddesses appear within the *process* of creation. They may direct the process by, for example, overcoming the forces of chaos, but they are contained within it.

The Jews of old used some of those stories in the five different accounts of creation in the Bible. But they changed them to make it clear that God is the one who initiates creation and who remains independent of it even when overcoming chaos and disorder. Moreover, God makes humans 'only a little lower than the angels' in the wisdom and skills that they possess.

The power of human wisdom led to a belief, in later parts of the Bible, that Wisdom works as the agent of God in creation as 'a skilled worker ... rejoicing in God's inhabited world and delighting in the human race'.

The belief that God creates all things with Wisdom is one of the two foundations of Western science, along with Greek rationality and science. From both together came the belief that the universe is consistent and reliable, open to investigation: apples do not fall off trees one day and fly to the moon the next; if not why not?

The reliability of God is seen in creation, but the opening chapters of the Jewish Bible show how the original goodness of all creation is disturbed by humans when they decide to pursue knowledge come what may, making decisions without much reference to God. As a result, fundamental relationships break down, between humans and God, husbands and wives, town and country, the God-fearing and those who are not, all culminating in the conflict of divided languages and nations after the building of the Tower of Babel (for this story explaining the origin of different languages, see *Genesis* 11:1–9).

The question then facing God is how to put this right – if at all. God almost decides to erase the entire document of creation, in the Great Flood: 'The Lord was sorry that he had made humankind on the earth . . . and he said, "I will blot out from the earth the human beings I have created"' (*Genesis* 6:6).

But the story of Noah tells how God nevertheless decided to make a new start with the one righteous man who was left, and it was with Noah and his descendants that God made a covenant, or agreement, of which the rainbow is to be a constant reminder.

In Jewish belief, this Covenant began the process of God's work of repair, showing how life ought to be lived and put right when things have gone wrong. The history of the Jews in the Bible becomes the history of successive covenants with key people, beginning with Noah and with the famous Ancestors, Abraham, Isaac and Jacob, continuing with Moses and the whole people, leading to the covenant with David and his successors. In this belief, the people are chosen by God to live in obedience to God's word and to show what it means to live in holiness set apart in order to be close to God (an underlying meaning of holiness): 'You shall be holy, for I The Lord your God am holy' (*Leviticus* 19:2).

The Covenant is not only the key to understanding the history of the Jews, it is also a belief that has changed the world. The basic idea of the Covenant is that God offers peace and prosperity on condition that people keep the terms laid down. Both social life and individual life depend for their success on living in ways that express justice and mercy. If God is to keep the Covenant promises that God has made, life on the human side cannot be turned into tyranny and oppression. Yes, sometimes it is, and the Biblical history of the Jews shows how God reacts in anger. But in general, people know how they should behave: they know what is required of them: 'to do justice, and to love kindness, and to walk humbly with their God' (*Micah* 6:8). The belief that covenants are the foundation of people living together in society condemns, as utterly destructive, sleaze and corruption in public life.

After the Covenant with Noah, God's Covenant with Abram and his descendants (his name was later lengthened to Abraham) established a particular and special relationship between them. It began with God's command to Abram to arise and go to a new land:

Now the Lord said to Abram, 'Go from your country and your kindred and your father's house to the land that I will show you. I will make of you a great nation, and I will bless you, and make your name great, so that you will be a blessing. I will bless those

who bless you, and the one who curses you I will curse; and by
you all the families of the earth shall be blessed. (*Genesis* 12:1–3)

The end of the book of *Genesis* and the beginning of the book of
Exodus tell how part of the kinship group descended from
Abraham (the *bene* Jacob/Israel) became economic migrants and
worked in Egypt, eventually as slaves. Jews believe that God rescued them from slavery and led them out (hence 'Exodus', Greek
for 'the road out') to freedom. The Exodus and the beliefs associated with it continue to change the world because they often
inspire those who rise against oppression. The cry of Moses, 'Let
my people go!' is still heard. In Christianity, for example, it
fuelled the long struggles against slavery, then against apartheid
in South Africa, and it was the foundation of Liberation Theology,
mainly in South America, but in parts of Asia as well. Liberation
Theology asked, in the words of one of its founders, Gustavo
Gutiérrez, 'how to tell the non-person, the nonhuman, that God
is love, and that this love makes us all brothers and sisters'.

After a period of testing in the wilderness, the people are
brought to the land that God had promised to give them. The
belief that God will rescue the chosen people has given hope to
Jews even in the worst persecutions. It was during the wilderness
period that God established through Moses the Covenant with
the Jewish people. Torah contains narratives, but it also contains
law codes and individual laws. In Jewish belief, it was through
Moses that God entrusted Torah to the people: its 613 commands
and prohibitions are the conditions of the Covenant.

Many Jews believe that all those laws were revealed through
Moses, but others believe that, while they are all associated with
Moses, some were added and organized later. What is therefore
at issue among Jews is the extent to which every law must be

obeyed as literally as possible (some are impossible because they refer to the now destroyed temple in Jerusalem), or the extent to which they can be adapted and applied to changing circumstances. The question is clear: while some laws are universal and must be obeyed, others apply to particular circumstances and must be interpreted and applied differently when circumstances change. But how is that to be done?

This issue is as urgent today as it has ever been, and it is urgent far beyond the boundaries of Israel. The issue is the status in ethics of the authority of the Bible or of any other Scripture (particularly when understood as the Word of God) in decision-making. In authoritative sources of that kind, some commands apply always and everywhere, and such commands are known technically as 'context-independent commands'. They are commands like, 'Be holy as the Lord your God is holy.' No matter what the context, that command has to be obeyed. The Ten Commandments were originally addressed to adult male Israelites only, but they came to be understood as moral law of that universal kind, even beyond Judaism, and that is why they were placed prominently in non-Jewish court-houses and churches.

Other commands, however, are very specific, and are really applications of those 'context-independent commands' to particular circumstances, and they are therefore known as 'context-dependent applications'. Thus the command to a woman to bring two turtle-doves or two pigeons to the priest to make atonement after her menstruation is context-specific, and might be interpreted and applied differently now.

This is a fundamental issue for all religions whose foundation documents – Scripture or any other claimed Revelation – include commands: it is to recognize how great the difference is between *independent commands* and *dependent applications*. If that difference is ignored, then many of the specific commands in revelation can only be obeyed by reproducing in the present day the circumstances in which the original commands were given. In that case, what happens is that the distinction in the original text is forgotten, and *dependent* applications are turned into *independent* commands.

An example of this at the present time is a tense issue in several religions. It is the prohibition against homosexual acts. Where the Bible is concerned, that was originally a context-dependent application, and for many believers it must be reassessed when the context changes, as now in terms of our better understanding of homosexuality. Others, however, have converted it into a context-independent command, so that homosexuality must always be condemned – hence the angry protest by Orthodox Jews against Gay Pride marches in Jerusalem.

Beliefs that change the world may therefore themselves change, at least in application, when it is remembered that not all the commands in the Bible or other revealed texts are context-independent commands: many are context-dependent applications which do not have to be repeated in the same way for ever. That is the contested issue, and the different answers given change very greatly the worlds in which people live.

From the Promised Land to the Exile

In the Exodus and the Wilderness the foundations were laid of the most fundamental Jewish belief, that there is only one God whose name and nature have been revealed to a people chosen out of all the nations:

When the Most High apportioned the nations,
when he divided humankind,
he fixed the boundaries of the peoples according to the number
   of the gods;
the Lord's own portion was his people,
Jacob his allotted share. (*Deuteronomy* 32:8f.)

The belief that there is 'only one God' does not sound startling now, but it certainly was in the ancient world, where there were many gods and goddesses who pursued their own lives and interests. In Jewish belief, God is the One from whom all creation comes, the unproduced Producer of all that is. There can only be *God*, not competing gods. This so-called *monotheism* (in Hebrew *yihud haShem*) is the foundation, not just of Judaism, but of Christianity and Islam as well, both of which acknowledge what they owe to this radical Jewish belief by understanding Abraham to be the father of all the faithful.

This basic statement of Jewish belief is summed up in a single verse in *Deuteronomy* 6:4: 'Hear O Israel, the Lord [YHWH] is our God, the Lord is one.' With other verses, this belief is recited twice daily in prayer, and from its opening word in Hebrew, *shema* ('hear'), it is known as the Shema. Jewish history in the Biblical period shows how this total allegiance to the One, and only one, who is God overcame all temptation to follow other – and false – gods.

The four letters YHWH are the name of God. That name became so holy that it cannot be spoken, so it is not known how the name (in Hebrew, *ha-Shem*) was pronounced. Because it consists of four letters, YHWH, it is therefore known, from the Greek for 'four letters', as the Tetragrammaton. In the written or printed text of Torah, the vowels from the Hebrew word *Adonai* ('my Lord') are inserted into the letters YHWH in order to remind readers that no attempt should be made to pronounce the Name. It follows that the name Jehovah is certainly wrong, because it simply adds the vowels from the Hebrew of 'my Lord' (*adonai*) which were put there in the first place only in order to warn any reader not to try to pronounce the Name. YHWH is conventionally rendered as Yahweh, translated as 'the Lord'.

As a reward for giving their allegiance to God, the Jews came to believe that they had been chosen by God out of all the nations to serve God and to keep faith with God, come what may. To be a chosen people in a Covenant with God involved far more by way of obligation and obedience (keeping the laws and the prohibitions of the Covenant) than it did of privilege, but it did at least carry with it the promise of a land where they would live, as we saw earlier in the Covenant with Abraham. The actual settlement in the land, however, required them, as a matter of obedience to the command of God, to drive out and if necessary kill existing populations, including women and children. An example of that command is in *Deuteronomy* 20:16–18:

> As for the towns of these peoples that the Lord your God is giving you as an inheritance, you must not let anything that breathes remain alive. You shall annihilate them – the Hittites and the Amorites, the Canaanites and the Perizzites, the Hivites and the Jebusites – just as the Lord your God has commanded, so that they may not teach you to do all the forbidden things that they do for their gods, and you thus sin against the Lord your God.

The belief that this is God's command has changed the world greatly. Many understand it as a context-dependent command belonging to a particular moment in the history of Israel. But there are some who see it as an expression of God's purpose and who still appeal to it in the conflicts in Israel/Palestine. The boundaries of the Promised Land are described slightly differently in different parts of the Bible, but they cover roughly the present state of Israel, including the West Bank. Today, therefore, it is for some Jews a commitment of religious belief to restore the boundaries of the Promised Land.

After the Exodus and the period in the Wilderness, the different members of the kinship group, the *bene* Jacob/Israel, followed their own lives, but they would come into alliance in a period of crisis, when, for example, one of them was attacked. Then leaders, known as 'Judges', emerged, not in hereditary succession, but because they seemed best able at the time to deal with the crisis.

This began to change when a particular enemy, the Philistines (claimed now by some to be the original Palestinians, for obvious political reasons) became a constant enemy and created a permanent crisis. Saul suggested the wisdom of having correspondingly permanent leaders, or kings, but the idea was too novel, and he was opposed. It was left to David to introduce changes in belief of far-ranging consequence. He captured Jerusalem, which was already a sacred city of the Jebusites, but which had belonged to none of the tribes. Because it was neutral, David made it the new capital city of the kinship group, and began the building of a Temple (completed by his successor, Solomon) to be the centre of Jewish faith and worship. Even more, he became king and established hereditary succession, and made the king a vital link in the chain that binds God to the people. The king was specially anointed for this task, and therefore became known as 'the messiah' (from the Hebrew for 'the anointed one', *haMashiach*).

Jewish belief in the Messiah was originally focused on the ruling kings and on what benefits and blessings from God they might bring to the people. It was only after the kings repeatedly failed them that the belief was shifted into the future, and the Jews began to await a figure who had yet to come who would bring into being God's rule on earth. The idea of a future messianic age, when there will be peace and plenty and 'the wolf will lie down with a lamb', not only sustained Jews in times of bitter persecution, but it also inspired visions (far beyond the boundaries of Judaism) of different kinds of Utopia. Utopia may never be attained (the underlying Greek means 'not a place'), but the dream of working toward it has certainly changed the world.

Belief in Jerusalem as the city chosen by God to be the centre of worship and pilgrimage did not diminish, even when, at the end of the period of the First Temple, the Temple was destroyed by the Babylonians (in 586 BCE), nor even when, at the end of the period of the Second (and rebuilt) Temple, it was destroyed by the Romans (in 70 and again in 135 CE). The Temple Mount was then taken over by Muslims when they captured Jerusalem in 638 (17 in Muslim dating), and on it they erected their own buildings, in particular the Dome of the Rock and al-Aqsa Mosque, both associated with their own beliefs and history. Part of an outside retaining wall of Herod's Temple remains where it is a focus for Jewish prayer. It is still a fundamental belief that the Temple will be restored in God's time, and is clearly a divisive issue between Jews and Muslims. Meanwhile Jews in the Diaspora pray facing toward Jerusalem and expressing the hope, when they celebrate Passover (the commemoration of the Exodus), that it will be 'Next year in Jerusalem'.

After Solomon died, kings continued as hereditary successors, but some parts of the kinship group refused to go on giving allegiance to the heirs of David: 'What have we to do with the house of David?' They split off to have their own kings in the Northern Kingdom, and a hostility began which sometimes even resulted in war. Remnants of the Northern Kingdom emerged much later as the Samaritans, a small number of whom remain to the present day, while the Southern Kingdom in Judaea became those whom we now know as the Jews.

During this period of the kings, there emerged people who believed that they were called and inspired by God to speak out directly in the name of God. They were called Prophets, and in both kingdoms, North and South, they spoke out fiercely against all those, including kings, who were breaking the ethical conditions of the Covenant: 'The Lord has sworn . . .: Surely I will never forget any of their deeds. Shall not the land tremble on this account, and everyone mourn who lives in it? . . . On that day, says the Lord God, I will make the sun go down at noon, and darken the earth in broad daylight' (*Amos* 8:8–9).

At the same time, they reminded people of the great promises that God had made of peace and of prosperity for those who remain loyal. The belief that God calls and inspires some people to speak up for the poor, and to speak against the wealthy and powerful who oppress them, changed the world far beyond the boundaries of Judaea and Israel. It has led many others to speak with a prophetic voice on behalf of the poor. It is why Karl Marx was called 'the last of the Hebrew Prophets' – though Marx as a prophet would have spoken out against Lenin, Stalin and his puppets as angrily as the earlier prophets spoke against rulers who abused their power.

The Southern Kingdom came to an end when it was overrun by the Babylonians in the sixth century, its Temple was destroyed, and the majority of the population was taken into captivity (i.e., the Exile) in Babylon. In the ancient world, it was believed that when a people was defeated, its gods had also been defeated. In the Exile, the Jews refused to abandon their allegiance to YHWH. They mocked the Babylonian gods staggering by, carried in procession and unable to walk or do anything else on their own. They remembered the Exodus and the promises that God had made, and they did not change their beliefs: 'If I forget you, O Jerusalem, may my right hand wither away' (*Psalms* 137:5).

But why, then, had the disaster of the Exile happened? It was easy to say that people in past generations had broken the conditions of the Covenant and that they deserved to be punished. But it was not those people who were being punished. It was people of the present generation. So why were they suffering in this way?

From that question broke forth one of the most profound Jewish beliefs: they believed that although they were innocent, they were bearing the sufferings that others had deserved. They saw themselves as the Suffering Servant: 'He was wounded for our transgressions, crushed for our iniquities; upon him was the punishment that made us whole, and by his bruises we are healed' (*Isaiah* 53:4f.). It was a belief taken up in an equally profound way in Christianity.

When the Jews were far away in exile, they could not continue the worship and sacrifices of the Temple, which had in any case been destroyed. They developed ways in which they could continue to keep faith with God. Their belief that the Sabbath must be kept for God and for the renewal of Jewish life was of paramount importance. The Sabbath is the seventh day on which, according to the account in Genesis, God rested after completing the creation, and on which therefore all work is forbidden. In the Exile, and in the Diaspora for all subsequent Jewish history, the

Sabbath marks out the Covenant relationship between God and the Jewish people. Beyond Judaism, the Sabbath extended into Christianity, where 'the day of rest' was transferred to Sunday, the day commemorating the resurrection of Jesus. For the Jews, the Sabbath recreates for a day the Garden of Eden, and it anticipates the final state of the world to come: 'More than the Jews have kept the Sabbath, the Sabbath has kept the Jews.'

After the Exile

The Exile ended in 536 BCE when the Persian ruler Cyrus, who had defeated the Babylonians, restored the exiles to Jerusalem. At first, there was confusion about what to do next, but eventually, under the leaders Ezra and Nehemiah, they set about rebuilding the Temple. In order to make sure that such a disaster would never happen again, they gave increased powers to the High Priest and the Temple authorities to interpret and apply the laws of the Covenant. There was a brief attempt to restore the line of David, but then kings were abandoned, and the hopes associated with them were transferred to the future.

That change was extremely important: it created the belief that the future belongs to God who will send the Messiah to establish God's perfect kingdom and rule. Works began to be written which claimed to reveal that future. Those works are therefore known as Apocalypses, from the Greek for 'revealing the hidden'. The word 'apocalyptic' has come often to mean 'catastrophic' because often the future predictions in the Apocalypses have been of disasters, even of the end of the world.

As a result, predictions in Apocalypses have led through history to foolish speculations that 'the end is nigh', but their real importance is that they insist, in a dream-like or even nightmarish way, that nothing in the end can defeat the power and the purpose of God. Beliefs of a similar kind occur in other religions, and they have an important consequence: wars, plagues and disasters will predictably occur, and they are not necessarily to be regretted. They may even be welcomed by those who see them as signs that the world is about to end. 'Apocalypse Now' may well be seen as a fulfilment of God's purpose.

During and after the Exile, the Jews began to assemble the books that have become the Bible. In doing this, they gave expression to their belief that history is not just a series of events unrelated to each other, but rather that it is a single and con- nected story telling how 'God is working his purpose out as year succeeds to year.' Where other nations kept a record of events in annals (i.e., year by year, from the Latin *annus*, 'a year'), the Jews saw a thread connecting all the years.

Moreover, since God is the author and only significant char- acter in the story, the Jewish belief that history is God's story meant that they could include all other nations, even when they conquered the Jews, as a part of the story. Equally, they did not have to pretend that their human heroes, such as David, were without fault. They shared with all of us the common faults of sin, error and failure, but they also showed how even the worst faults are not 'past redemption': the possibility of forgiveness and of reconciliation was a belief that profoundly changed the world. It also made clear the belief that even in the face of evil the purpose of God is not defeated. Those are beliefs that made a profound difference in the ways in which enemies and offenders are treated. The portrayal of heroes in the past in a way that did not evade their faults changed the human attitude to history in the direction of being completely realistic: ultimately it underlies the way in the modern world in which fault is not evaded – for example, in films, in soap operas on television, or in scandal-seeking biographies.

Not much is known of Jewish history in the period of the Second Temple until Palestine became a part of the Seleucid empire during the second century BCE. The Seleucids were one of the empires created out of the conquests of Alexander the Great. The Seleucids tried to unify their empire by making all their citizens follow their Greek ways – a process known as 'Hellenization'. Some Jews welcomed this, but others did not, because it involved them in doing things that were forbidden in Torah. When Jews were required to pay tribute in the Temple to the image (called by the Jews 'the abomination of desolation') of Zeus or perhaps of the Emperor, the Hasmoneans, a family of Jewish priests also known as the Maccabeans, started a rebellion.

Their initial success in driving back the Seleucids led to the rededication in 164 BCE of the Temple. That spectacular success is still commemorated annually by the feast of Hanukkah. Having secured religious freedom, they continued to fight in order to secure political independence. That was eventually achieved, and the Hasmonean rulers continued successfully until the last two (Hyrcanus II, 63–40, and Antigonus, 40–37) became mere puppets of the Romans who had conquered Judaea in 63 BCE.

In the early days of the revolt against the Seleucids, it so happened that the Seleucids made an attack against the rebels on the Sabbath. The rebels were fighting to keep faith with God and to resist being turned into Greek citizens, and it was therefore impossible for them to fight on the Sabbath. They were therefore slaughtered. This raised a profoundly difficult question: here were people manifestly doing what God had asked of them, and yet God had done nothing to help them. As in the Exile, so here:

how is God keeping faith with those who are slaughtered while they are keeping faith with God?

From that question developed the belief that those who are killed in this way, keeping faith with God even to the point of death, are martyrs (Greek *martureo*, 'I bear witness'), and that God uses the blood of the martyrs to achieve something beyond their own death for others – in this case the achievement of political and religious independence. After the Holocaust, there were some who interpreted in that way the establishment of the State of Israel in 1948.

Even more importantly, the belief emerged that God is able to reward those who keep faith, not only in this life, but also in a life beyond death. It is extraordinary and surprising that in the books of what became Tanach, the Jewish Bible, there is virtually no belief in a worthwhile life after death. Those books celebrate the constant faithfulness of God in creation and in history; they are full of praise, thanksgiving and penitence, and they are constant in reiterating the importance of the Covenant and of keeping the conditions of the Covenant. But none of that was done with the expectation or even the hope that there will be a reward for that recognition and celebration of God in a life with God after death.

There are a few passages in the Jewish Bible in which the beginnings of that hope can be seen, but it is really only in the Hasmonean period that the belief is fully established until, in works like *The Wisdom of Solomon*, it becomes fundamental: 'The souls of the faithful are in the hand of God, there shall no torment touch them; in the eyes of the foolish they seem to have died . . . but they are at peace.' (3:1–3). Belief in life after death is late in the history of religions, and it is certainly a belief that has changed the world immensely far beyond the boundaries of Judaism.

The end of the Hasmonean dynasty came about because of the expansion of the Roman Empire. The Romans needed to control the Eastern seaboard of the Mediterranean in order to secure trade routes and the supply of corn from Egypt. They controlled Judaea and territories immediately to the north by installing Herod and his descendants as puppet rulers, and they kept an eye on events by appointing their own procurators. There were several uprisings against the Romans, all on a small scale until a major rebellion began in 66 CE. This was eventually crushed by the Romans in 70, when they captured Jerusalem and destroyed the Temple.

During this period, Judaism was not a single and uniform religion. There were many competing interpretations of what it should mean to live in a faithful Covenant relationship with God – in other words, to be a Jew as God intended. Thus there were some who believed that history as God's story means that God gives power to nations in turn, and that consequently they should accept being subject to the Romans. But others believed that a Messiah would come to defeat the invading Romans and restore the kingdom of David, and that rebellion against Rome would initiate the messianic kingdom. It was that belief that led to the fatal rebellion in 66.

That, however, was not the only dispute among Jews at the time. Other disputes were even more closely connected to beliefs. Some believed that the high priest and the Temple authorities (the Sadducees) were corrupt and illegitimate, and they built alternative temples far away from Jerusalem (for example, in Leontopolis in Egypt), where they continued what they regarded as legitimate worship while waiting for the time when God would restore them to Jerusalem. Others shared their rejection of the Temple authorities in Jerusalem, but they simply removed themselves to a community at Qumran on the shores of the Dead Sea, where they could escape uncleanness and corruption, and could live in the condition of perfect holiness which God and the Covenant require.

But what does holiness mean in practice? Some believed that it involves doing exactly what the laws and prohibitions in Torah require, as closely and literally as possible. Others, however, realized that that cannot possibly be done by those who have to live everyday lives in the conditions of the Roman (or for that matter of any other) empire. They therefore introduced careful ways of interpreting Torah in order to make it liveable in changed and different circumstances. They were known first as the Hakhamim (the Wise) and later, after the fall of Jerusalem to the Romans, as the Rabbis (*rabbi* means 'my master' or 'teacher'). Because they were interpreters of Torah they were also known as *perushim*, i.e., Pharisees. Among them, however, were some who believed that now the law has been interpreted to make it liveable, people have no excuse for ignoring it or for not keeping it. They therefore applied rigorous interpretations of the law, and it is those extremists who came to be condemned, not least in the Christian Gospels, as Pharisees.

All those options and arguments were divisive and competing answers to the one basic question: what does it mean in practice to be a faithful Jew, living, believing and acting as God commands? It was the answer of the Rabbis that prevailed and became what is now known as Judaism. They organized themselves carefully to transmit their teaching and their interpretations from one generation to another, and they made much use of an institution that had first come into being in the period after the exile. That institution was the Synagogue (in Hebrew *bet kenesset*), and it was supremely in the Synagogue that the Jewish people remained together and sustained their beliefs and practices, even when Jerusalem and the Promised Land were no longer theirs. Synagogues express the belief that Jews need each other in order to worship God, to instruct children and the faithful, and to give hospitality to strangers and travellers.

The origin of the Synagogue is not clear, although it was traditionally ascribed to Moses. It certainly existed in the first century before the defeat of the Jewish revolt in 70, but it became supremely important after that catastrophe. During the long centuries when Jews had neither a Temple nor a Land, it was the Synagogue that gave them a home and an identity. As the scholar Solomon Schechter put it in 1909:

> Dispersed among the nations, without a national centre, without a synod to formulate its principles, or any secular power to enforce its decrees, the Synagogue found its home and harmony in the heart of a loyal and consecrated Israel.

An English rabbi, at much the same time, wrote of the Synagogue:

> The synagogue is the one unfailing wellspring of Jewish feeling. There we pray together with our brethren, and in the act become participators in the common sentiment, the collective conscience, of Israel. There we pray with a mightier company still, with the whole house of Israel.

From the Fall of Jerusalem to Maimonides

Although Jewish belief was profoundly shaken by the Fall of Jerusalem in 70 CE and the destruction of the Temple, it could not be destroyed. Jewish faith is preserved and transmitted in the family. Even then, that faith is not a matter of individual choice or decision: it belongs to the whole community as the people chosen by God to continue God's purposes in the world. Jews are defined, not by individual belief, but by having a Jewish mother.

With the Fall of Jerusalem, some among the many interpretations of Jewish faith and practice disappeared – the Sadducees in the Temple, for example, and the community at Qumran. What did not disappear was the belief that a Messiah will come and lead the Jews into the promised kingdom of God. In 132 CE, another rebellion against Rome was led by Simeon ben Koseba who was renamed Bar Kochba ('son of a star' from a promise understood to be messianic in the Biblical book of *Numbers*, 24:17). This rebellion was another failure: in 135 Jerusalem was razed to the ground, and rebuilt as a hellenistic city called Aelia Capitolina.

There were Jewish communities in many parts of the Roman Empire, and there were Jews also who continued to live in Palestine where the reconstruction of Judaism was led by the Rabbis. The central authority in Jewish belief and practice became the Sanhedrin whose leader was called Nasi (lit., 'prince'). Work was begun to codify the many interpretations of Torah which had been accumulating for centuries, but which, until then, had been transmitted from teacher to pupil by word of mouth. One codification of particular authority and importance is known as the Mishnah, and this in turn became the foundation for the even larger collection known as the Palestinian Talmud.

There were also Jewish communities outside the Roman Empire, especially in Babylon and Mesopotamia, where Jews had continued to live since the Exile. These Jews were led by a Resh Galutha ('head of the exile') who had authority like the Nasi in Palestine. In this community an even more extensive collection and codification of the laws (also based on Mishnah) was made that became the Babylonian Talmud, the authoritative foundation of subsequent Jewish life and belief.

In the seventh century CE, Muslims conquered the whole area from Egypt to Mesopotamia and Persia. The caliph Umar introduced the so-called Pact of Umar which, on the basis of the Quran, gives to Jews and Christians a special status, because in Muslim belief they received their own Scripture from God and are therefore 'Peoples of the Book'. They are known as *dhimmis*, or protected people: they have a limited religious freedom and are exempt from military service in return for paying a special tax and agreeing not to insult Islam or to try to convert Muslims. This gave to Jews considerable security in Muslim lands, though they were never exempt from persecution.

This still left open the question for the Jews as to why the disaster of the Fall of Jerusalem and the destruction of the Temple had happened. One group emerged who believed that it had happened because the Jews had wandered too far from the literal and strict text of Torah in the interpretations which had ended up in the Talmuds. In their belief, Scripture alone must be the foundation of Jewish life. This group emerged during the eighth century, and by the ninth they were being called Karaites (Hebrew, 'readers', i.e., of Scripture). They rejected the way in which rabbinic Judaism showed what the meaning of Scripture is in Halakah and (H)aggadah. Halakah is 'that by which one walks' (i.e., the interpretation and application of the laws). (H)aggadah ('narration') is the belief that life lived in the boundary of law must be illuminated by stories and anecdotes, and it is this that has led to the Jews remaining brilliant storytellers who give delight to many far beyond Judaism itself.

After Christianity gained political power in Rome (from the

fifth century onward), Jews and Judaism were increasingly attacked as those whose ancestors had brought about the cruci-fixion of Jesus – they were even called 'God-killers'. The Jews were useful economically, not least as moneylenders, but increas-ingly they were attacked, compelled to wear identifying clothes, and expelled from particular countries (from England in 1290, France in 1394, Spain in 1492). Some were compelled under threat of death to convert, such as the Marranos in Spain, though many of them returned to Jewish belief when the opportunity came to do so. That opportunity arrived when Jews began to migrate eastward to Poland, the Ukraine and Russia, in all of which countries many Jewish communities were established – even though there too they were subjected later to savage persecution. Jews in these areas are known as Ashkenazim, from the name in *Genesis* 10:3.

The Jews of Spain and the Mediterranean area are known as Sephardim. The emergence of the Ottoman Empire in the Muslim world gave protection to the Sephardim, and many new Jewish communities were formed in Mediterranean lands.

During the centuries of persecution, Jewish belief did not diminish in the fundamental authority of the Bible whose meaning was made clear in the subsequent traditions of inter-pretation. Moses Maimonides (1135–1204), a notable physician in Muslim employment, produced a new organization of Jewish law in his great Code. His purpose was 'so that the entire Oral Law might become systematically known to all without citing difficulties and solutions of differences of view, but consisting of statements clear and convincing that have appeared from the time of Moses to the present, so that all rules shall be accessible to young and old'.

Maimonides was also a supreme philosopher who affected the

development of Christian and Muslim belief as well. He also drew up a non-negotiable list of Jewish beliefs, known as the Thirteen Principles. They are printed in Jewish prayer books, and are the nearest the Jews have come to producing something like a Creed. The Principles are:

1. I believe with perfect faith that the Creator, blessed be his name, is the Author and Guide of everything that has been created, and that he alone has made, does make, and will make all things.

2. I believe with perfect faith that the Creator, blessed be his name, is a Unity, and that there is no unity in any manner like his, and that he alone is our God, who was, is, and will be.

3. I believe with perfect faith that the Creator, blessed be his name, is not a body, and that he is free from all the accidents of matter, and that he has not any form whatsoever.

4. I believe with perfect faith that the Creator, blessed be his name, is the first and the last.

5. I believe with perfect faith that to the Creator, blessed be his name, and to him alone it is right to pray, and that it is not right to pray to any being besides him.

6. I believe with perfect faith that all the words of the prophets are true.

7. I believe with perfect faith that the prophecy of Moses our teacher, peace be upon him, was true, and that he was the chief of the prophets, both of those that preceded and of those that followed him.

8. I believe with perfect faith that the whole Law, now in our possession, is the same that was given to Moses our teacher, peace be upon him.

9. I believe with perfect faith that this Law will not be changed, and that there will never be any other law from the Creator, blessed be his name.

10. I believe with perfect faith that the Creator, blessed be his name, knows every deed of the children of men, and all their thoughts, as it is said, it is he that fashions the hearts of them all, that gives heed to all their deeds.

11. I believe with perfect faith that the Creator, blessed be his name, rewards those that keep his commandments, and punishes those that transgress them.

12. I believe with perfect faith in the coming of the Messiah, and, though he tarry, I will wait daily for his coming.

13. I believe with perfect faith that there will be a resurrection of the dead at the time when it shall please the Creator, blessed be his name, and exalted be the remembrance of him for ever and ever.

Yet for all the achievement of Maimonides, other Jews felt that he had been too liberal in interpreting Jewish beliefs when he acted as 'a guide for the perplexed' (*Dalilat alHariain*, the title of one of his most famous works, better known as *Moreh Nebuchim*). He was condemned for offering metaphorical interpretations of the attributes or anthropomorphic descriptions of God (such as 'the hand of God') as well as bringing rational analysis to such fundamental doctrines as the resurrection of the body. It was Jews who encouraged Christians, particularly Franciscans and Dominicans, to burn the works of Maimonides, beginning in 1232 with *Moreh Nebuchim*. The Maimonidean controversy is an example of the way in which the content and nature of beliefs can evoke bitter conflict, not just between religions, but also within religions.

From Qabbalah to the State of Israel

The controversy about Maimonides did not stop others from working to elucidate and sustain Jewish belief. Of great importance was the work of Joseph Caro (1488–1575), who produced *Shulchan Aruch*, 'The Prepared Table', a codification of the Law which reflected developments among the Sephardim. Moses Isserles (*c*.1530–72) then added notes from an Ashkenazi perspective, and the result became a foundation for subsequent Jewish belief and practice – reinforced by the fact that it was one of the first Jewish books to be printed.

Jewish belief, however, is about much more than a code of laws. It is about the way in which people live with God and in the presence of God. It was out of this desire to understand something of the mystery of God that the beliefs and practices drawn together in Qabbalah or Kabbalah (*qabbalah* means 'a traditional rule of conduct' or 'a tradition') emerged in the sixteenth century, although Qabbalah claims to rest on much earlier traditions.

In Qabbalah, an attempt is made to reconcile two beliefs in the Bible that seem to contradict each other: on the one hand, God remains utterly distinct and different from all that has been created, but on the other hand, God is active in the world and in history. Qabbalah claims that 'what God is like' is completely unknowable, because God is En Sof ('without limit'), utterly beyond human comprehension. But from God flow forth ten emanations, known as Sefirot, and these bring the effect of God into the world as rivers bring water from the same spring. Qabbalah offers the key to allowing the powers of the Sefirot to enter into one's life. In that way, people can receive a blessing and become a blessing to others. The Hebrew word for 'blessing' is *berakah*, and that is understood as *beyrakah*, a pool or receptacle: by making oneself through Qabbalah a worthy receptacle, one is filled with the overflowing blessing of God, so that believers in Qabbalah become agents of God in the work of repairing the world.

The work of those followers of Qabbalah in repairing the world was understood as a preparation for the coming of the Messiah, and many appeared in the seventeenth century claiming to be the Messiah. Of these, Shabbatai Tzevi (1626–76) was for a time the most persuasive and successful. He was a Jew from Izmir in Turkey who lived when Polish persecution of the Jews was particularly fierce. Claiming to be the promised Messiah, he persuaded many Jews to sell all that they had and to follow him to the Holy Land, where he threatened to march on Constantinople and depose the Sultan. Not surprisingly, he was arrested, and he converted to Islam in order to save his life.

In contrast, though also connected loosely with Qabbalah, was an entirely different movement which emerged in eastern Europe whose followers are known as the Hasidim. They were led by Israel ben Eliezer (c.1700–60), who became known as Baal Shem Tov, also known from the initial letters as the Besht. He believed that the aim of Jewish faith is for the soul to achieve union with God, even in the midst of everyday life and in the most ordinary functions of the human body. This union is known as *devekut*, which means literally 'clinging' or 'adhering', as Jews are commanded to do in *Deuteronomy* 4:24.

Subsequently the Hasidim have been led by men of charismatic power known as Zaddiks (holy men). They and the Besht rejected political involvement based on messianic speculation, and taught instead a way of joyful involvement with God. This was based on careful observance of Torah, but it celebrated *simhat Torah*, the joy of Torah. There was a strong emphasis on personal devotion to God, celebrated in prayer, dancing and singing. Much of their teaching has been preserved in striking stories. For example, Rabbi Elimelekh said, 'I am certain to have a share in the world to come. When I am judged and they ask me, "Have you studied all that you should?" I shall answer, "No." "Have you prayed all you should?" "No." "Have you done all the good you should have done?" "No." Then they will pronounce the verdict on me: "You have told the truth. For the sake of truth, you deserve a share in the world to come."'

Anti-Semitism did not diminish in general, but it began to be accompanied by increasing political emancipation. Oliver Cromwell had reintroduced Jews to England in 1656, but that had not secured them equal rights. In the United States, the Bill of Rights (1791) guaranteed freedom of religious belief. Emancipation proceeded slowly during the nineteenth century in Europe.

That, however, brought back an old issue for Jewish belief, but now in a new form: should Jews still remain separate from the life of the countries in which Emancipation was becoming real, in order not to compromise the terms and conditions of the Covenant; or should they interpret and adapt the laws in order to make life liveable in these new conditions?

Different answers were given, creating movements within Judaism that continue to the present day. Orthodox Jews believe that Torah cannot be changed or compromised, although it is right within that limit for Jews to participate in the life of wherever they live, following the Talmudic principle *dina demalchutha dina*, the law of the land is the law. In the State of Israel, it is Orthodox Judaism that prevails.

In contrast, the Reform Movement aims to retain the essentials of Jewish belief and practice, but to modify the forms of

Jewish worship and to relate Jewish belief to the vast changes in understanding being brought about especially by science. The Union of American Hebrew Congregations (Reform) was established in 1873, followed by a series of Platforms, beginning with Pittsburgh in 1885, in which the Reform understanding of Judaism was set out.

In reaction to what seemed to be becoming a far too liberal interpretation of Jewish belief, a middle ground was sought in the creation of Conservative Judaism, which held to traditional beliefs and practices, but allowed some changes where these are not ruled out specifically by Torah. Even so, many of the Conservative rulings are not recognized by the Orthodox.

Through all those developments in Jewish belief, anti-Semitism continued, often combined with persecution. In reaction to increasing persecution (especially in Russia and Eastern Europe), attempts were made to find a safe refuge and homeland for the Jews. When it became clear that forged evidence had been used to condemn a French Jew, Alfred Dreyfus (1859–1935) to penal servitude on Devil's Island, Theodor Herzl (1860–1904) came to believe that the Jewish homeland must be in the land promised to Abraham. Through a series of Zionist Congresses, support rapidly grew for a Jewish homeland in Palestine.

This gained the support of the British government during the First World War (when Jewish support was needed) through the Balfour Declaration, which was nevertheless careful to state that nothing should prejudice the religious and political rights of the local Arab population, the Palestinians. On the other hand, through the McMahon correspondence the British (also needing Arab support) made a commitment to the Arabs. The seeds of conflict were sown.

The pressure to create a Jewish homeland in Palestine became irresistible when the German Nazis set out to make Europe *Judenrein*, 'free of Jews'. The Shoah ('calamity') or Holocaust has raised wrenchingly searching questions for Jewish belief. In the total destruction in Europe of Jewish life and society, along with all its memorable contributions to science, literature, music and the other arts, the questions were inevitable: 'Where was God while all this was happening?' And 'What remains of the Covenant now when people, many of whom were as faithful as the Maccabean martyrs, have been slaughtered, along with countless innocent children?' A range of different answers has been given, from the claim that God was punishing the people who have strayed far from Torah, to the belief that God becomes powerless so that history can happen in which Israel is still the Suffering Servant, to the belief that Hitler, like Cyrus before him, was the agent of God in restoring the Jews to the Promised Land, thus creating the State of Israel.

The Jews were not the only victims of Nazi extermination policies, but they were massively the major target. This strengthened the international will to establish the State of Israel. Britain, who had held the Mandate over Palestine during the inter-war years, handed responsibility for Palestine to the United Nations in 1947, and the State of Israel was declared in 1948. On 14 May 1948, David Ben Gurion, shortly to become Prime Minister, stood in the Museum of Tel Aviv and said:

> On this day that sees the end of the British Mandate and in virtue of the natural and historical right of the Jewish people and in accordance with the resolution of the United Nations General Assembly, we proclaim the creation of a Jewish State in Palestine.

Arab armies immediately invaded what they regarded as Palestinian territory, and in the subsequent war the envisaged partition of the land disappeared and more than half a million Arabs became refugees. Many Jews migrated to Israel in the Aliya (the traditional 'going up' to Jerusalem), and after two further wars (the Six Day War in 1967, and the Yom Kippur War in 1973) Israel took control of Jerusalem and further territory. The wars raised acutely the questions, How much territory? and What kind of control? In effect, that became a question of whether the West Bank is part of the Biblical Promised Land. One group active at that time was called 'the movement for the entire land of Israel' (*Hatenua leEretz Israel heShlema*) with which Gush Emunim was closely associated advocating settlements on the West Bank and calling themselves 'believers of the land of Israel' (*Ne'emanei Eretz Israel*).

Within a generalized support for Israel, there are divisions of belief among Jews: at one extreme are those who believe that there should be no return to Jerusalem until the Messiah comes and who therefore oppose the Zionist movement; at the other extreme are those who believe that every centimetre of the Promised Land should be a part of Israel. Between the two, parties like Likud contain within themselves divisions about pragmatic and strategic solutions. Meanwhile the Palestinians continue to resist, either as terrorists (according to one set of perceptions) or as freedom and resistance fighters (according to another). Here are beliefs that are truly changing the world.

Christianity

Overview

When Herod was king in Judaea, there were many different and sometimes conflicting interpretations of what it should mean to keep faithfully the Covenant with God. We have looked at some of those briefly. One among them began in Galilee and moved to Jerusalem. It was set forth in the life, works and teaching of Jesus of Nazareth. He spoke with authority and performed remarkable works of healing. There were other teachers and healers among his fellow-Jews at that time, so that in itself was not remarkable. What was different about Jesus was the dramatic nature of his healing and teaching, often reversing the received wisdom and values of his time, and even more the way in which he insisted that his teaching and works did not come from himself, but entirely from God.

Some who encountered Jesus believed that the hands-on involvement of God on earth, the kingdom of God, was coming into being through him. Others thought that he was badly and dangerously wrong, and that he was betraying Torah. Jesus went deliberately to Jerusalem where the high priest alone could decide whether he was a true teacher or not. When the high priest decided that he was not, he was handed over to the

Roman authorities under Pontius Pilate as a threat to the law and order of the Roman jurisdiction, and he was executed by crucifixion.

This was, to say the least, hardly a promising start for a new religion. But some followers and family of Jesus who persisted with him to the end were suddenly aware that, 'on the third day', he was as fully alive as he had been most certainly dead. Since Jewish days end and begin at sunset, 'on the third day' means about 36 hours after the crucifixion – this return to life is known as 'the Resurrection'.

The Resurrection is the foundation of Christianity. The first Christians could not in any way explain or even understand exactly what had happened in the Resurrection, but it sent them out into the world to live in the service of others and to spread the good news ('Gospel') that Jesus is alive after death, and that he offers to share this new life with others who come into it with faith and trust, and who live in the service of others.

This union with the risen Jesus was made real through the enacted signs of Baptism and the Eucharist. The Eucharist is the constant taking up by his followers of his promise, at the last supper before his crucifixion, that even after his death he will be present with them in a new covenant re-enacted through bread and wine taken as his body and blood.

This 'new covenant' was strikingly different from anything claimed or taught by any of the many other teachers and healers of the time. But it was not actually a 'new religion'. It was, in the belief of the early followers of Jesus, a fulfilment of all that God had promised and intended in the original covenant with the Jews. In their belief, Jesus is the one who brings in the kingdom of God on earth. Since that was believed among Jews to be the role of the Messiah, they began to call him the Messiah. The

Greek for Messiah is *christos*, so the followers of Jesus called him Christ[os] and began themselves to be called Christians in Antioch about 15 years after his death.

Christians realized that Jesus was much more than a human teacher and healer: as he had made clear, all that he did and said came, not from himself, but from God working in and through him. From the start, they continued to call him by his human name Jesus, but they believed that he was the reality of God in the world. From the earliest writings in the New Testament, Jesus is so closely associated with God that he is to be honoured and worshipped as only God can be. This led to the belief that Jesus is the Incarnation of God, and thus to the claim that Jesus is both God and man, a perfect joining together of those two natures in one person.

The history of the early Church shows how Christians at that time began to try to understand the meaning and the implications of this staggering claim. There was much argument and even conflict out of which eventually there emerged creeds and councils in which the boundaries of the truth about God and Christ were agreed.

The Church, embodying so often a joyful transformation of life and hope, spread widely in the Roman Empire, where it was sometimes persecuted when Christians refused to offer sacrifice or other homage to the emperors as a sign of loyalty. But Constantine in the fourth century accepted Christianity as one of the tolerated cults and religions of the Empire, and although there were still some further persecutions, Christianity slowly became the recognized religion of the Roman Empire.

The Empire was divided for administration between West and East, and the Christian Church began to reflect that division. Christians in the West increasingly regarded the Bishop of Rome, called like other bishops papa, 'Father', as the highest authority in the Church and called him Pope. Christians in the East did not accept that the Pope had authority over them, and so the deep divide between the Western Church and so-called Eastern Orthodoxy opened up.

In the East, the Church had to face the expansion of Islam from the seventh century onward, and many Christian lands fell under Muslim rule. The capital of the East, Byzantium, later called Constantinople, held out until it was captured by Muslims in 1453. Eastern Orthodoxy had spread north through the Balkans into Russia, but the Muslims pursued them, reaching the gates of Vienna under Sulayman I (The Magnificent, 1520–66).

In the West, also, lands were lost to Islam – including the whole of North Africa and much of Spain. The Muslim advance was stopped in southern France by Charles Martel at the Battle of Tours/Poitiers in 732. Under Muslim rule, Christians became subordinate citizens, but there was a creative cooperation which led to the rescue of Greek philosophy, medicine and science: translated into Europe, this was the foundation of science in the West.

There were other invasions of Christian lands by so-called 'barbarians', although some 'barbarians' had already become Christians themselves. During the early Middle Ages, Christian faith was sustained increasingly through the monastic orders. As Christian lands became once more secure, attacks known as crusades were made against those who had been a threat, including Muslims. Security, however, brought its own problems as the Pope sought increasing power, not only in judicial matters, but in spiritual as well. To some, the faith itself seemed to be changing from the teaching of Jesus and the early Church: it became clear to them that the Church was in need of reform.

The many attempts at reformation were not seeking initially to break up the Church. But the issues were so serious that the fracture of the communities of faith became inevitable. Ultimately the issue was one of authority: does the Pope have final authority over the faithful, or must that authority be sought in scripture alone?

The reforming of the Church led to what is known as 'the Reformation'. In fact there was no single 'Reformation', but many reformations. In other words, there was no single Church protesting (i.e., Protestant) against the Pope and abuses in the Church. There are thus many Protestant Churches resting on the appeal to scripture. Attempts to reunite Christians are known as 'the ecumenical movement', which led to the founding of the World Council of Churches in 1948.

Independence from the authority of the Pope led to an increasing emphasis in Europe on the authority of reason. Some Christians – including Roman Catholics – rejected this if it involved questioning of the Bible and/or the Pope, but it led nevertheless to an entirely different Reformation, in which the foundations of human knowledge began to rest, not on obedience to authority, but on experiment and argument. The development of Western science was deeply rooted in the Christian understanding of creation as 'a second book' of revelation, but conflict was inevitable with those who insisted on a literal understanding of the Bible.

During all this time, Christianity followed exploration and trade so that Christianity (in its divided form) is now found in virtually every country, making up about one third of the world's population. The history of Christianity is really the histories of Christianity throughout the world. Some are older than European Christianity – in India and Africa – many have developed their own ways of being Christian – in North America and East Asia. They cannot all be summarized in a book of this kind, but these 'local Christianities' are nevertheless often the beliefs that have changed the world.

Jesus

The history of Christianity as a religion began with a Jewish man called Jesus, the Greek form of the Hebrew Joshua which means 'Yahweh (the Lord) saves'. It came to be recognized that Jesus 'lived up to his name', and that he was, in a dramatic way, the act of God bringing salvation, not just to the Jews, but to all people for all time. This was a belief which entirely changed, not just the Roman Empire, but eventually the whole world.

Because Jesus was a Jew, Christians see their history going back to the origins of creation itself, and they believe that Jesus was the fulfilment of all that God had intended to do through the Jewish people as those who show how life should be lived in a covenant relationship with God. Christians therefore accept Tanach, the Jewish Bible, as the inspired record of how God has worked with and through the Jewish people.

Christians eventually called the Jewish Bible 'the Old Testament' (*testamentum* being a Latin word for 'covenant') and their own writings 'the New Testament'. Both 'testaments' make up the Christian Bible, even though Christians disagree about the books of the Old Testament because they had not finally been decided by the time of Jesus: Roman Catholics include more books than other Christians because the Vulgate, their authoritative translation of the Bible, was based on the Greek translation of the Hebrew known as the Septuagint; that Greek translation included books whose status in Tanach had not by that time been decided, and which were later excluded from the Hebrew Bible. Disputes about which books have the authority of Scripture, and about whether translation into other languages can be allowed, have contributed to the divisions among Christians.

So how did it come about that this obscure person from Galilee came to be recognized as the fulfilment of God's promises and purposes recorded in Jewish Scripture? More briefly, how did Jesus come to be called Christ?

The Greek word *christos* is a translation of the Hebrew *mashiach*, 'anointed one' – or, putting the Hebrew letters into English, 'messiah'. The messiahs (anointed agents of God) included the High Priests, but the term was applied particularly to the descendants of David who had originally ruled as kings over the Jews. But after the failure of the kings, it was believed that the Messiah would only come when God decided to send him to inaugurate God's rule on earth. Throughout Jewish history, there have been many who have claimed to be a messiah, as we have already seen, and that was true at the time when Jesus was alive: there were many who believed that a messiah could easily defeat the Romans who now occupied the land, and could restore the independent kingdom of the Hasmoneans that had flourished in the century before Jesus was born.

It was, therefore, not particularly unusual that some people might hope that Jesus was the Christ – i.e., the promised Messiah. But there were two major problems: first, Jesus insisted that he was not a figure of the expected kind; and second, Jesus died nailed to a cross, the death reserved by Romans for criminals, hardly the fate of a messiah. How could such a person be the Christ?

In answering that question, it is important to remember that when Jesus was alive there was no such thing as Judaism. As we have already seen, there were many competing and divisive answers to the question of how a Jew ought to live faithfully with God. The life and teachings of Jesus were also an answer to that question, but of a very different kind.

When Jesus was about thirty years old, he appeared in Galilee (in the territories to the north of Jerusalem and Palestine) as a wandering teacher who spoke of God as one who is open to those who seek God, and who overturns the values and standards of a ruthless world: God is one who sets the poor before the rich, sinners before the self-righteous, children before their teachers, peacemakers before statesmen and soldiers, the last before the first. Asked like other teachers of that time to summarize his teaching in a sentence, he said that it is the love of God with all one's being and of one's neighbour as oneself.

In practice, that means sharing God's unconditional generosity with others. The belief that love has absolute priority has changed the world immensely in countless practical ways. It is the reason why Christians have so often taken the lead in 'giving to the hungry and the thirsty what they need, clothing the naked, caring for the sick and visiting those in prison' (*Matthew* 25:31–46). It is what Paul called 'the more excellent way': 'Now faith, hope, and love abide, these three; and the greatest of these is love' (I *Corinthians* 13:13).

So Jesus did not lead a revolution against Rome. He claimed that the revolution which was already coming into being is God's kingdom now and in the future. The signs of that kingdom he made apparent, not just in the way in which he taught its meaning, but also in the way in which he healed people and pronounced that their sins have been forgiven. All this was completely unconditional: it did not depend on keeping the law, or on having the right ideas about God. For Jesus, openness to God in faith and love is fundamental (and is possible for non-Jews as well as Jews), but it is not a condition of God's works of healing and forgiveness.

What was disturbing about Jesus was that he acted and taught with a striking independence which he claimed came to him directly from God: he made real in the world things that only God can do – the healing of the sick, the forgiveness of sins, and the establishing of God's kingdom on earth. Those who met Jesus saw him as one through whom the power and effect of God were at work in the world in dramatic ways. Even his enemies did not deny that something extraordinary was happening in and through the person of Jesus: they simply said that he must be doing it through the power of the devil, Beelzebub, in order to seduce Jews from their true obedience to God.

God's power, therefore, was brought to vivid life by Jesus through teaching, forgiveness of sins, and healing of body, mind and spirit. Jesus never claimed to do any of these memorable things out of his own ability or strength: always he said that they came to him from God whom he called Father.

When, therefore, the first followers of Jesus saw or heard him, it seemed to be God who was speaking and acting through him in ways that lie far beyond human power, so that, in the words attributed to Jesus, 'anyone who has seen me has seen the Father' (*John* 14:9). And yet Jesus spoke *of* God, and also *to* God in prayer, as Father, as one distinct from himself.

This is the foundation of the fundamental Christian belief that God was wholly present in the person of Jesus without destroying or diminishing his human nature. The earliest Christian writings (before even accounts of Jesus were written in the Gospels) express the belief that Jesus was the translation into human life of the reality and effect of God without his humanity being in any way distorted or destroyed. This belief is known as the Incarnation (Lat., *in carne*, 'in the flesh/body').

So the teachings and the healings of Jesus were dramatic indeed, but the belief that they were the very work of God seemed to be totally contradicted by the way he died. He died on a cross as a criminal.

How and why did that happen? It happened because Jesus insisted that God was at work in and through himself, not as a special figure (an angel, for example, or a new age prophet, or John the Baptist brought back to life after his execution, or even as a Messiah), but as what he called 'the son of man'. That phrase is not a title. In the Bible it has two meanings: in *Psalms* and *Job* it means 'an ordinary human being who has to die'. However, in *Daniel* 7 it is also a figure standing for those holy ones who have kept faith with God and who are brought before the Ancient of Days to receive their 'dominion and glory and kingship'.

As the son of man in that first Biblical sense, Jesus died. But why on a cross? That happened because Jesus deliberately moved from the safety of Galilee to Jerusalem. It was only there, in the Temple, that the high priest could decide whether Jesus was a true teacher, or whether he was fundamentally wrong and therefore a threat to the Temple. If Jesus was not a true teacher, God's word through Moses (*Deuteronomy* 17:8–13) is very clear: he must be executed, because nothing will divide and destroy Israel faster than a false teacher.

In fact, when Jesus was brought before the high priest and was accused of threatening the Temple, Jesus refused to accept the authority of the high priest, and he remained silent. For the high priest, that was enough: it showed that Jesus was rejecting Temple authority, and he therefore handed Jesus on to the Romans as a subversive threat to Rome. To Pontius Pilate it was convenient to support the Temple authorities in order to maintain good order in Jerusalem. He therefore ordered the execution.

In this way Jesus as 'a son of man' did indeed die, as all humans must, but it seemed as though his belief was entirely wrong that as *the* son of man – the well-known one in *Daniel* – God's purpose would be fulfilled in him. He cried out, just before he died, 'My God, my God, why have you forsaken me?'

And yet those who had witnessed that desolation and defeat were suddenly and almost immediately overwhelmed by the unmistakable truth that God had not forsaken Jesus, but had after all 'given to the Son of Man glory and dominion' in an utterly unexpected way: they were certain that he had died; they were now equally certain that he was alive – that he had risen from the dead and that he now offers to share that victory over death with all people.

The Early Years

That was a literally life-changing belief, and it is a reason why early summaries of Christian belief were extremely simple – but also dramatic: that Christ died on the Cross to deal with human sin, that he was buried, that he was raised from the dead and appeared to his followers – on one occasion to more than 500 people (I *Corinthians* 15:3–5).

The belief that Jesus has risen from the dead is fundamental. The actual resurrection is not described, and some have argued that the resurrection never happened – that, for example, Jesus did not die and was revived after his terrible experience (as the Ahmadiyya claim, as we will see later); or that he died but that his teaching and inspiration lived on. Those attempts to explain away the resurrection cannot be true, because they do not explain the most obvious historical fact of all, the fact of the New Testament: what brought those unique and extraordinary documents into being?

The New Testament contains different kinds of writing, the earliest being the letters of Paul. There are also accounts of Jesus called Gospels ('good news'). The four Gospels were associated with Matthew, Mark, Luke and John (early followers of Jesus), but they are unlikely to have been written by them. The first three are known as the Synoptic Gospels, because when they are put side by side it is clear that they use much of the same material, although they use it in different ways.

It is usually thought (but not all agree) that *Mark*, the earliest, was used by Matthew and Luke, who also used an even earlier source containing sayings of Jesus and known as Q (German *Quelle*, source). *Matthew* and *Luke* then have material of their own. Each Gospel has its own purpose, so that the Gospels give different interpretations of what Jesus said and did. All the Gospels focus on the suffering of Christ in his trial and crucifixion (the Passion), giving only a brief account of the life and ministry that led up to it.

Along with the letters and the Gospels there is a history (Acts of the Apostles) of how the Gospel was taken into the Mediterranean world, and an interpretation of the meaning of that history written in the form of Jewish apocalyptic, known as The Book of Revelation.

The extraordinary historical fact of the New Testament is that it exists. Among all the many writings of the ancient world, the New Testament is unique: it contains lives and letters that resemble those written in the Greek world, and apocalyptic that is like other Jewish apocalyptic works. But each of the New Testament writings is completely different, because it is a consequence of the unique and utterly different life, and death, and life beyond death of Jesus.

Exactly the same is true of Jesus himself. In some ways he resembles other characters in the world of that time: he is not unlike a prophet, a wisdom teacher, a special messenger from God, a rain-maker and miracle-worker, a healer, a wandering ascetic, even a messiah. But in the end he is *different* from them all because those who met him realized that, in a unique way, he had brought the power of God into the life of the world through his own person. The writings of the New Testament are somewhat like other writings and yet are completely different because Jesus was somewhat like other people and yet was completely different. What made the difference?

It was the extraordinary impact that Jesus made on those who met him which continued after he had died. Through his crucifixion and resurrection, the power and consequence of God were no longer limited to those who happened to have met him in Galilee or Judaea: they were made universal – as he had intended. At the Last Supper before he died, he told his followers that all they had experienced of God through him would continue. He said this in an enacted sign, a prophetic action which was believed at that time to bring the future into being: he took bread to be his body, and wine to be the blood of the new Covenant: 'Remember, I am with you always, even to the end of the age.'

When they found all this to be true, they called him, not only Christos, but also the Son of God. The phrase 'the son of God' may mean simply 'one who obeys the calling of God'. But Jesus was called 'the Son of God' in a much stronger sense: one who is in a uniquely close relationship with God. They believed that this man, with whom they had lived and whom they knew so well, was God in their midst:

We declare to you what was from the beginning, what we have heard, what we have seen with our eyes, what we have looked at and touched with our hands, concerning the word of life – this life was revealed, and we have seen it and testify to it, and declare to you the eternal life that was with the Father and was revealed to us – we declare to you what we have seen and heard so that you also may have fellowship with us; and truly our fellowship is with the Father and with his Son Jesus Christ. (I *John* 1:1–3)

Some have thought that all this came much later in Christian belief – that an ordinary teacher and healer was gradually promoted until, as time passed, he became the Son of God. That is certainly wrong. The *earliest* writings of the New Testament give the highest status and titles to Jesus. They still call him by his human name, Jesus, but they claim that it is he who is 'a reflection of God's glory and the exact imprint of God's very being, who also sustains all things by his powerful word' (*Hebrews* 1:3). They believed that God had dwelt among them, full of grace and truth.

This belief led to the Christian understanding of God as Trinity, as absolutely and uniquely One, and yet as being a unity made up of the interrelatedness of the Father, Son and Holy Spirit, Creator, Redeemer and Sustainer of life. The Holy Spirit is God at work in the world in a way that Christians believe was set loose in a new way after the resurrection of Jesus.

The belief that God has been here on Earth, not in legend but in a historical life, totally changed the world. It is an extraordinary claim to make about a crucified man, and the history of the early Church shows the first Christians struggling to understand the breathtaking brilliance of what has happened.

Among them, Paul (a highly educated Jew first called Saul)

CHRISTIANITY   49

had a particularly clear insight. He had persecuted Christians as erring and subversive Jews. On a journey to Damascus, he had been practising, as did other Jews at the time, the visualization of the majesty of God through concentration on the 'chariot chapter' of the book of *Ezekiel* (ch.1), but in a stunning blow he felt that it was *Jesus* as God who was commissioning him to go to the rebellious house of Israel (*Ezekiel* 2:3) – and not just to Israel, but to the non-Jewish world as well.

Paul saw, as clearly as Jesus himself, that God had been in Christ healing and restoring the world, doing for humans what they cannot do for themselves, rescuing them from their fault and sin in order to make a new start. The cross demonstrates that God in Christ has faced the furthest limits of human wickedness, and has gone through that and the darkness of death into a new and risen life.

That life is now offered to all who want to make that new start. They experience it in vivid gifts of the Holy Spirit (God in action in the world) who transforms life into love. They enter into it through another enacted sign, that of baptism, which draws them into union with Christ through his death and resurrection. 'You are already dead,' Paul wrote to the Christians at Colossae (3:3), 'and your life lies hidden with Christ in God.' In Christian belief, this transfer from death to life is the free gift of God: it cannot be earned, it can only be received and entered into with gratitude and faith.

Immense issues faced Christians of the first five centuries as they tried to work all this out: how had it happened and what exactly did it mean? The major questions were:

- What is the nature of human fault, and how does the death of Jesus on the cross bring forgiveness and reconciliation to us?

Jesus certainly extended God's forgiveness to those whom he met, but how can that continue to happen after he is dead? Christians believe that forgiveness is extended through the cross which is understood as the act of God establishing that the gap between God and humans in their sinful rebellion has been closed. Consequently they can be once more at one with God. This is the belief known as the Atonement.

- How can the nature of God and human nature be combined in the one person of Jesus without the one being diminished and the other being overwhelmed and destroyed, so that Jesus as the Christ is the true reality of God united with a genuinely human life? That is the question of what is known as Christology.

- How can God be absolutely and uniquely one, and yet be Father, Son, and Holy Spirit? In other words, how can God be one reality (since God can only be whatever God is), and yet for that reality to have within itself relationships of love? Christians believe that the ways in which God is known as Creator, Redeemer, and Giver of the many gifts of spiritual life, reflect the fact that there is a relatedness within the being of God which is the Love 'that moves the stars' (Dante) and into which we are invited. As Augustine put it in the fifth century, when we come to understand that Holy Scripture is revealing a supreme love that is called God, 'then the Trinity begins to dawn on us a little, namely, the one who loves, the one who is loved, and love itself'. That is the belief in the Trinity.

Christians have never agreed on the precise definition of these basic beliefs – of Atonement, Christology/Incarnation, and Trinity – although they have agreed on the boundaries within which acceptable answers can be found. From the earliest days of the Church, Christians have been divided. The earliest dispute was whether new Christians must take on the laws of the Mosaic Covenant, as they must if 'Christianity' is a form of Judaism, or whether the New Covenant has set them free from the laws of the old.

The Church in the Roman Empire

That particular dispute (*Acts* 15) about whether new Christians should come under Jewish law, in which case they should be circumcised, was resolved with a compromise: they were to keep some basic (almost 'natural') laws, but otherwise they were free. That enabled Christians to take the Gospel (the good news) into the Mediterranean world, led by Paul who eventually reached Rome where, according to tradition, he was put to death during the persecution of Christians by the emperor Nero (64 CE).

As a small 'new religion' Christianity was no threat to the Empire. But the Empire was now vast. In order to secure allegiance and unity, vows and sacrifices were required of citizens to demonstrate their support of the emperors on whose favour and prosperity the Empire depended. Christians could not do this if it suggested that they were offering sacrifices to humans as though to God.

Christians who refused were liable to be imprisoned or killed – in the latter case, becoming, like Paul, martyrs (Gk., *martureo*, 'I bear witness'): martyrs were remembered and revered on the anniversary of their deaths, the lists of which are the beginning and first examples of the Christian calendar. Attacks on Christians were usually local and intermittent until the celebration of Rome's millennium in 248 when the Christian refusal to participate led to savage persecutions in 250 under the emperor Decius.

They became even more severe under Diocletian from 303 onward.

Far from destroying the Church, persecutions strengthened it. Tertullian (*c.*160–*c.*225) wrote: 'We grow just as much as we are cut down by you: the seed is the blood of the Christians' (often quoted as 'the blood of the martyrs is the seed of the Church'). Many even sought martyrdom since it seemed to promise a speedy access to heaven.

Through all this period, there were new divisions among Christians. One issue was whether those who had given way when threatened with punishment or martyrdom could be re-admitted to the Church. Rigorists like Novatian (d. 257/8) in Rome or Donatus (fourth century) in North Africa said that the lapsed (Lat., *lapsi*) could not be readmitted, or could only be re-admitted if they were baptized again. The Donatists continued in North Africa as a separate (schismatic) Church until the Muslim conquest of the region.

Another kind of division was created by those who followed a different interpretation of Jesus and of his relationship to God. Among these were the Gnostics (Gk., *gnosis*, 'knowledge') who developed several different systems of belief, ranging from philosophy to magic, claiming to hold secret knowledge only to be revealed to initiates. They believed that God is supreme and transcendent, far above the imperfections of creation. From God, a succession of agents emerges until one is powerful enough to create the world without involving God in creation. To have this knowledge (*gnosis*) is to realize how to find the spirit of God within the body and how to release it from the body to return to the pure spirit of God.

For Gnostics it was impossible to think of God involved in the sordid details of the world and of human life, so that Jesus, far from being the Incarnation of God, could only be one of the agents of God teaching the way of escape from the earthly body. He was not even a real human being, but only the appearance of one, so that he did not really suffer or die: from the Greek *dokeo*, 'I seem', this view is known as Docetism, and it survived in Arabia as the Christianity which Muhammad encountered.

Of the many Gnostic movements, only the Mandeans of Iraq survive, though many more recent cults claim to be the successors of the Gnostics. In the first three centuries, they were a serious alternative and challenge to Christians who held that the Incarnation was a non-negotiable belief.

The uncertain status of Christians began to change after the death of Diocletian. Because the Empire had become unwieldy, he divided it for the purposes of government between West and East, with himself ruling in the West. In 306, Constantine (d. 337) was proclaimed emperor by the army in the West, but there were other claimants as well. At the battle of Milvian Bridge (near Rome) in 312, Constantine defeated his last rival, Maxentius. Perhaps under the influence of his Christian mother, perhaps under the influence of a dream (of a cross and the words, 'In this sign conqueror'), he put on his standards the Greek letters χρ (an abbreviation of the word Christos) and won the battle.

It was a turning-point in Christian history. It meant that Christianity was now included in the toleration for all cults, and it meant also that Christians could play an increasing part in the government and administration of the Empire. It was a process that culminated in the Theodosian Code. This is a collection of Roman imperial constitutions from the time of Constantine to Theodosius II (401–50), assembled between 429 and 435. Book 16 deals with religious matters, banning paganism, penalizing heretics and laying down how Church and State should be related.

By the fifth century, tribes from the borders of the Western Empire began to assert their power. They were called, dismissively, 'barbarians' (country-bumpkins), but in fact they were already Romanized and Christianized. In 410 Alaric, a Visigoth who had previously served the Empire briefly, took over Rome – later, but inaccurately, called 'the sack of Rome'. Further attacks were made by Attila the Hun (d. 453), and by Gaiseric the Vandal after whom, in 476, Rome was taken over by rulers once regarded as barbarians.

Throughout this period, Christians responded in four ways that changed the Christian world: by canon, creed, councils and Church organization.

To try to answer the major questions summarized above, and in particular to deal with alternative interpretations of Jesus, it became important to identify the writings that have authority for all Christians – in other words, to agree on which writings should belong to the New Testament in addition to the Old (though some, like Marcion, (d. 160), rejected the Old Testament altogether). A Canon (Gk., *kanon*, 'rule') was finally agreed by the end of the fourth century.

Creeds were originally short statements of belief recited by those becoming Christians at their baptism. They were called 'symbols' (Lat., *symbolum*, 'token', 'pledge'), a word used also for a password in the Roman army. An example is the so-called Apostles Creed (though it does not go back to the Apostles) of the second century:

I believe in God, the Father Almighty, creator of heaven and earth. I believe in Jesus Christ, his only Son, Lord. He was conceived by the power of the Holy Spirit and born of the Virgin Mary. He suffered under Pontius Pilate, was crucified, died, and was buried. He descended to the dead. On the third day he rose again. He ascended into heaven, and is seated at the right hand of the Father. He will come again to judge the living and the dead. I believe in the Holy Spirit, the holy catholic Church, the communion of saints, the forgiveness of sins, the resurrection of the body, and the life everlasting.

Later creeds tried to find common ground between Christians disagreeing on the fundamental questions summarized earlier. Of those creeds, a major example is the so-called Nicene Creed from the fourth/fifth century (named after the Council of Nicaea although in its present form it does not come from that Council). It remains a summary of basic Christian belief accepted by all the Churches. Even so, some Churches interpreted the Nicene Creed differently, for example, the Oriental Orthodox Churches, including the Syrian, Coptic, Ethiopian and Armenian.

Councils seeking common belief were brought together, first by Constantine in 325 at Nicaea, later by the Church – of which the Council of Chalcedon (451) drew up a statement of faith (the Chalcedonian Definition) in which Christ is acknowledged 'in two natures . . . concurring into one person and one subsistence'. This is widely accepted as the basis of Christian belief, although the Oriental Orthodox Churches have never accepted it.

The first seven councils held before the division of the Church between East and West are known as the Ecumenical Councils and have authority for all the Churches in Christian belief and practice. Roman Catholics have separated and held fourteen further Councils which they regard as Ecumenical, the last three being Trent (1545–63), Vatican I (1869–70) and Vatican II (1962–5).

The separation between Roman Catholics and other

Christians goes back to the fourth response to the threats and challenges in the early Church, the organization of the Church. In the New Testament, Christians are described as the Body of Christ, with Christ as the head and all other parts being equally important in what they do. By the end of the first century, experience of the ways in which the Roman Empire and its army exercised authority led to the metaphor being changed: the Body became hierarchical, with bishops as the head, priests as the executive officers, and lay people as the foot soldiers. Gradually, the Bishop of Rome began to claim an even higher authority over all other bishops, so that, whereas in the early centuries any Bishop might be called *pappas*, *papa*, father (as the Bishop of Alexandria still is), by the sixth century the title was claimed by the Bishop of Rome alone – hence 'papacy' and 'pope'. However, this assumption of supreme authority was not accepted by all Christians, and the first of two massive divisions among Christians opened up.

The Orthodox Church

The first of these major splits followed Diocletian's division of the empire between East and West. When he did that, he was recognizing not only the complexity of governing such a vast territory, but also the importance of the Eastern territories. In 330, Constantine renamed the ancient city of Byzantium Constantinople (now Istanbul) and called it 'the New Rome', the capital of the Eastern (Byzantine) empire.

The Church in the East was made up of areas under Patriarchs, of which the Patriarch of Constantinople was the senior, with those of Alexandria, Antioch and Jerusalem coming next (this being recognized at Chalcedon in 451). Those and the other

Patriarchates in the East are all independent: none of them has claimed (or recognized in the case of the Bishop of Rome) authority over the others. Christianity in the East is known as Orthodox Christianity, but the independence of its parts is recognized through names such as Greek Orthodox, Russian Orthodox, and so on. They may prefer, though, to be known simply as the Orthodox Church, since the addition of 'Greek' or 'Russian' might imply that they are different churches

The relative independence of the Eastern Empire from the West became all the more important in the fifth century when Rome was attacked by the Visigoths under Alaric (who captured Rome in 410), by Attila the Hun (d. 453), and by Gaiseric the Vandal after whom, in 476, Rome was taken over by barbarian rulers. Increasingly, the Popes in Rome took on a political role to protect the interests of the Church.

The Byzantine Empire resisted the Goths in a long war (537–53), and began to extend its outreach to the north, establishing Churches throughout the Balkans and in Russia where, in 988, Vladimir of Kiev declared that Greek Christianity was to be the faith of the realm. In the fourteenth century, leadership moved from Kiev to Moscow, and independence from Greek Orthodoxy was established.

The division of the Roman Empire into East and West was reflected in increasing tension between those who accepted the judicial authority of the Bishop of Rome (i.e., Pope) and those who did not. For 600 years after the fall of Rome, relations between the Orthodox East and Rome grew increasingly bitter until in 1054 each side issued an anathema (a formal statement of exclusion from the Church) against the other. The Council of Florence (1438–45) achieved a brief reunion which lapsed when the Muslims captured Constantinople in 1453. The anathemas were withdrawn in 1965, but the separation between East and West continues.

The separation was powerfully reinforced when the Fourth Crusade turned aside from attacking infidels and sacked Constantinople in 1204 in an attempt to reunify West and East. Its main effect was to weaken resistance to the Muslims who captured Constantinople in 1453. Eastern Orthodoxy continued, but very much under the oversight of the Ottoman Empire. Long memories of all this contribute to the difficulties involved in the reunification of Cyprus and in the entry of Turkey to the European Union.

The beliefs of Eastern Orthodoxy are not dramatically different from those of Christians in the West, but there are differences of emphasis. From as early as the fourth century, Greek theologians were clear that 'what God is' cannot possibly be known, because God cannot be produced as an object like other objects in the universe, able to be described. We can only say 'what God is not' (the *via negativa*): God is not five feet tall and rather round. The recognition that no one can speak positively about 'what God is like' is known as 'apophatic theology' (from the Greek *apophatikos*, 'negative'). Gregory of Nyssa (one of three great theologians of the fourth century who are known from their place of origin as the Cappadocian Fathers) wrote:

God cannot be seen, since what we seek is beyond all knowledge, being wholly concealed in a cloud of incomprehensibility. Therefore St John . . . says that no one has seen God at any time [*I John* 1.18], meaning by this negation that the knowledge of the divine nature is impossible not only for humans but for every created intellect.

Of course it is possible to say a great deal about God on the basis of Scripture (including, therefore, the Incarnation where, in Christian belief, God is translated into the language of human life) and on the basis of the effects of God in creation. Those are often referred to as the Book of Nature and the Book of Revelation. Those ways of speaking positively are known as 'kataphatic theology', and on that basis it is possible to respond to the invitation of God to enter into a union with God of complete and perfect love, in prayer, worship and contemplation.

The belief that there is in human nature a profound restlessness that seeks to find enduring truth beyond the passing fashions and philosophies of the day was expressed searchingly by Augustine (354–430) in *The Confessions*. In that work, Augustine reflected on the way in which God had worked in and through his life even when he had been living in ways far removed from God. He came to realize that the fundamental issue facing all people is that of the human will and desire: what do I truly desire above all else? If it is God, then God is the only answer. 'My heart is restless,' he wrote, 'until it finds its rest in God.' It is a belief that completely changes the possibility and the direction of human life. So he wrote (*Understanding the Psalms*, 64:3): 'Our yearning sees far off the land we seek, it throws out hope as an anchor that pulls us toward that shore.'

This quest for God led increasingly to people leaving the world and going into the desert, as Jesus had done at the beginning of his ministry, to struggle against all that distracts from devotion to God. Antony had withdrawn in this way in *c.*285, and others had joined him, thus forming small communities. The Desert Fathers and Desert Mothers are the beginning of Christian monasticism.

Monasticism became immensely important in both the East

and West. In the West, large Orders of monks and nuns were organized from the tenth century onward, but in Orthodoxy each monastery is self-governing under its own abbot. To govern these communities, another Cappadocian Father, Basil, wrote two Rules which remain a guide to the present day. A major centre of Orthodox monasticism is the Holy Mountain, a peninsula in north-east Greece which leads at its end to Mount Athos. Here the Lavra was founded in 961/2 as a Coenobitic (Gk., 'living in community') monastery, although there are hermits as well.

This belief that life should be devoted to God issues also in the rich worship and liturgies of the Orthodox Church. At the same time, prayer can be extremely simple and quiet. Gregory Palamas (d. 1359) advocated 'the Jesus Prayer' (the constant repetition of 'Lord Jesus Christ, Son of God, have mercy on me, a humble sinner'). Because this kind of prayer creates quiet (Gk., *hesuchia*) concentration on God, it is known as Hesychastic prayer.

The same desire for worship created icons (Gk., *eikon*, 'image'). These are pictures, painted under careful rules, of Christian themes and people ranging from God, Christ and Mary to the saints. The more the apophatic way was emphasized, the more important icons became, because they opened the way to the realities of God and spirit which cannot be seen. Icons are *never* worshipped: they are the means through which worship becomes possible.

Even so there were those who thought that the icons *were* being worshipped, and in two periods (known as the Iconoclastic Controversies), 726–87 and 813–43, icons were banished and destroyed. When the Patriarch Methodios restored the icons in 843, a great feast was held to mark the victory of the icons, now celebrated each year as the Feast of Orthodoxy.

Icons and worship have also been prominent in Russian

Orthodoxy, where spiritual guides or directors became equally important. They are called *startsi* (sing., Staretz, the Russian translation of the Greek *geron*, 'elder'). When Paissy Velichovsky (1722–94) led a great revival of religion in the eighteenth century, he emphasized continual prayer and obedience to a Staretz, and some, famed for their holiness, such as Seraphim of Sarov (1759–1833) and Amvrosy of Optina (1812–91) were eagerly sought out. Amvrosy became the model for Zossima in Dostoevsky's novel *The Brothers Karamazov* (1880).

When Constantinople fell in 1453, Moscow's claim to be 'the Third Rome' was greatly enhanced, and the Patriarchate was established in 1589. Russian rulers kept a cautious eye on the Church, not wanting to concede too much independent power to it. In 1727, Peter the Great abolished the Patriarchate and set up a Holy Synod to rule the Church – whose twelve members he appointed.

The Patriarchate was re-established in 1917 in the first days of the Revolution, but after the October Revolution the position of the Church became extremely precarious. As a result, the Metropolitan Sergius signed an agreement in 1927: in return for supporting the State, the Church was given a recognized legal status. That compromise, resented and rejected by those who formed the Russian Church in Exile, did not stop the savage persecutions of Stalin. There was relief during the Second World War, when the Russian Orthodox Church did much to inspire resistance to the Nazi invasion, but attacks on the Church were resumed under Kruschev between 1959 and 1964.

The long experience of suffering among the Russian Orthodox has produced people of faithful endurance and works of penetrating power – for example, *Creative Suffering* (1940) by Iulia de Beausobre, who, from her experience of imprisonment in the

Lubyanka prison and in a labour camp, wrote *The Woman Who Could Not Die* (1938). Nor could the Church. Persecution could no more destroy Christianity in the Soviet Union than it could in the Roman Empire. In the spirit of Jesus who prayed on the Cross for those who were crucifying him, 'Father, forgive them, they know not what they do', Iulia de Beausobre wrote of her jailors:

> The jailors, the examining officers, and the even more sinister men of the Kremlin who are at the bottom of all this, they come nearer . . . Why this strange nearness to me, who belong to death, of them who belong to life? I do not know. And when at night I am a flame burning on an altar to the Christ, I pray for them. I pray that vision, truth and peace may come to them too one day. Even to those of them who do not know what they are doing.

The Western Church

Meanwhile the Church in the West had been following its own history. When Alaric seized Rome in 410, it felt to many like the end of the world. Less than a hundred years before, Constantine had begun the process of integrating Christianity into the Empire. Why, then, had God allowed its capital to fall?

One answer was given by Augustine (354–430), Bishop of Hippo. In *The City of God*, he argued that good and evil grow entangled together in the world like the wheat and weeds of Jesus' parable (*Matthew* 13:24–30). The final judgement between them lies with God: meanwhile, it is important simply to keep faith.

But that left Augustine with the question, where does evil come from? Since all creation is good (*Genesis* 1:31), evil can only be the absence of good (*privatio boni*). Humans are born into that defective condition known as 'original sin'. This is a radical fault (Lat., *radix*, 'root') not chosen by anybody, much as we might say that people are born into a particular family and society, with a particular genetic inheritance, none of which they chose, but all of which affect their lives.

In that sense, Augustine could say that all humans in any scale of justice would have to be found guilty: people are *massa damnata*, all to be condemned. But Augustine followed Paul in saying that God through the death of Christ has simply scrapped the charge and the condemnation: people are justified (i.e., are held to have no charge hanging over them) by faith in God's free gift or grace.

This belief changed the world entirely, since it meant that Christians were urgent to share this good news with others. It also meant that they could accept with trust, not only the attacks on Rome by Huns and Vandals, but those of Saxons on England in the fifth century, and of Franks on France, Germany and Spain.

For the next 600 years the contest for Europe continued. Some invaders were converted, but they in turn were then threatened. Thus many Saxons had become Christians by 663, but within a hundred years the pagan Vikings were raiding England and occupying, not only England, but also northern France and Sicily. In England, not much was left beyond Wessex where Alfred became king in 871. Remembered now for his burning of the cakes, his renewal of Christianity went far beyond dreams: apart from military resistance, he committed himself to education through the founding of schools and monasteries.

Monasteries played a key part in the resistance to pagan conquests. They were often plundered and destroyed, but at their best, they were lights of learning and devotion in what are popularly (but as a generalization inaccurately) called 'the Dark Ages'.

Monasticism in the East, as we have seen, had begun as an austere detachment from the world in order to be devoted only to God. Some, known as Stylites (Gk., *stulos*, 'pillar') had lived on pillars raised above the ground. This rigorous monasticism passed into Celtic Christianity, associated with the names of Patrick and Columba in Ireland and in Scotland, where the monastery of Iona was founded in 563.

In Celtic Christianity, the battle against evil and danger was fierce: monks stood in icy streams to pray and built their huts in places remote from other humans. God was such a powerful presence to them especially through the natural world, that barbarian invasions were trivial in comparison.

This, however, was too rigorous for all, and Benedict (c.480–550), who founded Monte Cassino in about 520, wrote a Rule for monks ('a little rule for beginners') to help them live their lives more gently in the constant presence and praise of God. On this Rule are based, not only the Benedictines, but other great monastic Orders like the Carthusians and the Cistercians.

From Scotland and Ireland in the north, and from Italy in the south, monks moved out to win Europe for Christianity. When those from the south (such as Augustine of Canterbury, d. c.604–9) met those from the north (such as Aidan, d. 651) they realized how different Celtic and Italian Christians were in their practices, even with different dates for Easter. Gradually agreements were worked out, laying the foundations for the great seventh-century monasteries of north-east England at Lindisfarne, Wearmouth and Jarrow. All this produced a new form of monasticism which made possible the conversion of Europe, and which still continues.

Even so, Christianity in Europe was precarious: the Viking raids, for example, destroyed Lindisfarne in 793 and 875, Wearmouth and Jarrow between 867 and 870. However, the campaigns of Charlemagne (c.742–814) and his reforms of government and education laid the foundations for a Christian Europe, and by the eleventh century (the Normans invaded England in 1066), most of Western Europe was sufficiently Christian to undertake its own campaigns against unbelievers (infidels, Lat., *infidelis*) on its boundaries.

These campaigns were eventually known as Crusades, probably from the Crux (Lat., 'Cross') worn as a symbol. The Northern Crusades reached into Scandinavia, the Eastern Crusades (1095–1291) had a particular aim to recover the Holy Land and Jerusalem from their capture by the Muslims.

The first Eastern Crusade was initiated when the Seljuk Turks defeated the Byzantines at the battle of Manzikert in 1071. The Byzantines appealed for help, and Pope Urban II (c.1035–99) proclaimed the first Crusade in 1095. The Crusade moved on to the Holy Land, capturing Jerusalem in 1099.

Crusader territories on the eastern edge of the Mediterranean were no threat to the Muslims, and in 1187 Salah udDin (Saladin, 1169–93) recaptured Jerusalem. The fourth Crusade (1202) set out to recover Jerusalem, but it first attacked Constantinople in order to establish a Latin empire in the East. This briefly reunited the Western and Eastern churches, but actually increased hostility and weakened the East until Constantinople fell to the Muslims in 1453. In the end, the Crusades gained little beyond the recovery of Sicily and Cyprus.

The Crusades were a religious commitment, even though politics and economics were paramount. Early Crusaders described themselves as being on 'a pilgrimage' (*peregrinatio*), and the soldiers were 'the army of Christ' (*militia Christi*, from whom the Knights Templar are descended). Crusaders were promised remission of penances for sins already committed.

The Crusades and the beliefs about them have totally changed the world. The word 'crusade' is now used of any urgent or energetic campaign, but it has remained also a word and a concept to summarize any conflict between religions. In particular, many Muslims continue to see Western politics and armies as a continuation of the Crusades.

The period of the Crusades (1095–1291) was also the beginning of a long period during which Christianity in the West was consolidated. Christians began to build – literally in the case of churches, cathedrals, abbeys and monasteries, but metaphorically also as they founded universities (Paris and Oxford late twelfth century, Cambridge early thirteenth) and started to construct a more systematic understanding of Christian faith.

Above all, Thomas Aquinas (*c.*1225–74), a Dominican, showed the benefits of the new universities (he arrived in Paris in 1246) and of the way in which in Muslim lands Greek philosophy, especially Aristotle, had been recovered and transmitted into the West. Aquinas wrote (among many other works) two great summaries of Christian faith, of which the *Summa Theologiae* became the foundation of Christian theology in the West for many centuries, as it remains for some Christians down to the present day.

Whereas Augustine and others had started with God's self-revelation in Scripture, Aquinas started with God's self-revelation in nature and creation. From this, he argued, reason can know *that* God is (and he offered Five Ways, *Quinque Viae*, to show this). But to know *what* God is requires Scripture. The supreme point is not to write good theology, because God is not the conclusion to an argument, but to be drawn in worship, prayer and service to God who is love, and to rest there for ever.

Ordinary people, of course, could not understand Aquinas – few of them could even read. Wall paintings and stained-glass windows in churches became their books, and the mystery and morality plays of Coventry and York and other large centres made vivid the story of their salvation.

The faith was also taught through preaching and sermons, and Dominic (c.1172–1221) founded the Order of Preachers (the Dominicans) in 1215 for that purpose. Dominic longed to spread the gospel and was committed to humility and rigorous poverty. The outreach to the poor and to those outside society was also fundamental for Francis (1181/2–1226). Francis stripped himself, literally, of everything in order to give himself to the service and praise of God in the poor and in all works of nature: 'For what are God's servants but his minstrels, whose task is to strengthen people and move them to the joys of the spirit?' The followers of both are called Friars (brothers).

The more the Church rebuilt itself, the more urgent it became to achieve some kind of agreement, not just over Christian belief, but over Christian practice as well. Kings or other rulers might wish to follow their own customs, and certainly might not wish to submit to the authority of the Bishop of Rome (i.e., the Pope). Attempts were therefore made to standardize Church discipline, founded on the twelfth-century Decretals of Gratian, the beginning of agreed Canon Law.

The Reformations

That, however, did not in itself resolve the issue of where obedience and authority lie in the Church, and as early as the fourteenth century signs of serious division in the Church began to emerge. Popes in Rome claimed that their authority rested on the statement of Jesus (*Matthew* 16:18) that he was founding his Church on the rock (Gk., *petra*) of Peter, along with the tradition that Peter was the first Bishop of Rome and had been martyred there. Orthodox Christians may respect the bishops of Rome, but they have never accepted their authority to determine all matters in all parts of the Church.

The extent of the Pope's authority was also contested in the West by Councils and by individual territories seeking to limit Papal power. An early example was the Investiture Controversy (1076–1122): who has the right to invest bishops and abbots with the symbols of the office, the king (or emperor) or Pope? In England, the kings and the archbishops of Canterbury worked out a way of coexisting until Thomas Becket (*c*.1120–70) insisted on the authority of the Pope over the king, and as 'that turbulent priest' was murdered in Canterbury Cathedral in 1170.

The issue of authority carried with it equally important issues of what exactly the Pope was authorizing – or demanding. Western Christianity had become a religion in which people escaped hellfire by living good lives, and, if they failed, by confessing their sins and doing penances, often in public. They could call on Mary the Mother of God and on the saints in heaven to help them, and if they could earn or pay for indulgences which draw on the merits of the saints, they could escape the due penalties of their sins. All this could extend beyond death, because after death those who still have to make expiation for outstanding sins could do so in Purgatory.

Purgatory is the belief that the dead before they enter heaven must be 'purged' from the penalty for all outstanding sins. However, they can be helped by the living who pray for them and earn indulgences for them. Many left money for priests to say masses for their souls in special chapels known as Chantries. Indulgences could also be bought from professional 'pardoners', and from bequests to churches and monasteries, many of which became extremely wealthy.

In these ways, Christianity seemed to have become 'a cult of the living in the service of the dead'. Some began to question whether this was the faith intended by Jesus. In England, John Wycliffe (c.1329–84), followed by John Huss (c.1372–1415) in Bohemia, raised questions, not only about authority in the Church, but also about some of the recently established beliefs. For example, Jesus had intended to be present with his disciples, through the enacted signs of bread and wine, as often as they remember him in this way. But how is he present? Using Aristotle, it was argued (by 1215) that the outward appearance (the accidents) of bread and wine remain but that the underlying substance (what is really there) is the body and blood – hence 'the real presence', a belief known as transubstantiation. Wycliffe among many others questioned whether Greek philosophy is the true way to understand how Jesus reaches his followers in the sacrament.

Wycliffe also strongly advocated the translation of Scripture from the universal Latin (the Vulgate) into English and other languages, holding that the Bible is the final authority in belief and practice. The Papal Church saw the threat, and the Council of Oxford (1407) prohibited any new translations or the use of any translation made 'in the times of John Wycliffe or since'.

It was too late. The invention of the printing press made wide circulation possible of Tyndale's translation of the New Testament (the basis of the Authorized Version) which appeared in 1525, and of Coverdale's 'Great Bible' which was ordered to be put in all churches in 1539. The Bible was no longer mediated through the priests who alone could read Latin: it was now an open book for all who could read. They could see, for example, that Purgatory is not described in the Bible.

Printing also made possible the rapid circulation of books and pamphlets raising searching questions about Christian belief and practice far beyond those of Wycliffe and Huss. The intention was not to divide the Church, only to reform it. Desiderius Erasmus (c.1466–1536) wrote fiercely against corruption and error in the Church without intending to break from Rome. The same was true initially of Martin Luther (1483–1546), and yet with him the break became inevitable.

Luther was an Augustinian friar who believed that Christianity under the Popes was wrong to have turned the faith into a kind of transaction through which the favour and forgiveness of God could be earned by good works or bought through the purchase of indulgences: 'So soon as coin in coffer rings, The soul from Purgatory springs.'

Luther went back to Scripture, and there found (as had Augustine before him) that salvation cannot be earned: it can only be received as a free and unmerited gift from God. Relying, therefore, on Scripture alone (*sola scriptura*) and not on teachings of the Church added on through the centuries, Luther insisted that people are 'justified' (i.e., cleared by God of all charges) by grace alone (*sola gratia*) to which humans respond by faith alone (*sola fide*). He circulated 95 Theses in 1517 questioning indulgences, but these were less important in effecting change than his sermons and books containing other arguments.

These were beliefs that changed Western Christianity for ever. In 1521 Luther was placed under a ban and threatened with excommunication. He was saved and smuggled into exile by

Friedrich, Elector of Saxony, and in this, as also in other reformations of the Church, the old and unresolved issue of authority between rulers and the Pope became vital. Rulers in Europe were inclined to say *cuius regio, eius religio* ('whose is the region, his is the religion'), a summary of the Peace of Augsburg in 1555, whereby rulers decided whether the religion of their own domain should be Roman Catholic or Lutheran.

Luther's protest led to Lutheran Churches which are formed on the basis of Luther's teaching, especially as that was summarized in *The Book of Concord* (1580). The emphasis is on Scripture as the sole rule of faith, and on the lost condition of human beings who cannot please God by human effort or moral achievements. Only by God's act of grace can humans be saved. Luther had not regarded parishes becoming Lutheran as a new Church, but as the Church in its reformed state, and the Augsburg Confession of 1530, a fundamental statement of Lutheran doctrine, was drawn up to show this. The only major break among Lutherans was that of the Moravian (or Bohemian) Brethren (Die Brüdergemeine), but they in any case were a continuation from the reforming vision of John Huss.

Luther was by no means the only Reformer. When Luther was in prison or away, his reformation was led by Philipp Melanchthon (1497–1560), who did much to take the Lutheran reform of the Church to ordinary people throughout the land. In Switzerland, Ulrich Zwingli (1484–1531) allowed the voice of the people to guide an entirely different reformation which repudiated transubstantiation and abolished the Mass in Zurich in 1525, and secularized monasteries and convents to fund the community. Attempts to draw Luther and Zwingli together in 1529 failed.

Different again was John Calvin (1509–64) in Geneva who denounced the religion of Rome as a legal tyranny and as entirely false when judged by the New Testament and by the way in which the early Church was organized. Bishops and priests had been a late development, and he replaced them with elders and deacons. In 1559 he published *The Institutes of the Christian Religion*, which begins in agreement with Aquinas that there can be a natural knowledge of God, but then argues that such knowledge only shows how far we are from living on the basis of that knowledge, and how useless it is to save us. Salvation is a consequence of God's unearned grace, and the Bible alone is the authority in living and reforming one's life.

The Reformed Church is derived from the reconciliation between Calvinists and Zwinglians in 1548. The tension between strict adherence to the teachings of Calvin and insistence on independence from state or other control led to a number of so-called Free Churches, including the Wee Frees of Scotland who refused to join the reunion of Free Churches in Scotland in 1900. Reformed Churches tend to identify with the countries in which they follow their independent life, as in Scotland, or in the Dutch Reformed Church (Hervomde Kerke), formed at the Synod of Dort (1618–19) with Calvinist theology and Presbyterian government.

Calvinism was taken to Scotland by John Knox (1505–72), and there became the foundation of Presbyterian Christianity in which congregations, and not a Pope, are responsible for faith and practice. Elders (Gk., *presbuteroi*) govern the Church in the New Testament, so that Presbyterians claim to be scriptural as well as sensitive to the necessity that the Church is always in need of reformation, a belief known as *semper reformanda*, 'always needing to be reformed'. Presbyterian Churches are Reformed in doctrine and Presbyterian in character.

Different again are the Baptists who are derived from the

Anabaptists ('re-baptizers') of the reformation who insisted that only believers can be baptized after personal confession of faith. Other Christians believe that baptism is the free gift of God which does not depend on individual response – hence the possibility of infant baptism.

In England, the reformation took a different form. The initial desire was more like that of Erasmus, to reform the Church without breaking from its beliefs. But when the request of Henry VIII (1491–1547) to annul his marriage with Catherine of Aragon was refused, the old issue of 'whose authority prevails?' came up once more. He repudiated Roman canon law and ultimately the Papacy itself. Key figures, especially Thomas Cranmer (1489–1556) and Thomas Cromwell (c.1485–1540), steered a largely reluctant king toward reform of abuses (especially in the dissolution of the monasteries), to a restatement of some teachings, and to ordering that a Bible in English should be placed in every Church (1539). But the Church in England remained Catholic in outlook while also reformed.

Henry's successor, Edward VI, took the Church much further in the direction of the continental reformations, while his successor Mary tried to return the Church to obedience to Rome. Each side in turn pursued the other in horrific persecutions, of which Roman Catholics commemorate their victims as 'the English martyrs'. When Elizabeth I (1533–1603) came to the throne, she set out to find a middle way (Latin, *via media*, a name often given to the Anglican Church) between the extremists on each side. The Elizabethan settlement was, in those violent times, an extraordinary achievement which eventually changed England into a society where some degree of inclusiveness and toleration could be attempted, even if not always achieved.

Rome and the Popes

From that brief summary we can begin to see why there was no single 'Reformation' but, rather, many attempts to reform different aspects of the Church in different ways. Attempts were made to heal the divisions, but there were too many different reformations for any single solution to be found. At the Council of Ratisbon (1541), an unsuccessful attempt was made to heal the divisions in the Western Church. Combined with politics, the divisions soon developed into conflict, either in the form of 'the wars of religion' or in the persecution of one side by another. Dean Swift famously observed (1714), 'We have just enough religion to make us hate, but not enough to make us love one another.'

The Wars of Religion (1500–1648) were often political campaigns to determine whether Protestants or Roman Catholics were to be the dominant faith in any particular country. The fourth of nine such wars in France included the St Bartholomew's Day massacre (1572) of Huguenots (French Protestants) by Roman Catholics. The power of Spain was repulsed from the Netherlands and frustrated by the defeat of the Spanish Armada against England in 1588. The final series of wars, the Thirty Years War (1618–48), resisted the ambitions of the Holy Roman Empire and drew in almost all the European states. The Wars of Religion ended with the Peace of Westphalia, but that peace did not reconcile Protestants and Roman Catholics, nor did it reconcile Protestants to each other.

Even if the initial aim was to reform and not to divide the Church, many of the issues, especially those to do with authority (for example, does it rest finally with the Pope or with Scripture?), were so serious that the break from Rome became inevitable. On the Reformation monument in Geneva are the words, 'One man with God is always in the majority.' For Rome that leads to chaos, but Rome did accept that some criticisms of the protesters (i.e., Protestants) were right (Erasmus said, 'I have a Catholic soul but a Lutheran stomach'), so its own process of reform and self-definition began.

This brought into being the Council of Trent, which met in three sessions between 1545 and 1563. It clarified Roman Catholic beliefs on disputed questions and reasserted traditional teaching on indulgences, Purgatory and the veneration of saints. It also authorized a new missal (the form and directions for celebrating the Mass, through which, in Roman Catholic belief, the sacrifice of Christ is made present) and office book (the form of the official daily prayers). This Latin missal is known as the Tridentine (of Trent) Mass.

The Council of Trent had been opposed by some on the grounds that it might suggest that the Council had more authority than a Pope. That was an old issue going back to the Conciliar controversy of the fourteenth and fifteenth centuries: the possibility of a heretical Pope suggested to some that the general Council of the College of Cardinals (the Sacred College of those appointed by the Pope to help him govern the Church) might have ultimate authority, but this was condemned by Pius II (1405–64). In fact, Trent greatly strengthened the position of the Pope and opened the way to a belief that Christians and the Church are best protected from error by a strong centralized authority in the Vatican under the Pope who is 'the Vicar of Christ on earth'.

An immediate result of this was the revival of the Inquisition. This body to protect believers from error and heresy goes back to the various Inquisitions first established formally by Pope Lucius

III in 1184 under individual Bishops. These proved ineffective, especially in dealing with the Cathars (Gk., *katharos*, 'pure') who were dissenters from the Church in the twelfth and thirteenth centuries. They claimed to be restoring the 'pure' original Church, and they seemed, like the Gnostics, to understand life as a dualistic struggle between good and evil.

Pope Gregory IX, therefore, appointed full-time Papal Inquisitors drawn mainly from Dominicans and Franciscans. They had no powers of punishment themselves, but simply handed convicted offenders over to the secular authorities, who might execute them or burn them at the stake – though this was not common. In 1252, Innocent IV gave permission for Inquisitors to use torture.

The Spanish and Portuguese Inquisition took on a more independent form, being particularly concerned with the genuineness of the faith of forcibly converted Jews and Muslims. Its severity became notorious, although still the actual burning of the condemned at the stake, after a public ceremony of condemnation called *auto-da-fé*, was done by the secular power.

The medieval Inquisition declined in the fifteenth century, only to be revived by Pope Paul III in 1542 as the Congregation of the Holy Office. In 1965, Paul VI charged it with the duty of promoting the faith as well as protecting faith and morals, and it is now called the Congregation of the Doctrine of the Faith. It continues the task of condemning and controlling those teachers in the Church who express beliefs deemed to be unorthodox. Under Cardinal Ratzinger, who in 2005 became Pope Benedict XVI, it operated secretively in ways that ensured the condemnation of those accused. In this way an attempt is made to secure conformity of beliefs. It is a fundamental Christian belief that freedom of conscience is paramount, but among those recognized by the Vatican as teachers and the like, conscience must be informed by its own teaching in order to protect the Church from error.

The concern of the Council of Trent to renew the Church was by no means confined to the Council. Already a new confidence had led to the reform of old religious Orders and the founding of new ones. In Spain, Teresa (1515–82) and John of the Cross (1542–91) showed how the Carmelite life could be lived, not in the lax way criticized by Protestant reformers, but in an intense union with God. It led Teresa into the kind of ecstasy portrayed memorably by the sculptor Bernini, and it led John into the exploration of the spiritual life and to movingly beautiful poetry expressing its inner meaning.

Among the new Orders was the Society of Jesus, whose members are known as Jesuits. It was founded in Spain by Inigo of Loyola (Lat., Ignatius). He went to Manresa to live in poverty and there his commitment to God was confirmed in a vision. He wrote what he had learned at Manresa in *The Spiritual Exercises*, a guided way of prayer and discernment used increasingly outside the Order. The Order was recognized by the Pope in 1540, and Jesuits, in addition to the three vows of poverty, chastity and obedience, make a fourth vow of obedience to the Pope. Jesuits will go to any place where God's glory can be proclaimed.

As a result, they were prominent in taking the Gospel to all parts of the world, immersing themselves in the culture and life-styles of the people they met. This was opposed by those who felt that faith and practice must conform to Papal (i.e., European) practice. In India, Japan and China, European rites were imposed, and in South America the Jesuit defence of indigenous peoples was overwhelmed by political agreements with Spain and Portugal. Hostility led to the Jesuits being banned for forty years

(1773–1814), but they survived with the same commitment to prayer, teaching and the poor.

By the end of the eighteenth century, opposition to the Papacy (and to Christianity in general) became much more than a questioning of beliefs. The French Revolution (1787–99) made its declaration of 'The Rights of Man' in 1789, nationalized the lands of the Roman Catholic Church in 1790, and reorganized the Church under French authority. This was condemned by Pope Pius VI in 1791 and resisted by many Roman Catholics in France, leading to attacks on the clergy. Although the conflict was ended by Napoleon's Concordat of 1801, the French had shown how political systems and states could free themselves from the authority and interference of Rome.

This strengthened the necessity, going back to the fifth century, for the Vatican to operate as an independent political state. This was eventually recognized in the Lateran Pacts which the Vatican made in 1929 with the Fascist dictator Benito Mussolini (1883–1945). Since then, the Vatican City State has participated in many intergovernmental and non-governmental organizations, although the revision of the Lateran Accords in 1984 abrogated the first article of the Treaty which had made Catholicism 'the only religion of the [Italian] state'.

The steady centralization of authority in the Roman Catholic Church was not unopposed. In France especially there was a long tradition of independence going back to the thirteenth century, when claims were made for the privileges of the Church in Gaul (*libertés de l'Église gallicane*, hence the name for this movement 'Gallicanism'). The constitutional decisions of the Council of Trent were not accepted in France, where Papal authority over national Churches (royal Gallicanism) and over Bishops (episcopal Gallicanism) was minimized.

Those, in contrast, maximizing the authority of the Pope were known as Ultramontanists ('beyond the mountains', i.e., the Alps). The issue was finally resolved at the first Vatican Council (1869–70) in favour of the Ultramontanists. The Council went even further in securing the Pope's authority by stating that the Pope is infallible in defining matters of faith and morals, without any need for the consent of the Church. The Council also established, through the Constitution *Dei Filius* ('The Son of God'), the basic beliefs of Catholicism with which to resist attempts to explore how traditional beliefs might be related to those of the modern world – attempts known as Modernism and condemned by Pius X in 1907 in the Decree *Lamentabili Sane* (the 'Syllabus of Errors' listing propositions to be condemned and proscribed) and the Encyclical *Pascendi Dominici Gregis* attacking 'the sacrilegious audacity' of the Modernists.

During (and in the years preceding) the Second World War, Pope Pius XII (1870–1958) protected the Church from the dictators – though whether he could have done more on behalf of their victims, especially the Jews, remains deeply controversial. He was succeeded by John XXIII (1881–1963) who convened the Second Vatican Council (1962–5), which inspired the Church to move in a new way into the modern world.

Vatican Council II met in four sessions between 1962 and 1965. It produced Constitutions, decrees and declarations, notably on the Sacred Liturgy, on the Church, on Ecumenism, on the Eastern Catholic Churches, on the Bishops' Pastoral Office, on the Renewal of the Religious Life, on Priestly Formation, on Christian Education, on the Relationship of the Church to Non-Christian Religions, on Religious Freedom, on the Ministry and Life of Priests, on the Church's Missionary Activity, and on the Church in the Modern World. Its hope that the Pope would work in and with the whole College of Bishops (a belief known as 'collegiality') revived the old issue of local and central Papal authority and was in effect abandoned by John Paul II (1920–2005) and by Benedict XVI.

But the commitment of the Council to peace and justice as the practical meaning of Christian faith led to a new Liberation Theology (also kept in its place by John Paul II who thought it too Marxist) in which God's 'preferential option for the poor' became the option of the Church working out of 'an ethical indignation at the poverty and marginalization of the great masses' of the world. It led to people committing themselves heroically to others, as with Mother Teresa or Oscar Romero (who was shot at the altar in 1984 for defending the poor) or countless people who live unknown lives in the service of those in need. When Benedict retired in 2013, his successor, Francis, made it clear that he also would protect the faith and order of the Church, but that he would endorse and practise the purpose of the Church to bring the love and encouragement of God to the poor, the persecuted, and the dispossessed.

Expansion into the World

The divisions of the Church remain severe, between East and West, between Roman Catholics and Protestants, and among Protestants. Since Jesus prayed that his followers might be one, reflecting the unity that lies within God, efforts are now made to recover unity. These are known as the ecumenical movement which led to the founding of the World Council of Churches in 1948. Reunion is complicated by the fact that the Orthodox Church and the Roman Catholic Church each regards itself as the true Church and thus as already the United Church which other 'churches' can join if they make sufficient adjustments of their beliefs and practices.

Despite these deep divisions, all the Churches believe that Jesus has given them this command: 'Go therefore and make disciples of all nations, baptizing them in the name of the Father and of the Son and of the Holy Spirit, and teaching them to obey everything that I have commanded you' (*Matthew* 28:19).

In obedience to that command, Christianity has spread to every country in the world, so that the history of Christianity is really the histories of Christianity: they are so many that they cannot possibly be summarized. In some parts of the world, Christianity is as old as it is in Europe. Thus the Christians of Malabar (on the south-west coast of India) claim that their Church in India was founded by Thomas (one of the Apostles), making Christianity an 'Indian religion' older by far than the Sikhs. The Church in North Africa was founded before the end of the first century (traditionally by Mark, another Apostle) and continues in the Coptic Church of Egypt.

More often, however, the spread of Christianity followed the expansion of exploration and trade from the fifteenth century onward, together with the consequence of these in empires and colonialism. The missionaries have therefore been attacked as agents of imperialism imposing Western culture on people regarded as 'the ignorant savage'. That is far too simplistic. Often missionaries were the only outspoken critics of colonialism, and it was almost entirely through missionaries that health and education, often in the form of hospitals and schools, were taken out into the world.

The Edinburgh Conference of 1910 attempted to draw the many missionary societies together in a more cooperative and unified endeavour, but without success – although it was the first step towards the World Council of Churches. In general, the expansion of Christianity into the world took with it the divisions and conflicts of Christendom.

This was particularly obvious in North America, where the vast territories enabled Christians of different kinds to make their own settlements – which they sometimes did as refugees from persecution in Europe. In 1620, extreme Puritans (Christians dissatisfied with the Elizabethan settlement in England) established a settlement at Plymouth (so-called from the port they had left) in Massachusetts, and became known as the Pilgrim Fathers.

Spain, France, England, Sweden and the Netherlands all claimed parts of North America. Spain and France established Roman Catholicism, the Spanish in the southwest and west, France in 'new Orleans' in the south, and in New France in Quebec and Canada, where conflict between Gallicans and Ultramontanists was as tense as it had been in Europe. The English settlement in Virginia attempted to establish a form of Anglicanism leading eventually to ECUSA, the Episcopal Church in the United States, when its constitution and canons were agreed in 1789. John Wesley (1703–91, founder of a renewal movement in the Church of England called Methodism, which became a separate movement) ordained Thomas Coke (1747–1814) to be superintendent over 'the Brethren in America' who became the Methodist Episcopal Church. The Quakers (the Society of Friends, followers of George Fox, 1624–91, who stressed the importance of the inner light of Christ as the guide to life) founded settlements under William Penn (1644–1718) in Pennsylvania.

The experience of conflict in Europe led to a determination that it should not be repeated in the New World. The

independence of the United States in 1776, profoundly reinforced by the quest for 'the rights of man' in the French
Revolution, led to a Constitution in which freedom to practise
religion was guaranteed, but in which state and religion were
separated.

These beliefs not only allowed the coexistence of religions,
they encouraged the creation of new religions. Some are vigorous
new expressions of Christianity, including those of African
Americans and of Pentecostalists who believe that the Church
should show signs of the outpouring of the Holy Spirit. Others
include Christian beliefs but in new forms. Many, for example,
believe that the second coming of Christ is imminent: Seventh
Day Adventists, derived from William Miller (1781–1849) predicted the end of the world in 1843–4, and believe that the
Advent is delayed because of the failure to keep the Sabbath and
proclaim the Gospel throughout the world – hence the urgency
of their proselytization. Jehovah's Witnesses, derived from
Charles Taze Russell (1852–1916), have also predicted dates for
the end of the world, not least 1914 which is now regarded as the
beginning of the end.

Others believe that their founders have been entrusted with
new revelation which extends the old. Examples are Sun Myung
Moon, founder of the Unification Church in 1954, or Joseph
Smith (1805–44), founder of the Church of Jesus Christ of
Latter-Day Saints, better known as Mormons: Smith claimed
that in 1822 the angel Moroni told him where gold tablets were
to be found on which God's words were written; he published a
translation of these in 1830 as the Book of Mormon.

By the end of the twentieth century, Christians in the different
Churches began to work much more together. A new division,
however, began to open up, between those who believe that the

Bible contains the literal and inerrant words of God, so that any text from any part of the Bible has equal authority, and those who believe that the Bible, like the Incarnation, is immersed in history, so that the Bible is written (concursively) with God, but every text must be interpreted in its context.

It may seem a remote and academic issue, but beliefs about how the Bible should be understood in relation to the initiative of God in revelation have proved deeply divisive. A sharp example is the emergence of Creationism over the last 150 years, particularly now in the form of Intelligent Design. Creationism is roughly the view that the universe and all things in it were created directly by God (much as it is claimed in Genesis and other comparable creation accounts in other religions) and are not the result of a long evolutionary process. The history and consequences of that belief, particularly in education, have been brilliantly reviewed by Ronald Numbers in *The Creationists* (2006). He was himself brought up in a fundamentalist Seventh Day Adventist family, but he decided 'to follow science rather than Scripture on the subject of origins' (p. 13). Obviously it is possible to follow *both* science *and* Scripture in understanding the cosmos and human nature, as many believers do, but it requires a different understanding of Scripture. Contested beliefs of this kind can be bitterly divisive. The purpose of Numbers' book is to develop better understanding. He concluded his Introduction with this sentence (p. 14): 'I think it is profitable to get acquainted with the neighbours, especially so if we find them threatening.' It is a thought which summarizes a major purpose of this book.

Islam

Overview

Islam is now the second largest religion in the world, numbering over a billion adherents. Its own history began with the revelation of the Quran through the Prophet Muhammad (570–632). There had been earlier revelations, but in Muslim belief these had been falsified and corrupted by those who received them, so that the Quran is the only (and therefore final) uncorrupted revelation, and Muhammad is the last of the Prophets.

The Quran is the foundation of Islam, but the lives of Muhammad and of his Companions show how the Quran is to be understood in practice, so that the Traditions (Hadith) about them are also fundamental in Muslim life and belief.

The life of Muhammad shows how he broke away from the idolatry of Mecca (his hometown in Arabia) and from the conflicting claims of Jews and Christians in order to establish a direct relation of trust and faith with Allah, God above the gods or deities of all other inadequate or false claims – Allah means roughly in Arabic 'the One who is God'. Muhammad's appeal to the people of Mecca to come into that relationship with God of security and peace (the meaning of the word Islam) fell on deaf ears. They drove him out and he moved 300 km north to Yathrib (known from that time as (al)Medina or Medina) in the 'exodus' known as the Hijra. Muslim years are dated from this event, AH, after the Hijra. Since the Muslim calendar follows a lunar, not a solar, calendar Muslim and Western years are not of the same length. Dates are therefore shown in this double form, AH/CE. So, for example, the death of Muhammad occurred in 10 AH, which is the same as 632 CE. The date is therefore shown as 10/632.

In Medina, Muhammad established a new political reality based on the revelations which he continued to receive from God. He made treaties with those who acknowledged him, and campaigned against those who did not, including the Meccans. Eventually Mecca was conquered and became the religious centre of Islam, to which the annual pilgrimage is still made.

When Muhammad died, his followers disputed about who should succeed him: should it be his own nearest descendant (his son-in-law and cousin, Ali, since Muhammad had no son of his own), or should it be the man recognized by consensus as best fitted for the job? The latter view prevailed in the choice of the first three successors (or caliphs), but the supporters of Ali did not give up. Ali became the fourth Caliph, but he faced rebellions and was finally assassinated in 40/661. His eldest son Hasan succeeded him, but after six months he was compelled to yield the caliphate to the powerful governor of Syria, Muawiyya, and was later poisoned (50/670). Muawiyya intended that his son, Yazid, should succeed him, but Husayn, who was another of Ali's sons (and thus the grandson of Muhammad), refused and was killed in battle at Kerbala, in Iraq, in 61/680.

This is the origin of the divide among Muslims between the Shias and Sunnis – between the party of Ali (*shiat Ali*, hence Shias) and those who follow Muhammad's customs (*sunna*, hence Sunnis). Shiites believe that Husayn died as a martyr (some believe that Ali and Hasan also died as martyrs), and that Shiites must be prepared to follow that example and, if necessary, die as martyrs. They also believe that the succession from Muhammad continued through their Imams (who mediated the Word of God to their communities), and they await the final Imam who will come to usher in the end of time. Shiites make up about 10 per cent of all Muslims, but they are strong in parts of Iraq, Syria, Iran and Pakistan.

Sunni Muslims rapidly spread across the known world: Islam reached from the Atlantic to China within a hundred years of the death of Muhammad. Over such a wide area, it was inevitable that many new dynasties of caliphs would emerge, even though, theoretically, there should be only one successor (caliph) in authority over all Muslims. In the eighteenth century, an already ruling dynasty of Turkish Sultans claimed to be Caliphs of that kind: from their ancestor, Uthman, they are known as the Ottomans.

The Ottoman rulers had begun their conquests much earlier, from the eighth/fourteenth century onward: they captured Constantinople, renaming it Istanbul, and large areas of the Balkans and the southern steppes of Russia – they even reached the gates of Vienna. Their empire stretched as far south as Egypt and along the North African coast. Originally these rulers gave themselves the title of Sultan, but with increasing European and Russian involvement in the Mediterranean, they claimed the title of Caliph in the eighteenth century in order to unify the Muslim response to the new threat.

That response was increasingly ineffective. The failure of Turkey's alliance with Germany in the First World War led to the abolition of the Ottomans as sultans, and then of the Caliphate in 1342/1924, when Kemal Ataturk established Turkey as a secular state.

The Ottoman Caliphate had been extensive, but it did not reach as far as India, where Muslim dynasties ruled large areas in the north. Of those dynasties, that of the Moguls or Mughals was the most powerful and extensive. Nor did it reach to South East Asia, where Muslim traders were more important than armies in establishing Muslim majorities in Malaysia and Indonesia – which has the largest Muslim population of any country in the world.

The conquest of many Muslim territories and their absorption into European empires during the nineteenth and twentieth centuries was followed by the imposition of new and often artificial boundaries. This has led to considerable conflict and unrest in recent Muslim history, especially in the Middle East. Its most serious consequences can be seen in what Muslims regard as the imposition of Israel on the Palestinian people and territory, and in the rise of groups such as Al-Shabab, the Taliban, Boko Haram, al-Qaeda and Islamic State who regard it as a religious obligation 'to make an effort' (*jihad*) to defend fellow-Muslims when they are attacked by non-believers – as, for example, in Iraq and Afghanistan. Islamic State (known in Arabic as *Dai'sh*, an acronym from *ad-Dawlah al-Islamiyya fi'l-Iraq w'ash-Shams*) has revived the belief that all people in the world should belong to, or be associated with, a single *Umma* (people of God) under one Caliph.

Muhammad and the Quran

The history of Islam (as a distinct religion) would seem to begin with the life of Muhammad (570–632 CE), the Prophet through whom the Quran, the revelation from God, was transmitted into the world. But in Muslim understanding, that history began with the creation of the world, because from the start it was the purpose of God to make known to all people the life-way that they should follow.

That 'life-way' is known as Din (Arabic *dīn*). It is a word often translated as 'religion', but it is a word that embraces (as does the practice of Islam) the whole of life. According to this belief, there cannot be any separation between religious and other aspects of life: all come from God, and all life, therefore, must be lived as God intends.

How is that intention known? Much can be inferred from observing the way in which God has created all things to exist or live in mutual balance and support. As a philosopher, al-Jahiz (third/ninth century) put it, 'We are created to comprehend creation, with all the signs and evidence that it has been created with design, purpose and harmony.'

This belief led Muslims of the early centuries to change our understanding of the universe through the advances they made in many sciences – for example, in astronomy, mathematics, chemistry, physics, geography, agriculture and medicine. They were reading God's book of nature.

Even more important, however, was the reading of God's book of revelation. In Muslim belief, God repeatedly sent Prophets to different peoples (including Moses to the Jews and Jesus to the Christians), but always the Prophets were rejected or killed and the message was corrupted. The final Prophet is Muhammad who transmitted God's message, the Quran, to a people, some of whom rejected Muhammad, but others of whom accepted the message without corrupting it, and thus in the Quran alone the details of God's intended Din (life-way) are made clear. What is that revelation and how is it related to the life of Muhammad?

Muhammad was born in Mecca, in Arabia. His father died before he was born, so that he was brought up by his grandfather,

Abd al-Muttalib. When he was young he had an experience of two figures (later identified as angels) who 'opened his chest and stirred their hands inside'. It was the first of several experiences which led Muhammad into a quest for the truth and the reality of God.

He pursued that quest when he was employed by a widow, Khadijah (whom he later married), to take trading caravans to Syria, because there he met Jews and Christians, and especially the monk Bahira who recognized in him the signs of a promised messenger. He was also helped by Zayid ibn Amr, who was one of a number of people in Mecca called Hanifs. They were people who, influenced by the Jews in Arabia, followed 'the religion of Abraham'. Zayid condemned the worship of idols in Mecca, and such practices as female infanticide. He used to pray, 'O God, I do not know how you desire to be worshipped: if I knew, I would worship as you desire.' At least he knew enough to condemn Muhammad for worshipping idols, and Muhammad said later, 'After that, I never willingly touched [to receive power from] idols, nor did I offer sacrifices to them.' Later, when Muhammad threatened unbelievers with the fires of hell, he said that God would have mercy on Zayid, non-Muslim though he was, because he had lived as God intended.

Like other Hanifs, Muhammad began to go into solitude (in Muhammad's case, to a cave on Mount Hira) in order to search for God behind the bewildering varieties of religion and idolatry. On one occasion, he had the strong sense of a presence, later identified as the archangel Gabriel, pressing on him and insisting three times, 'Read!' (or 'Recite!') – or in Arabic, *Iqra*, the word, or letters, underlying Quran. He then felt the first of the many words that make up the Quran being spoken through him.

Those words were recognized by Muhammad himself and

others as being entirely different from his ordinary speech. They are a kind of rhythmic and rhymed utterance, which Muslims believe are completely unique and cannot be imitated. The utterances are gathered in sections known as Suras, with each Sura having its own name. They are arranged in the Quran in order (roughly) of length, with the longest (from the latter part of his life when he was in Medina, hence known as the Medinan suras) at the beginning, and the shortest (known as the Meccan) at the end.

The Quran is the absolute foundation of Muslim life. It cannot be altered or negotiated because, in Muslim belief, it comes directly from God without the intervention of Muhammad. For that reason, the Quran cannot be translated: it can only be *interpreted* in other languages, since Arabic is the language chosen by God – a reason also why it is an act of merit to learn the Quran by heart even if it is not understood: one who does so is known as Hafiz. Exegesis by those who are qualified is allowed because the Arabic is not always self-evidently clear, and there are recognized and legitimate differences of interpretation.

The Quran is not the only revelation from God. In Muslim belief, God has revealed both word and will through earlier Prophets, such as Moses and Jesus. But the people who received those revelations (i.e., Jews and Christians) corrupted them by allowing stories about their Prophets as well as other material to be mixed up with God's word. Despite this failure, Jews and Christians are respected in the Quran as 'the People of the Book', who have a protected status in Islam and are known as *dhimmis*.

In contrast, the Quran is believed to have been received and preserved without corruption, so that the Quran, according to Muslim belief, is the final revelation, and Muhammad is the last of the Prophets, known as 'the Seal of the Prophets'. It is this belief that has made Muslims so antagonistic to those, such as Babis, Bahais and the Ahmadiyya (thirteenth/nineteenth century), who claim to have received an extension of that revelation.

Although the Quran comes directly from God (in Muslim belief, the so-called 'Mother of the Book' is with God in heaven) and is exactly the same in essence whenever it has been revealed, it is nevertheless related contingently to the circumstances of each Prophet: thus the Quran mentions people and incidents of Muhammad's time including the battles of Badr and Uhud (e.g., 3.11, 117–119, 8.5–19, 42–48) and Abu Lahab ('the father of flame'), a vehement opponent of Muhammad (sura 111):

> Perish the hands of the father of flame, may he perish,
> with no profit to him from all his wealth or from all his gains.
> Soon he will roast in a fire of blazing flame
> with his wife as carrier of the firewood;
> on her neck a rope of palm-fibre.

This also means that the Quran does not deal explicitly with every conceivable issue in belief or behaviour, although it does supply the fundamental principles which apply in all circumstances. The history of Islam is thus the history of the working out of how those fundamental principles are to be understood and applied in the changing circumstances of life. For example, the Quran requires women to be modestly covered in public, but it does not specify the scarf or veil (*hijab* or *niqab*) or the all-encompassing *burqa*.

The earliest interpreters were Muhammad himself and his Companions, because they were a living commentary on the meaning of the Quran as it was revealed. Traditions (*ahadith*, known collectively as Hadith) were gathered of their acts and sayings (and silences), and these were formed eventually (by the end of the third/ninth century) into six great collections known as as-Sahih, 'the sound' collections. They are the second foundation of Muslim life. Together with the Quran, they make up 'the path by which one should walk', or, in Arabic, Sharia. The word goes back to the Quran (45.18): 'We gave you a *sharia* in the Word, so follow it, and do not follow the passions of those who do not know.' Muslims therefore believe that they should live under Sharia. They also believe that since Sharia is clear, penalties for bad offences must be severe – for example, execution for those who leave Islam (apostasize), or the cutting off of the hand of a thief. On the Day of Judgement, the acts of each person will be weighed on an exact balance (tempered by the mercy of God): those in deficit will burn in Fire.

Quran and Hadith make up the Sunna, the custom or way for Muslims to follow. But because of the legitimate differences of interpretation, four major schools of Sharia were developed among Sunni Muslims (also by the end of the third/ninth century), with a different emphasis in each: should life be ordered as closely as possible to Quran and Hadith, or can interpretation be made by way of analogy or consensus or informed opinion? Each of the schools controls the practice of Islam in any area where it is dominant, with a major effect on the history of Islam in those areas. The schools, named after their founders, are those of the Hanafites (from Abu Hanifa, d. 767 CE), allowing interpretation to meet changing circumstances, and strong in Turkey, parts of Iraq, Syria, Afghanistan and nearby states, Pakistan, India and China; the Hanbalites (from Ahmad ibn Hanbal, d. 855), seeking to stay as close to Quran and Hadith as possible, and strong in Arabia, some of the Gulf States and increasingly in Africa; the

Malikites (from Malik b. Anas, d. 795), conservative but allowing consensus, and strong in the Maghreb (i.e., the northern coastline of Africa from Egypt to Morocco) and West Africa; and the Shafiites, from al-Shafii (d. 820), relying on Quran and Hadith with strict rules of exegesis, and strong in South East Asia.

From Muhammad to the Abbasids

Muslim life, therefore, is rooted in the Quran and the record in Hadith of the life of Muhammad. The biography of Muhammad is known from the Hadith supplemented by accounts of his early campaigns (the *maghazi* books) and from some details in the Quran. Since little is otherwise known of his life, some historians have doubted whether the early biographies, such as that of Ibn Ishaq (who lived a hundred years after the death of Muhammad), can be trusted. Muslims have no such doubts, because they have their own well-developed methods for testing whether any tradition is sound, suspect or invented.

On the basis of Hadith, therefore, the life of Muhammad falls into two parts, the Meccan period, and the Medinan. After his experience in the cave on Mount Hira (in the year 610), Muhammad's first thought was that he had gone mad (i.e., *majnun*, possessed by the *jinn* of the desert), and he tried to throw himself from a cliff. He felt a restraint, and he returned home where his wife, Khadijah, told him that he must trust God. Other revelations followed, but there was then a break, equally testing of his faith, known as the Fatra. After that, the revelations resumed, and Muhammad knew with complete clarity that if there *is* God, there can only be *God*, and not competing ideas about God, as among Jews and Christians, still less idols who are believed to represent God. As with the monotheism of the Jews, this was a belief that not only changed but also divided the world, a division between those who serve and worship the one true God and those who do not.

This passionate belief became the half of the first of the Five Pillars on which Muslim life is established: 'I bear witness that there is no deity except God [i.e., Allah].' The second half continues, '. . . and that Muhammad is his Apostle [*rasul*, one who is sent].' This belief is known as the Shahada, 'witness', and it is a belief that has dramatically changed the world, because it brings Islam into being. The Arabic letters in *islam* are those which appear in the Hebrew 'peace', *shalom*, and Islam is the condition of peace and security into which people come when they bear witness to God and his messenger – i.e., when they become Muslims, *muslimun*. Thus the word Islam took on the meaning of obedience and service.

Muhammad began to preach this clear and simple belief in Mecca, but it required that the Meccans should abandon and destroy their idols, and also that they should follow a life-way (Din) worthy of God. This life-way was eventually summarized in the five fundamental obligations known as *arkan al-Din*, the Pillars of Faith: the Shahada (bearing witness), Salat (formal prayer with set movements five times a day), Zakat (giving a proportion of one's wealth to the poor), Hajj (making pilgrimage to Mecca at least once in a lifetime), and Sawm (fasting from dawn to dusk during the month of Ramadan).

The early preaching of Muhammad met with little success beyond some of his family (for example, Khadijah and Ali, his cousin and later son-in-law) and a small number of others: Abu Bakr, who became the first successor or caliph after Muhammad, was the first non-family member to become Muslim. The Meccans became increasingly violent in their opposition, and when Muhammad was invited by the people of Yathrib (a town 330 km north of Mecca) to resolve a long-running dispute, he moved there in 622 with his followers.

This move is known as the Hijra, the 'emigration', and it marks the beginning of the Muslim calendar, with years counted 'from the Hijra', or AH. Yathrib became known as al-Madinah ('The City') or Medina. Muslims believe that they too in obedience to God must be prepared to move or emigrate wherever God commands them.

The opposition from the Meccans continued, not least because Muhammad supported himself and his followers by raiding their caravans. At the battle of Badr (2/623), he defeated with his small army a much larger army of Meccans, and this was believed to demonstrate how God supports those who are trusting. However, in the next year the Muslims lost the battle of Uhud, and that became a sign of what happens if Muslims lose faith in God. In 5/627, the Meccans tried to destroy Muhammad, but they failed to win the battle of the Trench, and after that Muhammad took the fight to his enemies and captured Mecca in 9/630, cleansing it from idols and making it the centre of Muslim life and pilgrimage.

Throughout this period, he organized life in Medina on the basis of the continuing revelations from God, and he tried to bring surrounding tribes and communities into this new life-way. Some of these treaties are gathered together in the so-called Constitution of Medina. This is a collection of agreements with different surrounding tribes – whereas in contrast those who refused to enter into agreement were attacked and dealt with severely. This twofold approach became the way in which Muslims subsequently dealt with those whom they encountered as they extended into the world.

It is this approach which underlies the Muslim belief that the world is divided into three parts. Two are well-known: Dar al-Islam, the house or domain of Islam, and Dar al-Harb, the house or domain of War. Less well-known and well-developed is the third domain, Dar as-Sulh, the house or domain of Treaty: in the territories in which Muslims are in a minority but are well-treated and allowed to practise their Din, treaties of mutual coexistence are encouraged. Muhammad himself frequently sought treaties rather than conflict.

It was this belief that helped the Ottomans to secure degrees of peace and coexistence in their larger empire between rival Muslim groups and with minorities. In multicultural societies today and in the tensions and conflicts between Muslims and non-Muslims, it is massively important that this third domain should be developed and applied in a new way that both parties can endorse. It would create an entirely different context in which the focus would be on the exact and practical contribution that people together can make to the building of a better society.

When Muhammad died in 10/632, there was no obvious successor to lead the Muslims. He had had several wives (and according to the Quran, Muslim men may marry up to four wives provided they treat them equally), but no son had survived. His nearest male descendant was his cousin Ali who had married one of his daughters, Fatima. At that time, however, there were two ways in Arabia in which leaders of communities were identified: according to one method, the man with obvious qualities of leadership was chosen and elected; according to the other, leadership was by inheritance (cf. the contrast between Judges and Kings in Israel discussed earlier).

Both these ways were tried when Muhammad died. According to the first, it seemed obvious that Abu Bakr should succeed, and he became the first Caliph (the word *khalifa* means 'agent' or 'representative': in the Quran, Adam, as the first man, is called the *khalifa* of God on earth). The next two Caliphs were Umar and Uthman. Uthman relied too much on his family and was accused of nepotism and corruption: in 35/655 he was murdered, raising the issue for Muslims whether a ruler who abandons the precepts of Islam has ceased to be a Muslim and can therefore legitimately be killed – an issue that remains important to the present day, as, for example, in the case of Saddam Hussein or more recently of Bashir al-Assad in Syria.

There were, however, some who endorsed the second way of selecting a leader and who believed that the successor of Muhammad should have been his nearest blood relative, Ali. This 'party of Ali', *shiat Ali*, became eventually the Shiite Muslims. During the lifetime of Muhammad, the term *shia* was used of 'the household of the Prophet' among whom Ali was obviously included. Shiites believe that Muhammad, on two occasions, specifically designated Ali as his successor. The first was at Ghadir Khumm on his way back from his farewell pilgrimage, when, according to Hadith, he took Ali's hand and stated that he would be the supreme authority (*mawla*) over the believers. The second occasion was on his deathbed: according to tradition he called for pen and ink intending to write a clear instruction 'which will be a cause of guidance for you and prevent you from being misled'. Those who supported the other way of selection chose Abu Bakr while the family of Muhammad were dealing with his funeral and later said that Muhammad's letter was written while he was delirious.

Much more was involved here than a contest over succession and power (though that was certainly involved). Shiites believe that God would not leave people without the guidance and authority that Muhammad had exercised. In their view, the successors or Caliphs would, through their descent from Muhammad, have inherited that same God-conferred and inspired authority. The Imams of the Shia have an innate relationship with God far beyond the authority that is claimed for the Sunni caliphs.

Although the first three Caliphs were not of 'the household of the Prophet', Ali did become the fourth Caliph. Even then, however, the issue was not resolved. Muawiyya, who had been close to Muhammad and was a strong administrator in Syria, rejected Ali as Caliph on the grounds that he had been involved in Uthman's murder, and that the murder had not been justified. After an inconclusive conflict at Siffin (35/656), Muawiyya suggested arbitration. When Ali agreed, some of his supporters (known as Kharijites, 'those who go out') abandoned him on the grounds that Islam requires total adherence to God, who cannot be submitted to arbitration: 'There is no judgement except the judgement of God.' This is a belief still held by those Muslims who obey what God commands in the Quran, and refuse to participate in arbitration or negotiation, with consequences that are evident in the contemporary world. It was a Kharijite who assassinated Ali in 40/661.

Hasan succeeded his father to become the fifth Caliph (but for Shiites the second Imam), but Muawiyya persuaded Hasan to surrender the Caliphate to himself. Having done so, Muawiyya then established the first hereditary dynasty of Caliphs among those Muslims who claim to follow Muhammad's example and customs (the word for 'custom' is *sunna*, so that these Muslims, by far the majority numerically, are known as Sunnis). Muawiyya required oaths of loyalty to be sworn to his son, Yazid, in the expectation that Yazid would be his successor without election.

Among many who refused the oath was Husayn, Hasan's brother and therefore also a grandson of the Prophet. Husayn led his supporters to Iraq where he was surrounded and killed at Kerbala in 61/680. The martyrdom of Husayn is commemorated each year on Muharram 10 with manifestations of grief and also of guilt that the Shiites of his time did too little to help.

Muawiyya came from the Umayyah family of Mecca, so that the dynasty he founded is known as the Umayyad dynasty. He established his capital in Damascus in 41/661, and under the Umayyads the Muslim empire increased rapidly, stretching within a hundred years from the Atlantic to the borders of China and India: the advance through Spain into France was halted by Charles Martel in 732.

The Umayyads were overthrown in 132/750 by the descendants of an uncle of Muhammad, al-Abbas, who are therefore known as the Abbasids. They moved their capital to Baghdad, and under their rule (which lasted until 656/1258), the arts, architecture, philosophy and science flourished – of immense consequence in Europe even though Islam was not accepted.

Shia Islam and the Sunni Dynasties

When the Umayyads and the Abbasids set out on their conquest of the known world, they were obeying a basic command in the Quran that people should make an effort on behalf of God. The word 'effort' translates the Arabic *jahada*, 'he made an effort', from which comes the word *jihad*. Jihad is often translated as 'holy war', but that is only one part – a less important part – of what effort 'in the cause of Allah' (*fi sabili'lAllah*) means, as Muhammad made clear when he and his troops were returning to Medina from a battle: he told them that they were returning from the lesser Jihad to the greater Jihad, by which he meant the constant effort to overcome in themselves all temptations to stray from 'the straight path' (Quran 1.6).

Nevertheless, Jihad 'in the cause of Allah' may include Qital ('killing') in the cause of Allah, and this is certainly envisaged in the Quran (2.190f.):

> Fight in the cause of God [*qatilu fi sabili'lAllah*] those who fight you, but do not be aggressive: surely God does not love the aggressors. And kill them wherever you catch them, and expel them from wherever they have expelled you. The testing persecution is more grievous than the killing.

The Quran thus makes it clear that such warfare can only be defensive (22.40f.):

> To those against whom war is made, permission is given [to fight], because they have suffered wrong; and truly Allah is their most powerful help – those who have been driven out of their homes contrary to justice simply because they say, 'Our Lord is Allah'; and if Allah did not hold back one set of people by means of another, there would have been devastation of monasteries, churches, synagogues and mosques where the name of Allah is so much remembered.

A defensive war can also be undertaken on behalf of the oppressed in general (4.77/75):

> What reason have you for not fighting in the cause of Allah and of those who are weak among men, women and children, who say, 'Our Lord, take us out of this town whose people are

oppressors, and give us from yourself a protector, and give us from yourself a friend.'

In both Quran and Hadith, clear limits are set on the ways in which war can be fought (see, e.g., 2.186/190ff.). Abu Dawud (one of the six 'sound' or recognized collectors of Hadith) recorded how Muhammad instructed those setting out on a campaign:

> Undertake Jihad in the name of Allah and in the cause of Allah. Do not touch the old close to death, women, children and infants. Do not steal anything from the spoils of war, and play your part in collecting whatever falls to you on the battlefield; and do good, for Allah loves those who are good and devoted.

Muhammad also gave clear instructions about the treatment of prisoners of war:

> They are your brothers. God has delivered them into your hands so let anyone who has his brother in his hands give him food to eat from whatever he is eating himself, let him give the prisoner clothes to wear from whatever he wears himself, and let him not impose any work that he would not be able to do himself. If you impose work of that kind, help them to do it.

The first Caliph, Abu Bakr, also gave specific instructions about Jihad for the army invading Syria:

> Wait, my people, while I give you ten rules for your guidance in battle. Do not act treacherously; do not stray from the straight path; do not mutilate the dead; do not kill children; nor women;

nor old men; do not harm trees; do not burn trees, especially those bearing fruit; do not kill the flocks of the enemy except for your own food; do not search out those who have given their lives as monks – leave them alone.

So killing in the cause of Allah is one way in which Muslims recognize the authority of Allah, and Jihad is an obligation on able-bodied Muslims whenever their fellow-Muslims are attacked (as, for example, in Iran, Chechnya, Iraq, Syria, Afghanistan). It is not an obligation on all Muslims. Apart from the fact that those involved must be Muslim, male, sane, past puberty, and able to maintain their families while away, it is also the case that other obligations may have priority. Both al-Bukhari and Muslim (revered collectors of Traditions) record, for example, how obligation to one's parents comes first:

Abu Huraira told how a man came to the Messenger of Allah (peace be upon him) and asked, 'Who deserves the best treatment from me?' He replied, 'Your mother.' He then asked, 'Who next?' He replied, 'Your mother.' Again he asked, 'Who next?' and he answered, 'Your mother.' He said, 'Who after that?' and he said, 'Your father.' . . . Abdullah b. Amr reported that a man came to the Messenger of Allah and asked to take part in Jihad. He answered, 'Are your parents living?' The man told him, 'Yes', so he replied, 'You should make all your effort in caring for them.'

Even so, the lesser Jihad is precious in the sight of God who favours greatly those who die during the course of it and thus become martyrs. Just as the Greek word *marturos* means literally 'one who bears witness', so the Arabic *shahid* is 'a witness', as in the fundamental 'witness' (*as-Shahada*). A Shahid who dies in the course of the lesser Jihad is exempted from the interrogation in the grave by the two angels and already has a privileged place in Paradise. Because martyrs are already pure and clean, their bodies do not have to be washed before burial – indeed, they should be buried in the clothes they were wearing when they died, since they will appear in Paradise displaying the wounds that killed them. They have no need of the help or intercession of others, and instead they become those who intercede on behalf of others.

Among Shiite Muslims, Jihad and martyrdom have an even higher value, because they believe that Husayn died as a martyr (some believe this also of Ali and Hasan). To join Husayn in a similar act of witness brings one straight into his company in Paradise, and Shiites commemorate annually Husayn and other martyrs at Kerbala (where he was slain, in Iraq) in dramatic acts of *taziya* ('condolence') involving the reenactment of his death and willingness to accept painful self-infliction of punishment. In Shiite belief, where no other weapons are available, one's own body and life must become a weapon, as with the so-called 'suicide bombers'.

Shiites are a small minority of Muslims (about 10 per cent of the whole), and they have divided into many smaller groups. All believe that the leaders of Islam should come from 'the House of Muhammad' (*Ahl al-Bayt*, 'People of the House'), i.e., they should be the descendants of Muhammad and Ali. These leaders are believed to be divinely inspired and able to reveal to their followers inner or secret truth (*batini*, hence the name Batinite given to some Shiite groups), and are called Imams.

Among Sunnis, imams are simply the leaders of a congregation (especially in Salat, the formal prayers on the weekly day of assembly) in a local place of assembly or mosque. Shiites believe that the Imam has much higher status and authority. It came to be believed that he exists in a state of sinlessness, and that his teaching is divinely inspired.

Some Shiites believe that the line of succession ended when Ismail, the eldest son of the sixth Imam, Jafar as-Sadiq (80/699–148/765), died before his father. Those Shiites believe that when Jafar died, Ismail nevertheless became the seventh Imam. They are therefore known as The Seveners (as-Sabiyya) or more commonly as Ismailis. They have divided into many groups among which are: the Nizaris whose Imam has been called the Aga Khan since 1818; the Fatimid dynasty in Cairo from 358/969 to 567/1171 (founders of the renowned al-Azhar University); the followers of one of the Fatimid Caliphs, al-Hakim (d. 411/1021), who declared him to be a manifestation of God on earth (from this comes the secretive Druze religion, mainly in Lebanon and Syria, believing in successive manifestations of God and therefore highly suspect among Muslims); the followers of al-Hasan b. as-Sabbah, known as Shaikh al-Jabal, the Old Man of the Mountains, who in the late eleventh century sent out warriors to kill his opponents: since they were given hashish to encourage them, they were known as *hashshashin*, hence the English word 'assassins'.

In contrast to the Ismailis or Seveners, other Shiites believe that the succession passed from Jafar to his eldest *surviving* son, Musa. From him, the succession continued to the eleventh Imam, al-Hasan al-Askari. When he died in 260/874, his son Muhammad succeeded, although in fact he had disappeared when he was four years old, in the year 260/873. Despite his disappearance or 'hiddenness', he is, for these Shiites, the twelfth Imam, so they are known as the Twelvers, or, from the Arabic for 12, Ithnaashariyya. They are are strong in Iran, and are found in Syria, Lebanon, some of the Gulf States and Pakistan.

Having disappeared before his father's death, Muhammad is believed to be the Hidden Imam, in what is known as *alghayba alkubra*, 'the greater occultation'. Shiites believe that the Hidden Imam is 'the Awaited Guide' (al-Mahdi al-Muntazar) who will return at the end of time to establish a dominion of perfect order and justice, and to take vengeance on the enemies of God.

Al-Mahdi means 'the guided one', and Sunnis also believe in the Mahdi, but they do not identify him with the Shiite Imam. This belief has led to many figures claiming to be the Mahdi and leading campaigns against the enemies of God. Notable among them was Muhammad Ahmad ibn Abdullah (1259/1843–1303/1885) of the Sudan whose campaign as the Mahdi led to the death of General Gordon at Khartoum in 1885.

Among the Shiites, one who claimed to be the Hidden Imam in 1501 was Ismail (1487–1524), a ruler in the Safavid dynasty in Persia/Iran. The Safavids had begun as a Sunni reform movement in the fourteenth century, but became Shiite. Ismail was called Shah (King), and Twelver Shiism became the official religion of Persia. The flourishing dynasty of the Safavids was defeated by the Afghans in 1736, who were in turn driven out by the Qajar dynasty in 1799. The Qajars ruled until 1924, when Reza Shah Pahlavi (1925–41) became the Shah of Persia, succeeded by his son Muhammad Reza (1941–79) until he was deposed by Ayatollah Khumayni (1902–89) who rebuilt Iran on the basis of the beliefs of Twelver Shiism.

Shiites and Sunnis hold most beliefs in common, but remain deeply divided in their understanding of authority and of its relationship to descent from the House of Muhammad. Among Sunnis, the original principle continued of finding the man most able to be leader, but they then combined this with succession, so that a large number of dynasties emerged.

- When the Abbasids overthrew the Umayyads, the Umayyad dynasty continued in Spain from 138/756–422/1031. When they were driven out in the Reconquista and Spain became Christian once more, they left behind the magnificent Alhambra in Granada, and the Mosque (now church) in Cordoba.
- The Fatimids (above) in Cairo were replaced by the Mamlukes in 648/1250 who continued until 922/1517.
- The Seljuqs ruled in Persia and Iraq from 429/1037–522/1157.
- The Ottoman dynasty was established in 699/1341, under Uthman I, also known as Osman, hence their alternative name, the Osmanlis.

The Muslim invasion of India led to independent dynasties, of which the most notable were:

- The Ghaznavids who first came to power in Afghanistan (366/976–582/1186).
- The kings of Bengal (737/1336–984/1576), a Muslim presence that led after Indian independence to East Pakistan and then to the independent republic of Bangladesh.
- The kings or Sultans of Delhi (from 602/1206), culminating in the Mughal emperors (932/1526–1276/1858).

The name Monghal/Mughal is derived from Mongol. The Mongols came from the steppes of Mongolia and, under Jenghiz (Genghis) Khan, spread with ferocious power into China and into Muslim territories. Hulagu captured Damascus, sacked Baghdad and set up the Il-Khanid dynasty in 654/1256. The Mongols became Muslim, and the dynasty lasted until 736/1336.

A descendant of Jenghiz Khan, Babur (888/1483–937/1530) seized power in Afghanistan and defeated the Sultan of Delhi at the battle of Panipat in 932/1526. His grandson, Akbar (949/1542–1014/1605) extended the Mughal empire from Afghanistan to most of northern India, annexing the kingdom of Bengal in 984/1576. His descendant, Shah Jehan (977/1569–1037/1627), built the Taj Mahal and the Red Fort at Delhi, on which is inscribed, 'If there is Paradise on earth, it is here, it is here, it is here.'

Mutazilites and Creeds

That somewhat bewildering list of Caliphs, Dynasties and Imams does at least draw attention to the extreme variety that exists in the Muslim world. At first sight, that seems to be a contradiction of the command of God that those who commit themselves to God and the Prophet should be a single people. According to the Quran, God created human beings to live as a single community – in Arabic *umma*. The conflicts among different nations *before* the time of Muhammad are a mark of their disobedience. In the Muslim understanding of history, God has repeatedly sent prophets to recall people to the intended and commanded Din (life-way), but they have refused (10.19):

> Humanity was a single *umma*, but they fell into divisions. If a word had not previously gone out from your Lord, the matter between them would have been decided, concerning which they disagreed.

In Muslim belief, all must now live as God intended – and the Quran contains many threats of punishment and hellfire for those who refuse. It is this belief which unites Muslims – if necessary, against the world: Muslims are thus under the religious obligation of Jihad to fight against those who attack other Muslims. More positively, Muslims must aim to bring the whole world into the single Umma.

Despite this, there have been frequent divisions among Muslims, as in the fundamental split between the Sunnis and Shiites. Muslims believe that they are at one in all essential beliefs but that they have interpreted and applied them in different ways. Those differences and divisions arise from the fact that the Quran is not a detailed manual of doctrine and practice on every conceivable issue, nor is the Arabic always able to be understood without question. Thus several fundamental issues of belief emerged early, some of which still continue to divide Muslims. Within a hundred years AH, a group came into being whose members believed that human reason should be used to adjudicate on the most divisive of these issues.

These people were called Mutazilites (from *i'tazala*, 'he separated from') because they separated themselves from extreme views and sought a middle way between sceptical unbelief and 'fideism' (fideism means accepting as a matter of faith even unlikely propositions if there is authority for them in revelation or tradition).

The major issues dealt with by the Mutazilites were: the status of a Muslim who sins (was it legitimate to kill Uthman?); the belief that the Quran is a human creation (an uncreated Quran is less open to challenge and interpretation); the statements in the Quran which attribute to God human-sounding features (these are known as anthropomorphisms, such as the statement that God sits on a throne); and the statements in the Quran which say that God determines everything that happens: 'Nothing will happen to us except what God has written for us.' It is this which underlies the phrase (taking nothing in the future for granted), *insh'Allah*, 'if God wills it'. In that case, it hardly matters how people behave, since their behaviour has been determined by God – and in that case also the attempt by imams and others to change people's behaviour by threats of hellfire and promises of Paradise are completely pointless.

Eventually, the Mutazilites became identified by Five Principles, a summary of their rational belief:

1. Strict monotheism and the rejection of anthropomorphism.
2. The absolute justice of God in dealing with humans who are free and accountable in their behaviour.
3. The promises and threats in the Quran are real and must be remembered in the forming of social and individual life.
4. The middle way between the Sunnis and Shiites, particularly in deciding who should be Caliph (descendants from Ali should be honoured, but only be Caliphs if they are the best for the job – in fact only one descendant of Ali ever became Caliph in that way).
5. Commanding the good and forbidding the evil in building up Muslim society: commands and prohibitions are needed because humans are free and responsible.

These may seem long-dead debates on obscure issues, but in fact they are at the heart of Muslim life and of how Muslims should behave, not least because the mediating and reconciling positions of the Mutazilites were rejected and repudiated. It was thought by their opponents that by seeking rational solutions to theological problems, the Mutazilites were making reason superior to revelation and therefore superior to God.

In all religions, this is a perennial issue of belief: what is the status (if any) of reason in relation to a revelation received from God? Since all texts that are believed to be revealed have to be interpreted, what is the scope and what are the methods of interpretation, and who may make those interpretations? The issues sound remote, but the different answers that have been given have been powerful in changing the worlds that religions create, and in dividing religious believers from one another.

In the Mutazilite case, it was decided that human reason can elucidate and explain the Quran, but can never adjust or contradict it. There can never be in Islam anything like the way in which most Christians for two centuries have come to understand the Bible as derived from the initiative of God (and thus authoritative) working in and through the realities of history and circumstance. In Muslim belief, the Quran is contingently related to historical circumstances, but in content it is the expression of God's eternal word.

Thus on the vital issue of 'predetermination', that is, of whether God determines everything in advance of it happening, the conservative theologians (especially al-Ashari, 260/873–324/935, and al-Maturidi, d. 333/944) rejected the rational claim of the Mutazilites that if people are to be judged by God on the Last Day, they must have had freedom to act as they decide. The opponents of the Mutazilites argued that the will of God determines all things by creating all possibilities. But humans are accountable, because they have the freedom to acquire one possibility rather than another. It is as though God creates all the possibilities in a supermarket, with humans having the freedom and responsibility to buy one thing rather than another. On this view, humans are responsible for the punishment or reward they receive, depending on what they choose to acquire. This belief is known as 'acquisition', and it affects Muslim education and behaviour down to the present day – a reason why Muslims want their own faith schools.

In the end, the so-called 'rationalists' were defeated, and the Caliphs increasingly looked for conformity in belief, at least among officials in the empire. The Abbasid Caliph, al-Mamun (198/813–218/833) set up a kind of Inquisition (*mihna*) to examine those whose religious orthodoxy (or conformity) was in doubt. He, like other Caliphs, supported the Mutazilite view that the Quran is created, because an *uncreated* Quran would give it authority over the Caliphs, and yield too much separate power to judges and imams. Some authorities refused to submit to the *mihna*, including the leading conservative theologian of the time, ibn Hanbal – from whom is derived the most conservative of the major Schools of Sharia.

In these conflicts of belief, it became increasingly common for leading teachers and authorities to draw up a statement of belief, showing where they stood in matters of controversy. These are usually referred to as 'creeds', but they are unlike the Thirteen Principles of Maimonides or the creeds of the Christian Church. The basic Muslim creed is the Shahada. The later statements of faith are too long to quote here, but there is a short version of the creed of ibn Hanbal which will give an idea of what these statements of Muslim belief are like:*

1. Approval of the decree of God, submission to his command, patience under his judgement, acting in accordance with

---

* Taken, with slight changes, from W. M. Watt, *Islamic Creeds: A Selection*, Edinburgh: Edinburgh University Press, 1994, p.32.

what has been commanded and refraining from what has been prohibited.

2. Belief in God's predetermination [both] of what is good and of what is bad.

3. Avoidance of dispute and argument in respect of religion.

4. The moistening of the sandals [a dispute between Sunnis and Shiites about whether, before prayer, the bare feet must be washed, or whether moistening the sandals is sufficient].

5. Jihad with every caliph, [whether he is] upright or sinful.

6. Formal worship on behalf of one of the People of the Qibla [the direction in which Muslims turn for prayer] who has died.

7. Faith is [expressed in both] speech and action; it increases by acts of obedience and decreases by acts of disobedience.

8. The Quran is the speech of God, uncreated, sent down on the heart of his Prophet Muhammad.

9. Patience under the standard of the ruler, both when he acts justly and when he acts unjustly.

10. We do not take up the sword against rulers, even when they are unjust.

11. We do not declare anyone who asserts that God is One to be an unbeliever, even when he commits great sins.

12. We refrain from discussing what was disputed between the Companions of the Messenger of God [disagreements among the Companions are recorded in Hadith].

13. The most excellent of the people after the Messenger of God were Abu Bakr, Umar, Uthman, Ali [the first four caliphs, known as ar-Rashidun, the upright or righteous].

14. The calling for mercy on the Companions of the Messenger of God, on his children, his wives and his sons-in-law.

The defeat of the Mutazilites meant that reason in relation to belief could elucidate and explain the Quran, but not challenge it. Philosophy was thus important in early Islam to reinforce faith – and Muslims did much to revive great works of Greek philosophy which had fallen into neglect in the West. But ultimately, faith is more important than philosophy. Even so, the spirit of the Mutazilites was never extinguished, and it became important for Islam in the modern world.

Sufis and Islam in the Modern World

Under the Umayyads, Basra in Iraq became an important centre of study, especially under Hasan al-Basri (21/642–110/728), who was called 'the Third Master' (after Muhammad and Ali). Hasan was a key figure in developing Sufism (Tasawwuf), so important in the history of Islam. Sufis are those who seek a close and personal experience of God by forgetting the world and putting God first in all ways. Sufi Orders exist to teach the ways to do this.

Some contrast Sufis (as a spiritual Islam) with the theologians and jurists who developed a legalistic Islam. That contrast as a generalization is wrong. Hasan al-Basri was immersed in academic and legal questions, and he regarded an orthodox understanding and practice of Islam as the foundation and precondition of the Sufi way – as did most other Sufis after him. There were certainly some for whom the union with God was all that mattered, and they were regarded by others as outside the boundary of Islam. But in general there is no essential opposition between the two.

Nevertheless, it certainly looked as though there could be, because of the way in which Sufis abandoned the importance of this world in order to gain the world to come. Hasan wrote: 'Sell this present world for the next world, and you will gain both of them completely, but do not sell the next world for this one, or you will lose both of them completely.'

Sufis developed into adventurous explorers of total devotion to God as they sought a kind of death in this world (called *fana*, 'extinction') in order to live only with God. Many of them (such as Dhu'l-Nun al-Misri, d. 247/861, and Rabia of Baghdad, d. 185/801) continue to guide and inspire, not only Muslim lives, but the lives of non-Muslims as well.

To gain that guidance, people began to gather round a chosen Sufi teacher or guide, known originally as a Shaykh (sheikh) and later, in Persia and India, as a Pir. Many of these teachers set up a house (*khanaqah*) or fraternity for their pupils who were known as *salikun*, travellers, following the path (*tariqa*) of their guide or Pir. From about the sixth/twelfth century onward, these Turuq (paths, the pl. of *tariqa*) were organized in schools of transmission, many of which continue to the present day.

Among the most important of the Turuq (with approximate date of origin) are:

- the Qadiriyya, founded by Abd alQadir Jilani (470/1077–561/1166) who emphasized how indispensable it is to follow the law laid down in Sharia as a precondition of entering into the true knowledge of God. Because he regarded it as more important than entering into states of ecstatic union with God, he is known as the founder of 'sober Sufism' who demonstrated through his own life that God is not an idea or a philosophical abstraction, but is the presence in whom people can learn to live and from whom each moment of life is then transformed.
- the Kubrawiyya, founded by Abu al-Jannab Najm ad-Din Kubra

(*c*.540/1145–618/1221), known as 'the Maker of the Friends of God'. He based his teaching on visionary experiences of God, and insisted on absolute dependence on the Shaykh, or teacher, as the director and interpreter of the disciple's way: that way is a journey inward, discovering and dealing with realities that are talked about as external (e.g., devils, angels and eventually even God) within the reality of one's own being.

- the Chishtiyya, founded by Khwajah Muin ad-Din Hasan (*c*.536/1141–633/1236) (from Chisht in Afghanistan). He insisted on austerity and poverty: one should neither earn nor borrow money, and if one receives a gift, it should not be kept beyond the dawn of the next day.

- the Shadhiliyya, founded by Abu al-Hasan ash-Shadhili (593/1197–656/1258). He wrote special litanies of prayer to bring people into a full realization of the truth of God. Through the constant remembrance of God (a form of prayer known as Dhikr) people can learn to detach themselves from the world, so that when this world disappears, they will remain attached to 'all that remains', i.e., God.

- the Nimatullahi, founded by Shah Nimat Allah (731/1331–834/1431). He was a farmer who believed that people should not detach themselves from the world but work in such a way that God's possession of their lives would become manifest through their generosity and service of others.

- the Naqshbandi, founded by Khwaja Baha ad-Din Muhammad Naqshband (717/1317–791/1389). He described in detail the path that people should follow in developing a spiritual know-ledge of God, including obedience to the laws of Sharia, so that their knowledge of God might penetrate the whole of society.

- the Mevelevis or Mawlawis, followers of Mawlana ('our Master'), Rumi: Rumi was a supreme poet of the soul's relation to God, who encouraged his followers to engage in rhythmic and whirling dance in order to fly from the world and attain God – they are therefore known by outsiders as 'the Whirling Dervishes'.

- the Alawiyya, named after an Algerian Shaykh, Ahmad al-Alawi, strong in North Africa and present also in Syria where they prefer to be called Shadhilis so as not to be confused with the Alawites to whom the ruling family belong.

The Turuq run through the whole history of Islam, a reminder that the history of religion is told, not only by great leaders and events, but also by ordinary and often unknown lives. Even so, the great events have their effect, even on the most hidden lives. That has certainly been so in the recent history of Islam, because, from the nineteenth century onward, many Muslim countries became part of the empires or the administrations of non-Muslims – from North and West Africa, through the Middle East and India, along the southern steppes of Russia, to the Pacific Islands.

This remains painful for Muslims because they are supposed to live under Sharia, and although in some countries Sharia law was continued, it was not ultimately administered by Muslims. The political ideal for Muslims has sometimes been described as a theocracy – direct rule by God. In fact, it is rule by humans guided by God through the Quran. Provided the principles and practice of Sharia are maintained, different forms of that human rule are possible. At the least, the ruler should be advised by a council, Shura, representing the people. A Western-style democracy is one possibility, but the recent US goal of foreign policy to establish *only* that kind of democracy is, according to Muslim belief, insulting and absurd. The failure to understand this has inevitably made much of Western policy maladroit.

When Muslims regained independence during the twentieth century, they were in a new political world. The Ottoman Empire disappeared, and Turkey became a republic with a secularizing agenda. In contrast, Pakistan was created in 1947 as an Islamic Republic in areas of India where Muslims were reckoned to be a majority – as the name implies: P from Punjab, A from Afghania in the north-west, K from Kashmir (allocated to India in 1947, hence the continuing conflict), S from Sindh, Tan from Baluchistan, the name together meaning Land of the Pure. New kingdoms were established, as in the Hashimite kingdom of Jordan (Hashimites are those who can trace their descent from Muhammad's family of Hashim), and older ones were reaffirmed, as in Saudi Arabia.

In the confusing history of the recovery of Muslim independence, two major themes have been involved, often in tension and conflict. Both go back to the fundamental beliefs already reviewed.

The first theme is that of legitimate exploration and reform. This is rooted in the pursuit of rationality among the Mutazilites, and the exuberant thrust of work by Muslims under the Abbasids in science and philosophy. Egyptians such as al-Afghani (1839–97), Muhammad Abduh (1849–1905) and Taha Husayn (1889–1973) dreamt that Egypt might once again be a centre of civilization. In India, Ameer Ali (1849–1928) turned against blind reliance on authority and encouraged education, Abdullah Yusuf Ali (1872–1953) made a lucid interpretation (paraphrase) of the Quran, and Muhammad Iqbal (1873–1938) argued that Islam is the next stage of the world's philosophical thought.

In contrast to reform, the second major theme is one of return to the foundations laid fundamentally in Quran and Hadith: the way forward is the way back to strict obedience to the Word of

God. Insistent on this are the Wahhabis, brought into being by Muhammad ibn Abd al-Wahhab (1115/1703–1201/1787). They are based on Hanbalite Sharia and are strong in Saudi Arabia. The Ikhwan alMuslimun (the Muslim Brotherhood), founded by Hasan alBanna in Egypt in 1928, also aims to return to the fundamentals of Islam, and these two conservative organizations have trained many of the leaders of al-Qaeda and the Taliban – movements which believe that God will show favour only to those who adhere strictly to the Word and the commands of God. For these groups and for later developments like Boko Haram and Islamic State the obligation to defend the true and orthodox Islam leads them to attack, not just infidels but also 'Muslims' who do not conform and obey. The tension between those extremes is reinforced by the division between Sunni and Shia Muslims, and by the different answers that are given to the question, Who is the true Muslim?

The extreme complexity to which all this gives rise can be seen in the stark and tragic conflicts in Syria. After the end of the Second World War and of the French mandate in 1946, various different forms of government came to an end when an army general, Hafez al-Assad, seized power in 1970. His family belong to a religious group known as the Alawites. The word *'alawi* means basically 'supporters of Ali'. It would seem, therefore, that the Alawites are a branch of Shiat Ali, the Shia. The Alawites, however, absorbed beliefs and practices from other religions, and as a result many Muslims, both Sunni and Shia, do not regard them as being Muslims at all. Sunnis made several attempts to overthrow Assad, culminating in their bloody defeat at Hama in 1982. The uprising in 2011 was originally a continuation of that rejection of the Assad family, but it was rapidly joined and taken over by far more conservative Sunni-based groups including al-Qaeda and Islamic State. That evoked considerable support for Assad in Syria among minorities that had lived in Syria for centuries and had been protected by Assad. Perhaps surprisingly at first sight, that support included Shias who in general terms do not consider the Alawites to be true Muslims. But better Assad than Islamic State!

To the complexity of those shifting patterns of alliance are then added the interventions of non-Muslim states, not just in Syria but in other countries with majority populations of Muslims. Given the religious obligation to defend Muslims if they are attacked, it is not surprising (going back to the two extremes summarized earlier) that the conservative is now gaining increasing power. This has been exacerbated by the US-led support for Israel and the failure to find any just solution for the displaced Palestinians. From a Muslim perspective, Israel was imposed on Palestine after the Second World War, in 1947, when the territory, under the United Nations, was partitioned between Jews and Arabs. That partition was destroyed in the immediate outbreak of fighting, and Palestinian land was appropriated by Israelis, with many Palestinians becoming refugees – though some remained in Israel. Two attempts by Arab states to recover Palestine (in the wars of 1967 and 1973) were defeated by the overwhelming skill and strength of the Israeli army. UN Resolutions (242 and 3236) calling for occupied territory to be returned remain only partly fulfilled.

Since the Israelis are allies of the US and possess nuclear weapons, the Arabs face an asymmetrical war. That, however, is exactly what they faced at Badr, and yet they prevailed by trusting in God. This belief means that Palestinians and the organizations that support them (for example, Hamas and Hisbullah) will use such weapons as they have in seeking to recover what they regard as their own land. As freedom or resistance fighters ('terrorist' is only applicable if the rules of Jihad have been abandoned), they will make use of whatever weapons they have including their own lives. The obligation of Jihad continues by whatever means are possible. Whether that includes firing rockets at civilians is, to say the least, an obvious issue. Those who believe that it is justified point to the indiscriminate way in which Gaza was subjected to bombardment in 2014, and more generally to the way in which Israel with the support of the US (who nevertheless were unable to impose a two-state solution on Benjamin Netanyahu, the Israeli prime minister) continues to seize land and life from Palestinians.

Jewish perceptions, with the promise of the Land and memories of the Shoah, are utterly different. Some Muslims now accept the reality of Israel, but others believe that the abolition of Israel is a necessary (because religious) goal, although Jews could still be citizens in a Palestinian state. Such beliefs will not disappear while world powers say that Israel has a right to exist and defend itself, but never say that Palestine has a right to exist and defend itself, even though most of its land has been taken away or occupied. Coexistence *might* be achieved, but only if the underlying *religious* beliefs on both sides are understood. These are certainly beliefs that are changing the world and will continue to do so.

Developments from Islam: Ahmadiyya, Babis and Bahais

Returning to the question, 'Who is the true Muslim?', it has already been pointed out that throughout the history of Islam, some interpretations have been developed which other Muslims regard with suspicion, or with outright rejection so that they have become, in effect, new religions. Suspicion can easily arise in the case of a Sufi Order (*tariqa*), because the guide (Shaykh or Pir) may lead his followers into his own interpretation of Islam.

An example of this is Ahmad al-Tijani (1150/1737–1231/1815). When young, he had originally joined three different Sufi Orders (Turuq), before founding in Fez the Order named after him, the Tijaniyya. In the thirteenth/nineteenth century, the Tijaniyya spread rapidly in West and North Africa, where, appealing to Jihad, it became a powerful resistance movement to French colonialism. Later, some members co-operated with the French, but only as a means to the same end: the expulsion of non-Muslim invaders from Muslim lands.

None of that is particularly unusual. Resistance of the Tijaniyya to French colonialism is repeated now in the widespread Muslim resistance to the neo-colonialism of the US and others in their invasions of Muslim lands. Jihad requires that defence of fellow-Muslims. Recently, some commentators have claimed that the motives of the resistance fighters and the suicide bombers (whom they call terrorists) are political and not religious, but that claim is blindly and dangerously absurd: Muslim beliefs and motives cannot be disentangled in that way, as the history of Islam demonstrates.

What was certainly unusual, and what has made the Tijaniyya suspect in the eyes of other Muslims, was the claim of Ahmad al-Tijani to have seen Muhammad in a vision and to have received from the Prophet a direct commission to establish his Order. The Tijaniyya is thus the only Order to trace its descent from Muhammad himself, and not through a chain of teachers and guides. The Tijaniyya have therefore repudiated the other Turuq, and their followers are forbidden to join any other Order.

It is this belief (that Ahmad al-Tijani received a direct

commission from Muhammad, along with particular prayers for his followers to use) that has made the Tijaniyya suspect to other Muslims. Nevertheless, the Tijaniyya is extremely strong in Africa, where for many it is the only Islam they know, and their devotion to their founder is great.

It is in this way, by personal allegiance, that some of these suspect interpretations have become in effect new religions, although often they have claimed to be the fulfilment of what Islam is intended by God to be.

That claim of fulfilment was made by Shaykh Ahmad al-Ahsai (1166/1753–1241/1826), a Shiite from Persia who shared the common Shiite belief that the Hidden Imam chooses a *bab* ('door' or 'gateway') whenever he needs to communicate with his followers. He believed himself to be that *bab*, and, not unlike the Mutazilites before him, developed a rational understanding of Islam, rejecting, for example, the Muslim belief that there will be a resurrection of this body, and believing instead that there will be a resurrection of our spiritual essence. It was not so much his beliefs as the authority he claimed for them that made him suspect to other Muslims.

Among the Shaykhis was a young Punjabi, Ghulam Ahmad of Qadi (1250/1835–1326/1908). Many Muslims believe that at the turn of each century, someone will appear, known as *mujaddid*, who will renew Islam. As the years approached 1300 AH, Ghulam Ahmad came to believe that he was that *mujaddid*, renewer of the faith. In 1307/1889, he announced that he had received a divine revelation that he was the true caliph (successor) of the Prophet, and in 1309/1891 he declared that he was not only the awaited Mahdi, but also the Messiah of the Jews and the Avatar (manifestation of God) of the Hindus. In other words, he claimed that he was the fulfilment of the dreams and hopes of all religions. In some ways, he followed the Shaykhis in reform, while remaining insistent on the absolute validity of the inerrant Quran – so that, for example, he supported polygamy and the veiling of women.

On the basis of the Quran, he shared with all Muslims the belief that Jesus did not die on the Cross. Sura 4.156 states that the enemies of Jesus claimed to have killed Jesus, but 'they did not kill him and they did not crucify him, but his likeness [appeared] to them.' Thus Muslims believe that the likeness of Jesus appeared on the Cross, but that Jesus himself was rescued by God and was neither crucified nor killed. In fact, the Arabic of that verse in the Quran is ambiguous, because the relevant proposition can mean 'its' as well as 'his'. So the verse could mean, '*its* likeness [appeared] to them': in that case, it could be a straightforward statement of the resurrection: they *thought* they had brought about the death of Jesus, but they had failed to do so because he rose from the dead. All Muslims, however, accept the first interpretation. Ghulam Ahmad introduced a variant, that Jesus was indeed crucified but that he survived and went to India where his teaching was continued by Ghulam Ahmad. Jesus eventually died and was buried in Srinagar, where his tomb can still be seen.

When Ghulam Ahmad died, his followers split between those based in his home town of Qadi, the Qadiyani, and those based in Lahore, the Lahori, who have continued the reforming tradition. Both groups have been zealous as missionaries throughout the world.

For other Muslims, all this raised the sharp issue of where this teaching had come from, and of whether Ghulam Ahmad was claiming to extend Muhammad's teaching. If so, he would be challenging the belief that Muhammad was the Seal (i.e., last) of the Prophets. Ghulam Ahmad and his followers believed that only Muhammad had received the absolute and complete attributes of a Prophet, but that God reveals some prophetic gifts and words to others, and especially to one who is, like Ghulam Ahmad, a *mujaddid*. Other Muslims rejected this belief emphatically, and still do. After Ghulam Ahmad's death, there were violent conflicts between his followers, the Ahmadiyya, and other Muslims, until in 1974 the Constitution of Pakistan was amended to state that the followers of Ghulam Ahmad are not Muslims, and are debarred from holding public office.

A very different claim to be the completion and fulfilment of Islam (and all other religions) began also in the thirteenth/nineteenth century, but in Persia, not in India. This was the claim of Ali Muhammad of Shiraz (1819–50) to be the Bab through whom the Hidden Imam communicates. He had originally been a Shaykhi (above), but he moved far beyond them when he claimed that he was himself the Hidden Imam and the Mahdi. He also claimed that he was the Point, Nuqta, of a new revelation from God.

As he began to attract many followers (known as Babis), so the authorities began to take alarm. At a gathering at Khurasan in 1848, the Babis seceded from what they regarded as the corrupt Islam of their day. The response was a series of ferocious persecutions, culminating in the execution of the Bab in 1266/1850.

The Babis then split: some gave their allegiance to the Bab's designated successor, Yahya Nuri, who was known as Subh-i Azal, Dawn of Eternity, and these Babis are known as Azali Babis. Others gave their allegiance to his half-brother, Husayn Ali Nuri, who was known as Baha'ullah, the Splendour of God: he became a founder of the Bahais.

Baha'ullah, as one of the earliest disciples of the Bab, suffered greatly in the persecution of the Babis. He went into exile in Iraq, and there, in 1863, he declared to a small group of followers that he was the figure predicted by the Bab, 'The One whom God will Manifest'.

Bahais believe that God is unknowable in essence, but that God becomes manifest in many ways – for example, in the creation of the world which is a continuing process, and in Prophets who have appeared in a sequence beginning with Adam and leading up to Baha'ullah. Other religions are non-prophetic, but their founding figures, such as the Buddha, represent the manifestation of God in the ways appropriate to their times and circumstances. Bahais believe that since all religions are part of God's plan, they must be respected, even if the Bahai faith is the culminating point of that plan – at least so far: Bahais believe that there will be Prophets in the future related to circumstances at present unforeseeable. It is these beliefs which have made Bahais an energetic force in seeking reconciliation between religions as well as peace and harmony in the world.

For Muslims, however, all these claims, from Ahmadiyya to Bahais, have gone far beyond the limits of Islam. They are beliefs that have changed the world for many people, but not the world of Islam.

India

Overview

The majority religion of Bharat, more commonly called India, is known as Hinduism, but this name gathers together many related religions. The history of religion in India is really the history of many independent systems of belief and traditions of practice, so that it is, in effect, the history of several religions. Nevertheless, they share many concepts and beliefs, even if they make use of them differently. They have much in common, and clearly belong to the same family, even if they often live apart. Some have even left the family home and become independent religions. This happened particularly in the case of Buddhists, Jains and (much later) Sikhs. Organized traditions of teaching, practice and belief are common in India and are known as Sampradayas.

The word Hinduism comes from the Sanskrit *sindhu* (Greek, Indus), the river in the north-west. The area around the river Indus became known in Persian as Hindustan (taken into Greek and Latin as India), and Muslims, after their conquest of northern India, called the non-Muslim population Hindus – the name adopted also by the British in the nineteenth century who also used 'Hinduism' for the religion(s) of the Hindus. The terms

'Hindu' and 'Hinduism', although not terms used originally by Indians themselves, will be used in this book for convenience for the peoples of Bharat and their interrelated, though differing, beliefs.

Hinduism goes back to the Indus Valley civilization (from about 2500 BCE to about 1500 BCE) and to the Dravidian and tribal cultures. The Indus Valley civilization, known from archaeology, was affected by a people known as the Aryans. It was once thought that they invaded and imposed their beliefs, but it is now thought by many that they settled in the area (c.2000 BCE onward) and made changes to Indus Valley beliefs from within. In that case, Indian beliefs (i.e., Hinduism) long predate the Aryan influence – an issue that has become politically important in recent years. Between 1200 and 600 BCE they spread from the Punjab to most of north India.

The consequence of this was the development of beliefs based on the Vedas, i.e., Vedic religion. Little is known of the history of the Vedic period (c.1500–600 BCE), but the Vedas, believed to be timeless revelation, have survived to give insight into beliefs at the time, along with texts known as Brahmanas and Aranyakas (composed c.900–600 BCE) recording chants, rules for sacrifice and ritual, and explanations of their meaning. They also have continuing authority as Shruti (*śruti*, 'that which is heard'), the eternal and timeless revelation which is extended in Smriti ('recollected'), texts whose authority is derived from Shruti; to that extent they are secondary, yet, nevertheless, they include texts that are of fundamental importance in Indian belief.

During this time there were reactions against the religion and life-way based on sacrifice and ritual (the religion of the ritual experts, brahmans, hence often referred to as 'brahmanic religion' or as Brahmanism). The reaction produced ascetics who renounced the world. Among these developed the new religions of the Jains and Buddhists (sixth century BCE).

In contrast, Vedic religion committed itself to the living of life in the world. Since everything that they observed in the world around them follows an ordered rule and process, it seemed obvious that human life and society should be comparably ordered. From that belief developed an understanding of Dharma as the way in which the life of individuals, families and society should be formally organized. It was a belief that transformed Indian life. It produced, for example, the basic divisions in society known as Varnas (*varna*, 'colour'), with brahmans as the ritual experts, and with others in designated social roles as advisers or warriors (*rajanaya, kshatriya*), traders and farmers (*vaishya*), and servants (*sudra*).

Alongside the classification of *varnas* there developed the overlapping but separate classification of people by birth. This is the caste system, known as *jati*, 'birth', with brahmans and the twice-born at the top and Untouchables (or *dalits*) at the bottom. This belief has had a major effect on Indian society, because there cannot be social mobility from one caste to another except through rebirth in another life. Since Independence this has been modified but not abolished.

The post-Vedic period of history is one of dynasties and empires in local areas, often in conflict with each other or with invaders from outside (for example, from Greece and from Central Asia). A dynasty of powerful rulers was that of the Mauryans (*c*.320–185 BCE), among whom were those who favoured Jains (Candragupta, *c*.392–297) or Buddhists (Ashoka, third century BCE), so that 200 BCE–200 CE was the period of greatest Jain and Buddhist influence in India.

The hierarchical system of society in Brahmanic religion was paralleled in the hierarchical structure of kingdoms, from local rulers up to kings and emperors. There were many of these, with their own separate histories. One of them became extensive, the Gupta empire, c.320 CE–540, founded by Candragupta I, which covered the north and much of central India.

After the Gupta dynasty, when Indian architecture and art flourished, there was a break-up into smaller kingdoms and military aristocracies, such as the Rajputs in northern and central India, and there were frequent changes through alliances and conflicts.

Throughout this long period, from c.1000 BCE–700 CE, the great texts and foundational expressions of Hindu belief were written – the accounts of how life and society should be organized, the Puranas and Epics telling the stories of the Deities and the world, the philosophical reflections culminating in the Upanishads.

At the same time, the independent traditions of southern India became strong. They are characterized by their loving devotion (known as Bhakti) to God. Brahmanical religion from the north spread into the south, but it was assimilated without the southern beliefs and traditions, especially in Tamil-speaking areas, being destroyed. In this lies the foundation for present-day claims in the south for greater autonomy, if not independence. The search for a Tamil state has spilled over into the conflict between Tamils and the mainly Buddhist population of Sri Lanka.

Despite the shifting patterns of conflict and alliance, India did not fall apart: the unity of India was maintained, partly because of the strength of shared religious beliefs (even though they existed in very different forms), and partly because of the strong sense that the whole of India belongs together as a sacred unity, even though it may happen to be divided among different rulers. In one of the Epics, *Mahabharata*, the whole of India is regarded as a place of pilgrimage.

During the period from the fifteenth to the seventeenth centuries, this sense of religious unity was powerfully reinforced by groups of people known as the Sants. They saw different religions as different but equal ways to come to God, and this belief was expressed in lives and poetry of great beauty. From this background came Guru Nanak (1469–1539) and the Sikh religion.

This vision and practice of unity was, however, threatened, not by internal wars, but by the invasions of north India by the Muslims. These began in the eighth century, but became more extensive from the eleventh century onward. A Sultanate was established in Delhi in 1206, which, after much interior strife and bloodshed, extended at the beginning of the sixteenth century from the Punjab in the West to Bihar in the east. The Mughal or Mogul dynasty was founded by Babur (d. 1530) and flourished until the death of Aurangzeb in 1707. The empire continued until 1858, but in a weak and ineffective form.

Part of the weakness came from increasing European involvement in India. Initially concerned with trade, rivalries between the French and the British led to the dominance of the British East India Company, particularly when led by a military adventurer, Robert Clive. In order to secure the Company's position, he defeated the local Mughal ruler at the battle of Plassey in 1757, enabling the Company to gain control over the riches of the Ganges valley and over Bengal.

The British government was drawn into undertaking direct rule instead of leaving it to the Company. Lord Cornwallis, governor-general from 1786–93, laid the foundations of a separate administration less open to corruption. Just under half of India was still controlled by local princes or maharajas ('great rulers'), with whom the British entered into various forms of alliance and indirect rule, even after the Indian Mutiny of 1857–8.

Indian nationalism began in the first half of the nineteenth century as an attempt to reform British rule and to associate Indians with it. The Indian National Congress was founded for this purpose in 1885, but by 1907 a more radical group emerged seeking *swaraj*, independent rule. At that time, the large Muslim population in India became wary of Hindu dominance and founded in 1906 the Muslim League.

The move toward independence was led by Mahatma ('great soul') Gandhi (1869–1948), the strength of whose own beliefs, deeply rooted in the Indian tradition, made the process less violent than it would otherwise have been. He hoped to keep Muslims and Hindus together in a single independent state, but the Muslims, led by Muhammad Ali Jinnah (1876–1948), were determined to achieve a separate Muslim state, to be named Pakistan. In 1947 the British withdrew, and India and Pakistan achieved independence.

The Vedic Period

The early religion of India is known as Vedic religion because it is based on the Vedas ('sacred knowledge'). Vedic religion was based on sacrifice and ritual to which the four Vedas are related in different ways. Rig Veda collects hymns and chants, many of which are used on ritual and sacrificial occasions, and some of which probe profound questions about the meaning and origin of life; Yajur and Sama Vedas contain instructions on what has to be done; Atharva Veda contains further hymns and chants concerned mainly with the satisfying of particular desires and with the warding off of specific threats or ills, chants and spells, and offers explanations and interpretations of what the sacrifices mean. The Vedas are believed to have no human origin and to have been transmitted originally by word of mouth. They have been written down only since humans have lost their original powers and have needed this assistance.

The Vedas are addressed to Devas, heavenly beings that dwell in their own domain above those of atmosphere and earth. The words *deva* and *devi* are often translated as god or goddess, but they are connected to the word *daeva*, 'shining/exalted', and they can be used of many things that seem to come from a more-than-human origin. They are, therefore, Beings with emotions and desires who live in a different realm. They have powers and responsibilities in the cosmic order and in the world in which humans live. People can interact with them, particularly through sacrifices, in order to make their lives more secure in a hazardous world. The Devas can even be invited to the ritual meals that accompany the sacrifices that are offered to them.

It used to be thought that the Vedic deities were personifications of features in the natural world, such as Fire (Agni), the Sun (Surya), the Wind (Vayu) and so on. Many do indeed have control over the natural world, hence the importance of being in a good relation with them. But there are others who are not connected with specific natural features. Varuna, for example, was believed to protect good order in society and in the cosmos, accompanied by Mitra, the guardian of contracts in society.

It was believed that human life depends on the natural order in which it is set. From a very early stage (the exact date cannot be known) this belief was summed up in reverence for the *go*, 'the sacred cow'. The cow sums up the generosity of nature, and the five gifts from the cow (milk, curds, ghee, urine and dung) were used in worship: to kill a cow is equivalent to killing a brahman. For Gandhi, the sacredness of the cow is the gift of Hinduism to the world, because it is a constant reminder that all living things are interdependent, and that human life depends on the non-human.

This dependence was expressed in the Vedic period particularly in sacrifices through which the natural order of the cosmos is acknowledged and sustained. From the earliest time, Hindus have believed that the cosmos is governed by a fundamental order and balance. It is basically reliable, even though events of chaos and apparent disorder certainly occur. This order and balance is known as Rita (*rta*), a word related to *rtu*, the seasons which recur with a regularity that is reliable but certainly outside human control.

This belief that Rita must be maintained is of particular importance now as the world faces the consequences of increasing population and of climate change. It is Rita that must be observed and sustained in all ways, but especially through sacrifices and other rituals. Sacrifices express the belief that the entire universe is food and the eater of food: plants and animals are killed in order to produce food, but the one who eats food becomes food for another: 'This whole world is just food and the eater of food.'

In this process, Agni (Fire) plays a vital part, because Fire consumes whatever is put on it, and the smoke carries its subtle consequence up to the heavens to sustain the gods. The very first hymn in Rig Veda is addressed to Agni:

> I magnify the Lord, the divine,
> the Priest, minister of the sacrifice,
> the offerer, supreme giver of treasure . . .
> To you, dispeller of the night,

> we come with daily prayer
> offering to you our reverence.
> For you are Lord of sacrifice,
> enlightener, shepherd of the world,
> who wax mighty in your own abode.[*]

Fire, therefore, is of paramount importance in Indian belief and ritual, especially in the home and in the rituals for marriage. Equally, it underlies the belief that the bodies of the dead should be cremated and not buried. In the Vedic period, there was no belief that there will be a life after death of any worthwhile or substantial kind: traces of the dead continue, but they are only vague shadows of a memory. Only later did Hindus come to believe that there will be continuity from one life to another, but even then the existing body is not necessary for that process.

In the Vedic period, it is already becoming clear that the family is the foundation of Indian life and belief. Although women had a restricted role in public life, their role in the home was paramount in transmitting to children beliefs, values and practices. Ideally, it came to be expected that an individual life would fall into four stages known as *ashramas*: being a student, then a householder establishing a family, after that retirement from involvement in the world, followed by a complete withdrawal as a *samnyasin*, one who gives up all dependence on the world and moves into the acceptance of death.

During the active stages of this process, there are four equally

---

[*] Translation by Raimon Panikkar, *The Vedic Experience: Mantramañjari: An Anthology Of The Vedas For Modern Man* (Berkeley: University of California Press, 1977).

legitimate goals that high-caste Hindus can pursue, known collectively as *purushartha*. They are Dharma, knowing how people including oneself should behave; *artha*, material goods and wealth; *kama*, enjoyment of the senses including sexuality (hence the *Kama Sutra*); and Moksha, release from rebirth in the world (on which see more below).

Of those four goals, the belief in Dharma is particularly important in every aspect of Indian life. The word *dharma* comes from the Sanskrit root *dhr* which underlies words meaning 'hold', 'uphold', 'sustain' and 'protect'. Dharma refers to the way in which all things and all people ought to behave if the Rita (the order) of the cosmos and of individual and social life is to be maintained. 'Hinduism' (i.e., that family of related religious beliefs and practices) is really a map of Dharma, a map of how people should behave appropriately in whatever circumstances they find themselves. In fact, an Indian name for its own religion is Sanatana Dharma, everlasting Dharma.

Arthasatra of Kautilya, dealing with the organization and governance of society, makes clear that Dharma is deeply rooted in the Vedas (1.2; it refers to the Threefold Veda, Trayi, but includes Atharvaveda as of the same authority): 'The Threefold Veda makes definitively clear the respective obligations of the four Varnas and of the four goals of life [*purushartha*].'

To ignore or disregard Dharma, therefore, is to disturb the order of the cosmos. Not surprisingly, there are many texts in which the details of Dharma and its application are laid down, but it is in the family that they are transmitted most effectively from one generation to another. That is why many Hindus (including many women) do not think that the role allotted in Dharma to wives and mothers makes them inferior. One, Mrs Pancholi, claimed that women have a far more important role than men: 'Women are the transmitters of culture in Hindu tradition, and this role lies in the hands of women, and I don't think a man has time, or even the patience, to do that.'*

The meaning of Dharma is also brought home in the many stories that Indians tell to each other – and even now, the village storyteller can still be found as a revered figure. But supremely the practical implications of belief in Dharma are explored through the great Indian Epics, *Mahabharata* (very approximately 400 BCE–400 CE) and *Ramayana* (in several versions from about the same period), and through texts known as Puranas which traditionally deal with five clusters of Indian belief: genealogies of the gods and the great ancestors (where have we come from?); the periods of fourteen ancestors of humans, the Manus; the dynasties of the cosmic rulers from whom human kings are descended; the origin of the universe; the destruction and subsequent re-creation of the universe, exemplifying the Indian belief that each universe goes through four stages known as Yugas: a golden age when Dharma is perfectly observed, an age when Dharma declines and the Vedas have to be written down, an age of further decline when the Vedas are forgotten or ignored, and a final age, the Kali Yuga when disease, anarchy, warfare and despair prevail. In Indian belief, we are now living in the Kali Yuga, a belief that changes considerably one's perception of the world as it now is.

Embedded in book 6 of *Mahabharata* is a section where the question of Dharma is central. This section of 700 verses, often printed separately, is known as *Bhagavadgita*, 'The Song of the Lord', and for many Hindus it is their most revered book, the epitome of their beliefs.

---

* Quoted in John Bowker, *Worlds of Faith: Religious Belief and Practice in Britain Today* (London: BBC Books, 1983), p. 213.

In the context of the whole Epic, *Bhagavadgita* comes at a moment when Arjuna, a warrior, finds that he is opposed in battle by members of his own family: should he fight and perhaps kill them or not? To answer that question, Arjuna is offered the assistance of God in the form of Krishna. Arjuna accepts and receives instruction on what he should do. The instruction forms the main part of *Bhagavadgita*.

Basically he is told that he must obey the duty of his Dharma as a warrior. But he is then taught how all human actions must be undertaken without calculation of the consequences for oneself. It becomes a fundamental Hindu belief that only those deeds that are done with insight and without attachment to consequences and through devotion to God, can lead to the final goal of union with God. Krishna then instructs Arjuna in the ways that lead in that direction. Any way that leads to the goal is known as *marga*, and *Bhagavadgita* groups them in three categories known as Trimarga: Jnyanamarga (the way of knowledge and insight), Karmamarga (the way of action without attachment to consequences), and Bhaktimarga, the way of devotion to God. Each of the three contains many different ways to proceed, any of which can be followed depending on a person's circumstance in any particular birth. It is a fundamental Indian belief, as we will see, that individuals are reborn many millions of times in a process known as Samsara, 'wandering'.

The Epics, the Puranas and *Bhagavadgita* come from a period after the Vedic foundations had been laid, a period (*c.*1000 BCE–200 CE) during which major developments in Indian belief took place, and commentaries and reflections on the meaning of the Veda were taught and written down. Among these reflections are works known as Upanishads, which were written over a long period. There are more than a hundred of them, though the ones having authority through their direct connection with the Vedas are fewer in number, perhaps about eighteen. They are listed in my *The Message and the Book*.* They are supremely important in understanding fundamental Indian beliefs.

The word Upanishad is made up of three words meaning 'sitting down near', and imply the transmission of teaching through an instructor with a group of students. In the Upanishads themselves, the word means 'secret knowledge' or 'secret teaching'. In Hindu belief, the Upanishads are the foundation of true understanding. Basic to that understanding is Brahman. In the Vedas, *brahman* means 'prayer' or 'sacred word' and the power that these contain. From this, the word came to mean the power that brings the universe into being. In the Upanishads, Brahman is the source of all appearances, the unproduced Producer of all that is. That might be equated with God as Creator, but the Upanishads make clear that Brahman lies behind even the appearance of God or gods. Thus the Upanishads say that Brahman is 'One without a second', 'beyond anything that can be known', even 'beyond the unknown'. In other words, Brahman is so distinct from this or any other universe that Brahman cannot be described: in this sense, Brahman is without attributes, without any characteristics that can be described.

Yet Brahman does become known. How can this be? It is partly because something can be inferred about the nature of Brahman from the world that has been created (though that requires well-trained eyes to see!), but even more because the reality of Brahman pervades the world as soul, or Atman. Thus

* John Bowker, *The Message and the Book: Sacred Texts of the World's Religions* (London: Atlantic Books, 2011), pp. 171f.

Brahman can be discerned in and through the universe not least through Atman residing within us. These were beliefs that completely changed the Indian world, and in the Upanishads exploration is made of the nature of Brahman, the source and originator of all appearance, and of the relation of the universe (and of humans within the universe) to Brahman.

Basic Beliefs

The Upanishads claim that since Brahman brings all things into being, Brahman cannot be an object like other objects *within* the universe, and is therefore not open to direct observation and description. If a description is wanted, all that can be said is negative – that Brahman is not three feet wide and four feet tall, is not more square than oblong, and so on. All that can be said is 'Neti, neti', not this, not this (or more literally, No! No!). Brahman beyond any kind of description is known as 'Brahman without attributes' (Brahman *nirguna*).

Something, nevertheless, *can* be said of Brahman, because the universe is the consequence of Brahman, and the reality of Brahman penetrates the universe – indeed, some Hindus believe that the universe is the body of Brahman and must therefore be treated with reverence: this is a belief that powerfully reinforces the quest for Rita and Dharma already discussed. It is possible, therefore, to say something of the nature and consequence of Brahman, and Brahman with attributes is known as Brahman *saguna*. In the Upanishads, the claim is made that the true reality of Brahman is within life as Atman.

In the Vedas, *atman* is a word meaning 'breath', or it may even simply be a way of talking about 'oneself'. In the Upanishads Atman has become the real Self that a person is, the underlying reality in all life which cannot die because it is identical with Brahman.

Humans with intelligence can come to know this, and they can therefore come to realize that the Atman within themselves (and others) is nothing other than Brahman. To realize this, and to live on the basis of this all-important truth, is to be set free from believing that this body and this world are important. They, after all, come into being and pass away, but Atman, being Brahman, cannot die. That is why in the Gita Krishna tells Arjuna that when he does his duty (Dharma) as a warrior and kills his cousins he cannot kill the immortal Atman in them.

To realize that I in my real self am nothing other than Brahman is to realize that 'I', like Brahman, cannot be touched or affected by anything, least of all by death. This belief is summed up in the Four Great Sayings (Mahavakyas) of the Upanishads: 'You are That'; 'I am Brahman'; 'All this is truly Brahman'; 'This Self is Brahman'.

This belief gives to all living things a profound worth and value, and is a reason why many Hindus, in addition to never eating meat from the *go*, the 'sacred cow', are vegetarian. However, in every individual there is an ordinary life tangled up in the world and completely unaware of this identity with Brahman. The everyday self is known as *jiva*, and the two 'selfs', Atman and Jiva, are said in the Upanishads to be like two birds sitting on the branch of a tree: 'Two birds, companions, always united, cling to the same tree. Of these two, the one eats the sweet fruit, while the other looks on without eating.' What Hindu beliefs offer are ways to disentangle the two birds, to disentangle Atman from the world so that it can realize that its true nature is Brahman.

Brahman is immortal, but humans and all other living things are not. How then can the immortal Atman/Brahman within us not die when the entangled life of Jiva does? Only by realizing its identity and escaping altogether from this world and this life (the escape is known as Moksha or Mukti), or, far more often (because of the way that most people are attached to this world too much), by being reborn again in another body in order to try again.

So began the far-reaching Hindu belief in rebirth, Samsara. In that belief, the Atman will be reborn as often as it takes until it learns to give up its entanglement in this world. We may in fact have to be reborn many millions of times before we learn that, however much we enjoy the attractions of this world, there is something offered to us that is better than even the best of these attractions: it is our escape from this world and this body to find our true union once more with Brahman.

The belief that there is a greater good than even the greatest good things of this life is common in other religions as well. It has changed the world greatly. It is to affirm the good things of life and to love them – the beauty, the food, the sex, the friend-ship, and so on – and *also* to say, But I have an even greater love than these. Certainly it has been common for some religions and for some religious believers to go to an opposite extreme and to insist that those good things must be denied as destructive temp-tations. But in Indian belief they have not been set against each other, but have an equal value in their appropriate time and place, exactly as we saw in the four goals of life summarized earlier.

The ultimate goal, nevertheless, lies beyond the long sequences of rebirth in this world. The goal is to find that greater love in the final escape or release known as Moksha ('liberation'). The many different ways of being Hindu are simply different ways of moving toward the same goal, or of achieving it. This is the fun-damental belief that has made so many Hindus tolerant of each other and indeed of other religions. Hindus are as capable of violence and intolerance as any other religious believers. In some circumstances it may be the Dharma of some particular Hindus to fight against threatening enemies, as it was in the case of Arjuna and as many Hindus now believe when they face militant Muslims. It is the reason why, for example, Bal Thackeray, who died in 2012, founded Shiv Sen (Śiva's Army) to defend the integrity of Hindutva against outsiders, initially Communists but later Muslims in particular. He spoke of Muslims as a cancer needing cutting out and he advocated fighting fire with fire: 'Islamic terrorism is growing and Hindu terrorism is the only way to counter it. We need suicide bomb squads to protect India and Hindus.'

Even so, the overriding imperative is to recognize that in the sequence of many rebirths, there will be many different ways in which to make progress toward Moksha. It is why Hindus are inclined to say that there are many different roads leading up a mountain but only one summit at which we should all eventually arrive; there are many different rivers but they all lead to the same ocean. This belief has meant (among much else) that India has had as President not only Hindus, but Sikhs and Muslims as well. The equivalent of that has never happened in Pakistan, nor could it, because of specific Muslim beliefs about authority and revelation, as we have seen.

The history of India may seem to contradict this tolerance, because Hindus have often been involved in bitter conflicts among themselves or with outsiders, and Hindus are not indifferent or casual about their beliefs when they are threatened – Gandhi was assassinated by a devoted Hindu. Nevertheless, Hindus can remember that even if people are in error and are, so to speak, religiously or politically wrong, they will have many opportunities in future lives to learn the truth and to practise it.

The point is that in Hindu belief, as we have just seen, life is a long process of lives through many rebirths. The process of Samsara is not random or arbitrary. It is governed by Karma ('action' or 'deed'). The forms in which the soul can be reborn are many, ranging from animals to humans, from devils to gods. Exactly how the soul is reborn, for good or for ill, depends on present behaviour, and the outcome depends on Karma.

Karma is sometimes loosely translated as 'punishment and reward' but it is in fact entirely neutral. There certainly are rewards and punishments in the ways in which people are reborn, but Karma itself is simply the moral law in the universe which is as certain as the law of gravity: it makes the consequence of behaviour (for good or for ill) as certain as a fall to the ground for anyone who steps off a cliff.

The process of working through the effects of Karma acquired in a previous life may be a long one. It may be that Moksha will not happen during or at the end of this particular life. But provided people live according to the Dharma of the particular circumstance in which they have been born, they will work out the consequence of the Karma that lies in their past, and will be reborn closer to that final goal. They will attain Moksha or release as they become finally and for ever what in truth they already are – Brahman, the one and only Reality that there is.

From all this, it will be clear that Hindus take a long view of things – indeed, a *very* long view. Time, in Hindu belief, is not a relatively short process with a beginning and an end. Time unfolds in stages of immense, almost unimaginable, length in successive periods. As we have seen briefly in connection with the Puranas, any sequence of periods has four parts, each of which is known as a Yuga ('age'). The first is the golden age (*krita-yuga*) in which the cosmos rises to a condition of order and harmony which nothing disturbs; the second is the *treta-yuga*, when righteousness begins to decline and sacrifices become necessary to maintain good order; the third is the *dvapara-yuga*, when the Vedas have to be written down but few in any case study them; the fourth is the *kali-yuga*, the furthest point of decline, when disease, despair and wars prevail: this is the age in which, according to the belief of Hindus, we are at present living, so the chaos and conflicts in the world do not surprise them. When the universe reaches its lowest point it begins to rise again.

All these beliefs were developed just before and through the period of the Upanishads. They changed the Indian world for ever. Combined with the belief in Dharma, they mean that every life has the opportunity to gain release (Moksha) from the constant round of rebirth (Samsara). All that is required (though for those entangled in the world it is a big 'all') is an understanding of what is on offer and of how they should proceed. In other words, they must find a way of overcoming ignorance, *avidya*. Hinduism as Sanatana Dharma ('everlasting Dharma') is the coalition or family of the many different ways (known as Margas) by means of which it is possible to move toward the final goal. It may be through guides and gurus, through ascetic renunciation of the world, through the four stages of life, through joining a particular temple or by being devoted to a particular god or goddess.

God, Gods and Goddesses

To anyone visiting India it seems obvious that Hindus worship many gods and goddesses. There are many temples and shrines dedicated to different Deities, and it is said that there are about two major festivals for each day of the year. The worship of many gods is called (from two Greek words) 'polytheism', so it would seem clear that Hinduism is polytheistic. In fact it is not, because the way in which Hindus understand the nature of the Deities is a belief which has completely changed the human understanding of God.

Since Brahman is believed to be the source and originator of all appearances, the unproduced Producer of all that is, it follows that Brahman brings into being, not only living creatures in their myriad forms of appearance, but also the gods and goddesses in all their variety. These Deities perform many functions. For example, the so-called 'Hindu Trinity' (Trimurti, or Three Forms) is fundamental in the process of time and creation: Brahma creates the universe, Vishnu sustains it, and Shiva destroys it, after which the process begins again. Other Deities are more specific in their function. For example, the elephant-headed Ganesha brings wisdom and good fortune. Others again may be extremely local, concerned with the protection of particular villages.

The belief here is that Brahman without attributes (Brahman *nirguna*), of whom one can only say 'not this, not this', is too remote and inaccessible. By bringing into being appearances in the form of Deities, Brahman creates God as a real presence with whom people can interact in worship and prayer. In fact, most Hindus believe that Brahman is best understood *as* God, the unproduced Producer of all that is, who creates Deities as agents in the world. Brahman as God will still remain far beyond description, but because God becomes manifest in so many different forms of the various Deities, the attributes of Brahman (Brahman *saguna*) can be known, and God becomes a real presence in the world, able to be approached in worship, love and devotion. It is a belief that has changed profoundly the Indian way of living in the world.

The Sanskrit word for 'devotion' is Bhakti ('to be loyal', or perhaps 'to separate'). Bhakti is one of the Trimarga (Three Ways) described in *Bhagavadgita* by which one can make progress toward Moksha or release. *Bhagavadgita*, a fundamental text for all Hindus, was written at a time (probably somewhere around 200 BCE) when Indian religion was in danger of splitting into various parts. The Jains and the Buddhists had already become separate traditions or religions, and the Gita seems to have been written to show that the three different ways (Margas) of knowledge, action and devotion are all legitimate and can exist together. But the Gita makes it clear that the way of devotion to God, or Bhakti, is the most direct, and that it is open to all: 'Whoever takes refuge in me, whether they have been born in sin or are women or traders or even labourers, they too reach the highest goal.'

The Gita also develops another fundamental Hindu belief. This is the belief that God in the form of Vishnu (see further below) can become manifest in different forms, both of animals and of humans, when the world is in trouble (*Bhagavadgita* 4.7–8): 'Whenever there is a decay in Dharma and an increase in unrighteousness, I throw myself into birth. To protect good and to destroy the evil, and to establish Dharma, I am born from age to age.'

This manifestation of God in the world is known as *avatara* ('descent'), sometimes translated as 'incarnation', but that translation obscures the fact that the manifestation of God is not limited to being *in carne*, 'in the body'. For example, *arcavatara* is the manifestation of a Deity in a temple image; and it may be applied to the divine infilling of inspiring individuals, such as Gandhi, Jesus or

Muhammad. To this day, spiritual guides and gurus can be recognized as Avatars. A notable example is the Vaishnavite Sahajananda who, at the beginning of the nineteenth century, founded the reforming Swaminarayan movement, now widespread around the world. In the past, however, Avatars are particularly associated with the manifestations of Vishnu in Rama and Krishna.

One of the major traditions of religious belief in India is known as Vaishnavism, because it is devoted to the worship of Vishnu and of his Avatars. But the word 'it' is misleading if it implies that there was just one tradition. Vaishnavism is a complex tapestry of interrelated ways of being related to Vishnu, drawing on traditions from both north and south India. All that can be attempted here is to indicate some of those that have 'changed the world' in different parts of India.

Krishna is the Avatar of Vishnu who comes to the help of Arjuna in the Gita, but he was clearly worshipped as a god long before that time. He may even have been a historical character who later came to be recognized as God. In the Gita he says that he was worshipped by some people as Vasudeva. This reflects a time, from about 500 BCE onward, when devotion to a Lord who is personal to the worshipper became increasingly widespread, and by the second century BCE, Vasudeva and Krishna had become merged as one Deity, as the Gita says. The worshippers of this single Deity called him Bhagavan, the 'one who receives his share' of offerings and honour, and in return is constantly concerned for human wellbeing. Those who worship Bhagavan are known as Bhagavatas, and this tradition became widespread and strong when it was supported by the Guptas, a ruling dynasty in northern and central India, during the fourth to sixth centuries CE. From this point on, the names Krishna, Vasudeva, Vishnu and Bhagavan refer to the same personal Deity.

This does not mean that all Vaishnavites agree. Some (for example, the Shrivaishnavites) believe that Krishna is subordinate to Vishnu because he was simply one among many Avatars. But others (for example, the Gaudiya Vaishnavites) maintain that Krishna is superior because he had already been active in the world and gave Vishnu a helping hand in order to do for Vishnu what Vishnu could not do for himself. Gaudiya Vaishnavites focus on Krishna and Radha (see below), and celebrate the exemplary devotion of Chaitanya (c.1485–1533), from whom the International Society for Krishna Consciousness (ISKCON), more popularly known as the Hare Krishna movement, comes.

The Shrivaishnavites were founded by Nathamuni (tenth century CE) and flourished in Tamilnadu where they taught complete dedication to Vishnu with reliance on his grace. In about the fourteen century, a division of emphasis took place between the Vatakalai of the north who taught that humans must work at their dedication and devotion, and the Tenkalai of the south who taught that everything depends on the free gift or grace of Vishnu and requires surrender to that grace – the two are known as 'the cat and the monkey' schools, since cats carry their young in their mouths (total grace), but the young of monkeys cling to their mothers (make some effort).

Among another tribal group, the Abhiras, Krishna was known as Gopala, the protector of herdsmen and cattle, who patrolled the forest of Vrindavana, still an immensely important centre of devotion to Krishna. Many of their stories have been merged with other stories to create the figure to whom so many Hindus are devoted – stories, for example, of how Krishna danced and made love with the women guarding the cattle, the Gopis: there were 16,000 of them, but each thought that she alone was the love of Krishna. The way in which Krishna loves all as though each one is unique, and the way therefore in which Krishna becomes the universal love of all, form the foundation of the outpouring of ecstatic devotion in which sexual imagery and emotion are embraced – superbly expressed in Jayadeva's *Gitagovinda* of the twelfth century CE where the poet describes the love between Radha and Krishna epitomizing the supreme bliss of the union of the soul with God (12.23.10):

> So the encounter in love began,
> when the shuddering of bodies
> hindered firm embrace;
> where the joy of contemplating one another with searching looks
> was interrupted by blinkings;
> where the mutual sipping
> of the honey of each other's lips
> was impeded by the utterances
> of small love-cries.
> Yet even these seeming hindrances
> enhanced the delight in love-play . . .
> Though entwined in her arms
> though crushed by the weight of her breasts
> though smitten by her fingernails
> though bitten on the lips by her small teeth
> though overwhelmed by the thirst of her thighs
> his locks seized by her hands
> inebriated with the nectar of her lips
> he drew immense pleasure from such sweet torments.
> Strange indeed are the ways of love!*

---

*   Translation by D. Mukhopadhyay, *In Praise of Krishna: Translation of Gitagovinda of Jayadeva* (Delhi BR Publishing, 1990).

Krishna meets all who are devoted to him in Bhakti with a corresponding love, but his favourite among the Gopis is Radha. The love between them is made up of two themes, separation and union. In one of the stories of Krishna, he hides himself from the Gopis who become almost desperate in their grief to find him. The belief that God withdraws his presence from those who seek him, in order to draw them further and deeper into devotion and love, issued in Virahabhakti, devotion to God even in the absence of God. It is a belief that appears in other religions where, as here in this poem by Mirabai (a sixteenth-century Rajput princess), it helps people to keep faith even when they feel abandoned:

> Sharp and piercing is my pain
> Through the absence of this night:
> When will gently arise again
> Shafts of dawning light?
> The moonlight – O deceiving foil –
> Brings no comfort to my heart;
> I wake – and still the same turmoil
> Anguished while from you apart:
> Lord of mercy, Lord of grace,
> Glimpse me blessings from your face.

The theme of union is, however, equally important, and the two together become major themes of Vaishnavite (and of all Hindu) prayer and worship, producing poetry of extraordinary beauty, especially in south India. A group known as the Alvars (the name means 'drowned in devotion') wrote much of this poetry between roughly the sixth and tenth centuries and are believed by many to be Avatars of Vishnu's attributes and companions:

> God, the infinite mystery,
> who on that distant day
> measured the world with his stride,
> this day has come to me.
> How? I do not know;
> but life is swooning in sweetness.

The Hindu belief that God becomes present in the world in many manifestations of Deity means that Hindus are not compelled to worship one form only. In other words, they do not *all* have to be Vaishnavites; and even if they are, they can recognize and worship other manifestations of Deity. Each Hindu can have his or her own personal form of Deity, known as Ishtadevata, and there are many indeed, both gods and goddesses, among whom they can choose.

Shiva and the Shaivites

There is, however, another major tradition which has had a history and a following for as long as the Vaishnavites. These are the worshippers of Shiva, who are known as Shaivites. God in the form of Shiva is worshipped by Shaivites, who form the second major tradition in India, each of which has its own long history. Where Vaishnavites can be recognized by vertical marks on their foreheads (often two or three parallel lines), Shaivites are distinguished by horizontal lines (often two curved or three straight).

The history of Shaivite traditions is even more complex and varied than that of the Vaishnavites. The worship of Shiva may go back as early as the Indus Valley civilizations if one of the seals found there is correctly interpreted as being Shiva as Pashupati, the Lord of the Animals – but that is disputed.

In the Vedas, Shiva appears as a description of Rudra, meaning 'auspicious'. But as Rudra declined in importance, so Shiva emerged as a (and for many 'the') supreme Deity, and Shiva attracted to himself the worship of other, earlier deities. For this reason, Shiva ends up with many apparently contradictory features:

- he is the great ascetic, generating immense power through his asceticism, and yet he is also the erotic, fervent lover;
- he is thus the model of faithful and creative love, and yet his consorts are often fierce and destructive, transmitting to him the power to destroy;
- he is therefore the all-powerful Lord, and yet without the female power transmitted to him he is helpless, and he is often shown lying inert beneath the feet of a Goddess;
- with his third eye he has burned away all Desire (Kama), and yet he seduces the wives of those seeking wisdom; he combines within himself both male and female and is often shown in androgynous form (*ardhanarishvara*).

These many contradictions, however, are only apparent, because Shiva gathers into himself *all* the features that are otherwise scattered among the many different manifestations of Deity in India. Thus the Hindus in general believe that the three constituent parts of the universe (creation, sustenance, and destruction) are the work of the three Gods in the Hindu Trinity. But Shaivites believe that Shiva does all three himself – and that is why he is often portrayed with three faces.

In this way Shiva is, like Brahman, the unproduced Producer of all that is, and yet he is equally present in the universe, above all in his famous dance which turns the wheel of creation and of destruction. Shiva is Nataraja, the Lord of the dance, and he also dances the dance of death in cremation grounds and the dance of the gods in the Himalayas. He is believed to dance at the centre of the universe at Tillai in south India (now known as Chidambaram), where his temple is still the home of the dancing Shiva.

His other 'home' on earth is at Varanasi (Benares) or Kashi, the City of Light. Here, Shiva is united with his beloved Ganga, the river Ganges, the flowing form of female energy which pours through Shiva's hair to give life to the world. Shaivites believe that if they can die in Kashi, their past Karma is abolished and they are carried by Shiva over the flood of death.

From all this it can be seen that Shiva is worshipped in as many different ways as there are different beliefs about him. This means that the history of Shaivite beliefs cannot be summarized because they have flowed into so many different traditions, each with its own history. However, in the development from the Vedic period, one of the Upanishads (*Shvetashvatara*, fifth or fourth century BCE) is important for them all because it marks the transition from Brahman as the remote source of all appearance to God as creator of the universe, who is above all things (transcendent) and yet lives in the lives of those who love him (immanent).

During the Gupta dynasty (*c.*320–500 CE), the main Puranas were being written through which we gain insight into so-called *pauranika* or puranic religion. Puranas focus on different deities (the famous *Bhagavata Purana*, for example, on Krishna) and some therefore focus on Shiva. The Shiva Puranas divide Shaivites into four groups, Shaivas, Pashupatas, Kapalins and Kalamukhas.

Among the Shaivas, some remained a part of the mainstream religion of the brahmans, but others pursued separate paths. Of those, some attempted, through extreme forms of asceticism, to break out directly from the round of rebirth (Samsara), others attempted a more gradual progress through the attainment of special powers (*siddhi*). In the Shaivite texts, the first of these ways, or Margas, is known as *atimarga*, 'the outer path', which strikes out, if necessary, far beyond the ordinary considerations of life according to Dharma. The second is known as *mantra-marga*, 'the mantra path'. Since this is more gradual, it envisages a long process of rebirth through higher worlds in which great pleasure can be found.

The Pashupatas, who appeared at least by the second century CE, have divided into many sects. In general, they were ascetics who had to be high-caste brahmans and celibate (known as *brahmacharya*). To achieve liberation (Moksha) they had to move through three stages: they had, first, to live near a Shaivite temple covered in Shiva's ashes, worshipping Shiva in dance and song; second, to leave the temple and live in socially repellent ways, acting as if mad and attracting abuse from passers-by, thereby attracting good Karma; and third, to withdraw into isolation, for example into a cave, meditating on sacred sounds (*mantras*) and on the Sound which is the supreme Being and which permeates the universe, Aum or Om: in that meditation and repetition of the primordial Sound they become a part of the music of the universe. Only if they pass through those stages could they then move on to live in a cremation ground, subsisting on whatever, if anything, comes to hand, before dying and gaining union with Rudra (*rudrasayujyam*).

Kapalika Shaivites have also divided into many sects, but in general they worshipped the fierce and destructive form of Shiva, known as Bhairava, and his consort, the equally ferocious Kali. The energy with which Shiva creates and sustains is the same energy which destroys: with the same energy a tigress suckles her young and kills her prey. Kapalikas believe that we have to learn, through many rebirths if necessary, to live as faithfully with destruction as with construction since both are equally the work of God. The name Kapalika means 'people of the skull', because they carry a skull-top staff, use an empty skull as their begging bowl, and live in places where cremations take place. Few Kapalikas remain today apart from the Aghoris who are found mainly in Varanasi.

Kaula Shaivites are those who join themselves to the families (*kula* means 'family') of the yoginis, the servants of various Deities. Some Kaula Shaivites attach themselves to the servants of ferocious Deities, others (the majority) to the beautiful and inviting Deities, such as Lakshmi, who is worshipped in Shri Vidya.

Kaula Shaivism appeared in Kashmir after Vasugupta (*c*.875–925) had a dream in which Shiva told him to go to Mount Mahadeva (in Kashmir), and there he found inscribed on a rock the *Shiva Sutras*. These are the foundation of Trika ('threefold') practice through which, at its heart, initiates purify their bodies by destroying them symbolically in order to recreate them through the energy of sacred sounds (Mantras); they then seek union with Shiva by visualizing Shiva's trident entering and pervading their bodies; finally, they complete the union through constructing and entering the sacred diagram known as Mandala, in which the whole universe is compressed into a small space with Shiva at its centre.

As the Muslims began to establish their rule in northern India, many Hindus migrated south with their beliefs. Among these was yet another group of Shaivites who have persisted in south India to the present day. They are known as Shaiva Siddhanta. In the north, Shaiva Siddhanta had taught that there are three distinct kinds of existence: Pati, the Lord Shiva the source of all creation;

pashu, the indestructible soul which belongs to Shiva but is distinct from Shiva, and which is now entangled in the material world; and *pasha*, the cosmos made up of mind and matter. Shaiva Siddhanta offers to believers the way to remove impurity and entanglement from the soul in order that it may regain its proper union with Shiva: souls and Shiva become a complete unity in which nevertheless they remain distinct from each other.

When Shaiva Siddhanta migrated south (in about the eleventh century CE), it retained that threefold structure, but now it absorbed (as did Vaishnavism) the strong emphasis in the south, especially in Tamilnadu, on Bhakti, utter devotion to God. Between the sixth and eighth centuries, poets had wandered through south India visiting temples devoted to Shiva, where they encouraged others to join them in singing their Tamil hymns of praise and love. The poets are known as the Nayanars ('leaders' or 'guides'). Three major poets among them, Campantar, Appar and Cuntarar, are known as 'the first three Saints', and nearly 800 of their hymns are gathered in *Tirumurai*, which is regarded by Tamils as revealed Scripture, the equivalent of the Vedas. According to Appar, the poems of praise are worth more than any offering or sacrifice:

> Flowers make ornaments,
> and so does gold;
> yet if our Lord who sweetly abides in Arur
> were to desire an ornament for himself,
> simple heart, let us honour him
> with the ornament of Tamil song!*

---

* Translated by Indira Vishwanathan Peterson, *Poems to Śiva: The Hymns of the Tamil Saints* (Princeton, NJ: Princeton University Press, 1991).

At first sight this proliferation of organized beliefs and practices in India must seem bewildering. But the variety of different beliefs exemplifies a fundamental belief which has characteristically changed the world, not just in India, but far beyond as well. It is the belief that the cosmos and human life within it are both invitation and opportunity. Humans, whether now or in the past, are invited to make explorations and discoveries. Those explorations can be made, not just into the world outside, but also into the world within. Religious beliefs and practices in all religions help and encourage people to discover truths within them which give them new understanding of who and what they are, and which are capable of completely transforming their lives.

The exploration and discovery of what lies within can result in people living lives of detachment from the world. One great Indian teacher withdrew so far that he abandoned speaking to his disciples, and yet they still learned everything from him. Equally, however, other people are led to greater devotion to the God whom they have found and who has found them.

That devotion in India, as we have already seen, is summed up in the word and practice of Bhakti, often expressed in poetry of moving devotion. In the tenth to the twelfth centuries, that poetry was developed by a further group of poets known as *vacana* ('something said') poets among whom Basavanna was outstanding. It was he who became the leader of a new way of practising Shaivite belief.

Goddess and Tantra

Bhakti is a belief that changes the world for many people, because it holds that *all* people can be devoted to God, irrespective of birth or caste or gender. That belief was taken to a new extreme

by one of the Vacana poets, Basavanna, who founded a movement known as the Virashaivites, 'the heroes of Shiva'. Women
and men were regarded as equal, and women were no longer
regarded as unclean at the time of menstruation. They banned
child marriage, and supported the remarriage of widows. They
even abandoned caste, and they practised no rituals apart from
their own.

The Virashaivites are also known as Lingayats because they
believe that the linga is the only sign and presence of Shiva that
they need. The word *linga* means 'symbol', and for Shaivites, and
especially for Lingayats, the linga is the supreme symbol of the
energy flowing from Shiva and sustaining life in the world. The
linga is the penis, the male organ of generation, and it is therefore often found with the yoni, the female counterpart. Shiva and
his consort Shakti (see below) are the energy which creates, sustains and destroys all things. Together they are the fundamental
power that brings all things into being.

The linga became supremely important for Basavanna when
Shiva appeared to him in a dream and commanded him to leave
the temple in which, until that time, he had worshipped.
Basavanna protested that he would not know how to worship
without the temple, so in another dream Shiva gave to Basavanna
a linga, and Basavanna knew that Shiva would always be with
him in the linga, no matter where he went. As a result, Lingayats
always wear a linga round their necks, a reminder that the body
is the true temple, and that they have no need of any other temples or rituals.

The linga and the yoni are the male and female counterparts
in the creation and origin of life. Just as both are required for the
creative energy which brings life into being, so also both God
and Goddess are necessary in Hindu belief. The female source

of energy is known as Shakti, and those who worship the manifestation of Shakti as Goddess are known as Shaktas. Shakti is the power that all the gods need in order to bring anything into being or effect: without Shakti, the gods are powerless, and that is why the gods have their consorts.

Shakti herself can be approached in worship through the forms of Mahadevi (Great Goddess) or of Bhagavati (Supreme Goddess). But Shakti/Mahadevi also becomes manifest in the form of many goddesses who bring female energy to bear in the universe in two directions, either to create or to destroy. In the case of the former, she appears as Lakshmi (also known as Sri, auspicious) or as (among many others) Parvati; in the case of destructive energy she appears as, for example, Durga or Kali.

The power of sexuality to unite human beings with each other is a fundamental realization, in Hindu belief, of the necessity for the union of what might otherwise seem opposites in order to bring anything into being. That is why sculptures on Indian temples often portray gods and goddesses in sexual union (*maithuna*): from this union the same energies flow forth from the temple as those that create life and sustain the universe.

Not surprisingly, therefore, the power of sexuality, with all its associated emotions, not only unites human beings with each other, it also unites them with Deities. This belief found its fullest expression in Tantra. Tantras are texts which contain, often in secret form, the beliefs and practices which make up Tantra. Tantra is found in all Indian religions, in so many different forms, that is almost a religion in itself. Once again, it is impossible to write a history of Tantra, because it divided into so many sects and movements, all of which have their own histories, and it attached itself, not only to the Vaishnavites, Shaivites and Shaktites (among others), but to Jains and Buddhists as well.

In general terms, however, Tantra is founded on the belief that the energies which constitute the universe flow through the human body as well. Indeed, the human body is regarded as a miniature version of the entire cosmos. The aim of tantra is to teach practitioners the ways in which the divine energies can be located and channelled within the human body, especially by bringing into union the male deity (often Shiva) and his Shakti, the Goddess Kundalini.

An Indian holy man, Pandit Gopi Krishna (1903–84), has left us a description of the experience of Kundalini as 'a dreadful burning effect of devouring fire within':

> With my mind reeling and senses deadened with pain, but with all the will-power left at my command, I brought my attention to bear on the left side of the seat of Kundalini, and tried to force an imaginary cold current upward through the middle of the spinal cord . . . Then, as if waiting for the destined moment, a miracle happened. There was a sound like a nerve thread snapping and instantaneously a silvery streak passed zigzag through the spinal cord, exactly like the sinuous movement of a white serpent in rapid flight, cascading a shower of brilliant vital energy into my brain, filling my head with a blissful lustre in place of the flame that had been tormenting me for the last three hours.

Kundalini yoga releases the power coiled like a serpent at the base of the central channel of energy in the human anatomy of Tantra. The Tantrika (the one who practises tantra) is then liberated (Moksha) into that union. On the way to that final union, the Tantras teach the way to achieve both extreme bliss (*bhoga*), and great powers (*siddhi*). Because in Indian belief the energies in the cosmos run as much in destruction as in creation, tantra may lead the Tantrika to seek those energies in places and practices that are abhorrent to those who live in appropriate ways – i.e., those who live according to Dharma. According to a Tantric text, 'By the same acts that cause some people to be born in hell for a thousand years, others gained their eternal salvation.' Those acts include five acts known from their initial letters as the five 'Ms', including alcohol and ritual sex, including intercourse with the dead.

It follows that the journey of the Tantrika is dangerous, because the energies let loose in the body may be overwhelming unless they are properly controlled. Access to the practice of tantra, known as Sadhana, requires initiation or *diksha* and must be guided by an accomplished teacher known as a Guru. Gurus are not confined to Tantra. They appear widely in Indian religion and are often organized in traditions, each of which has its own history.

In the unfolding history of Indian religion, it will be obvious that Deities have played a central part. And yet at the same time there have been traditions which have accepted that Deities occur among the many appearances in the universe, but that they are not of central importance. Two of those traditions, Jains and Buddhists, broke away to become separate religions. Others remained as philosophical reflections within the main family of Indian religion.

Of these, Samkhya was one of the earliest, appearing in about the ninth century BCE, and becoming a systematic philosophy, Karika Samkhya, in about the fourth century CE. Samkhya did not deny the reality of Deities, but accounted for the emergence and existence of the cosmos without requiring any action or input from God.

In Samkhya belief, Purusha ('man' or 'person') is the absolute and unchanging Consciousness which is aware of the changing history of the universe, but is not involved in it. That changing history is a consequence of Prakriti ('making first') which is the unconscious cause of all that appears and happens. The relationship between Purusha and Prakriti is described as a lame man with excellent sight (Purusha) being carried on the shoulders of a blind man with strong legs (Prakriti).

Samkhya offers a way of understanding the relationship between Purusha and Prakriti, and of finding a way to the freedom of Purusha through yoga – especially in the Samkhya-yoga of Patanjali (second–third centuries CE), to whom is attributed the *Yoga Sutra*, a system of 'eight-limbed yoga', the eight limbs being different techniques for disentangling Purusha from Prakriti. On the basis of Samkhya, many other systems of yoga (from *yuj*, 'to yoke', 'to unite', or 'to control') were developed which, through various different practices, lead to a transformation of consciousness, in which concern for the world and o ther impediments to freedom, such as greed or hatred, are eradicated.

In Samkhya, it can easily be seen that Deities are not necessary for the creation or sustaining of the universe, but they are nevertheless allowed in Samkhya as one of the many effects of 'blind Prakriti'. This belief that gods and goddesses exist but that they are not necessary for the explanation of the universe still has important implications for the Indian understanding of the relation between science and religion.

If, however, God is not needed for creation (and many Hindus would certainly dispute that), why *is* God needed? Samkhya-yoga answered that God as the supreme Lord (Ishvara) is a special 'outpost' of Purusha who has never been entangled in Prakriti and is therefore a bridge to Purusha, across which a

person moves to become the entirely free person known as
Kaivalya ('alone', 'unique'). It was that answer which changed the
beliefs of Indians in subsequent history, both in practice, and
also as it was explored by the great philosophers.

Philosophy, Reform and Modern India

Yoga is an example of the belief found extensively in Indian and
many other religions that spiritual exercise is as necessary as
physical exercise in maintaining health – in fact, even more so
because the body will fail in health until eventually it dies, but
the interior truth endures beyond the death of the body.

But what is that 'interior truth'? What is its character and to
what does it lead? Those are questions that religions answer and
to which philosophy attends. Philosophical reflection is known
in India as *darshana* ('viewing' or 'viewpoint'). In the post-Vedic
period, six *darshanas* were recognized as being within the family,
and were known as *astika*, of which Samkhya was one. Others
were thought to be too far out because they denied the authority
of the Vedas, and were known as *nastika*. They were regarded as
still belonging to the family even though they were aberrant
members of it. Jains and Buddhists are an example, as also is
another early system (*c.*sixth century BCE) called Lokayata *darshana* because it restricted truth to this world (*loka*) only, and
was a version of materialism.

Later than the *astika* viewpoints were the philosophical reflections on the revealed texts, including the Vedas and the
Upanishads, known collectively as Vedanta. Among these systems, three remain particularly important: the first is Advaita
('non-dualism') which claims that there is only the one reality of
Brahman and nothing beside it; the second is Vishishtadvaita

('qualified non-dualism'), which accepts that there is only one reality, but that within the nature of that one reality there is relatedness of God and souls; the third is Dvaita, which believes that God is utterly distinct and transcendent, but that souls can enter into a union with God in which they remain distinct in their final state.

Advaita is particularly associated with Shankara, who lived in the eighth/ninth centuries CE. Taught by a pupil of Gaudapada (sixth or seventh century CE), he argued that there is only one absolute and unchanging reality, Brahman. All else comes and goes and is, in comparison with Brahman, unreal. But Brahman can be discerned in the world and within ourselves as Atman, so that a wise life seeks simply to realize the simple truth, 'I am That'. Shankara summarized his viewpoint in one sentence: 'Brahman alone is real, the world is appearance, Atman is nothing but Brahman.'

If the world as we see it is a transient appearance, how come that such things as mountains and mice look extremely real? It is because all things come from Brahman as a kind of dream that Brahman conjures up. Brahman does this through Maya, which means 'the power to bring things into being'. We then look at the dream and suppose that it is real. So Maya becomes illusion because out of ignorance (*avidya*) we superimpose our own ideas and believe them to be true. So what has to be overcome, in Shankara's viewpoint, is not so much evil and sin as ignorance.

That is why, at the end of his life, Shankara made the 'Tour of Victory' (*digvijaya*), defeating in debate rival points of view. He also established at the four points of the compass centres of learning and instruction in order to send out teachers of Advaita known as Dashanami Samnaysins ('world-renouncers'). The learned men in charge of them are known as Shankaracaryas who are still regarded with honour and authority by observant Hindus of a traditional kind.

Shankara recognized the importance of Deities (and restored several temples), but he saw them as agents of Brahman who help and support people on the long road to truth. Ultimately, they are no more real than any other appearance. To another philosopher, Ramanuja (eleventh/twelfth centuries), that was too dismissive of the human experience of devotion to God. Ramanuja lived in southern India and knew well the ways in which Bhakti had changed the world of so many people – he knew at first hand the beliefs and practices of the Shrivaishnavites.

Ramanuja agreed with Shankara that Brahman is that which truly is, but he did not agree that all else is the projection of *avidya* (ignorance). He believed that individual selves are real, but that they are always dependent on Brahman for their exist-ence and functions. Selves are the instruments of Brahman, and so this view is a qualified non-dualism – i.e., Vishishtadvaita. There are two ways to liberation (Moksha), the monkey and the cat: by effort in Bhakti and by complete surrender to the grace of God.

The third of the three major schools of philosophy is that of Madhva, who was a Vaishnavite and lived at some time between 1199 and 1317. He believed that there are five distinctions or dualities, hence his school is known as Dvaita['dual']-vedanta. The distinctions which cannot be destroyed are between God and the soul, God and matter, souls themselves, the soul and matter, and the constituent components of matter. The final union of the soul with God is not one of being absorbed, or of souls and God retaining their identity but in one reality. It is one of a relationship between a lover and the one who is loved.

All these viewpoints have continued to be life-changing to the present day. For example, Sarvepalli Radhakrishnan (1888–1975), President of India from 1962 and 1967, interpreted Indian religion to the world outside India (where he was a professor at Oxford and an ambassador to countries including the Soviet Union) as basically Advaita. He argued that Maya means (as we have seen earlier), not illusion, but the power to bring things into being. In that way he hoped to reconcile Indian beliefs with Western science.

This attempt to show the harmony between Indian and European beliefs had begun much earlier and is particularly associated with Ram Mohan Roy (1772–1833), sometimes called 'the father of modern India'. Learning much that he admired from the British presence in India, he opposed social evils which he did not regard as an essential part of Hindu beliefs – such things as caste, the prohibition against the remarriage of widows, discrimination against women, and *sati* (suttee, the requirement that a widow should burn herself on the pyre of her deceased husband).

In 1828, he founded Brahmo Sabha to foster these aims, which became Brahmo Samaj in 1843 under Debenranath Tagore (1817–1905): he was the father of Rabindranath Tagore (1861–1941), the first Indian to win a Nobel Prize (for Literature in 1913) who wrote the verses which became the Indian National anthem after independence. Dayananda Sarasvati (1824–83) agreed with the protest against social evils, but he believed that the correct way to eradicate them was not to make an alliance with European values, but to return to the fundamental Indian values and beliefs contained in Vedic religion. He founded the Arya Samaj in 1875 to promote the view that the Vedas are the source of all human wisdom, including the natural sciences, and that the Vedas themselves insist on such social reforms as the emancipation of women and the abolition of the abuses of caste.

The belief that Indian values are the foundation of life as it should be lived began to change attitudes to India and Indian religion in Europe and the United States, where people began to think that there is perhaps a finer wisdom to be found in India and Asia: *ex oriente lux*, 'from the East light'. This belief was spread widely in the West by Vivekananda (1863–1902), especially after the World Parliament of Religions in 1893.

It was a belief that changed the lives of many young Indians at the time as well, who began to feel a confidence and pride in India. From the Arya Samaj came a political party known as Hindu Mahasabha committed to the idea of Hindutva (of being Hindu in distinction from all foreign, including Muslim, beliefs). Hindutva is 'the quality of the Hindu way' found in the entire entity of land, people, beliefs and practices, and it was introduced by V. D. Savarkar in 1923: 'A Hindu is he ... who above all addresses this land, this Sindhustan, as his *punyabhu*, as his Holyland – the land of his prophets and seers, of his godmen and gurus, the land of piety and pilgrimage.' A member of that party, K. V. Hedgewar (1890–1940) founded the Rashtriya Svayamsavak Sangh (RSS), a nationalist volunteer organization, insisting on the idea of a Hindu nation. That belief was shared by the Bharatiya Janata Party (BJP), founded in 1980, which began as, in effect, the political form of RSS. In 2014, the BJP under the leadership of Narendra Modi, the Chief Minister in Gujarat, won the general election and became the government of India. Modi ended his letter of thanks to the electorate with these words: 'Let us begin the journey towards "Ek Bharat, Shreshtha Bharat" and create an India our founding fathers would be proud of.'

That same pride in India was felt by Mahatma ('Great Soul')

Gandhi (1869–1948), but he attempted to include rather than exclude others as he joined the struggle for independence from British rule. From the fundamental Indian belief in Ahimsa ('not harming' any sentient creature) Gandhi developed what he called Satyagraha, 'truth force'. This manifested itself in non-violent resistance to the British, but it embraced much more than that. It meant for Gandhi that all are equally the same under God who is Truth. He therefore called the Untouchables (the lowest in the caste system) Harijans, 'the children of God', though to them this title is empty and they call themselves Dalits, the Oppressed.

Gandhi made every attempt to include Muslims in the new India, but the pressure to create a separate Muslim state was too great. Ironically, Gandhi was assassinated by a member of the RSS who believed that Gandhi had made too many (mainly monetary) concessions to the Muslims. Beliefs that change the world can be divisive in the extreme.

Jains

Jains and Buddhists belong to religions which emerged in India during the Vedic period, though they see their origins going back to the beginning of time. Both religions are rooted in the quest for Enlightenment, but they became separated religions because their founders found Indian religion in their day to be a failure and an impediment in the quest for that goal.

Their own background seems to lie in individuals known as *shramanas* ('those who make an effort'), or by Jains (in Prakrit) as *samanas*. Shramanas were those who rejected the structure of the Varnas, along with the injustices and immoralities of society. They also rejected the sacrificial rituals of the brahmans as a way to overcome them and to find one's own peace and enlightenment. They therefore withdrew into the forest and pursued their own Enlightenment with an increasingly severe asceticism. The brahmans concluded that they had abandoned Dharma (appropriate behaviour) and were outside society altogether. This belief fuelled the many subsequent conflicts between Hindus on the one side, and Jains and Buddhists on the other.

Of the shramanas, some attained enlightenment by their own efforts, and without the help or guidance of teachers. Those individuals are known as Paccekabuddhas (Pali; in Sanskrit, Pratyekkabuddhas). Their enlightenment gave them complete self-understanding of the reasons why people (including themselves) live wrongly, and how that can be put right through ascetic renunciation of the world and its ways.

That may sound self-centred, but the earliest descriptions of the shramanas and Paccekabuddhas stress how deeply they were moved by compassion (*anukampa*) for those who are still lost in the world, and how urgently they gave help to others. In particular, they had achieved peace, and they therefore extended that peace, not just to humans, but to all sentient beings.

The belief that we should live at peace, not just with ourselves, but with the whole world, is the foundation of the Jain and Buddhist commitment to non-violence, Ahimsa. Ahimsa is not just a theoretical belief. It must be accompanied by 'a putting into action of that truth', *saccakiriya*: Gandhi, who was much influenced by a Jain friend, made powerful use of these combined beliefs in his own way.

Jains first appeared in about the eighth or seventh centuries BCE, in the area of India now known as Bihar. Jains believe that there are two forms of existence, Jiva and matter. Jiva is, in Jain belief (in contrast to Hindu understanding of Jiva), the spiritual reality which originally possessed complete bliss and understanding. Now it is weighed down by Karma. Karma is not the law of consequence, as elsewhere in India. It is the weight of wrongdoing which pervades us and which holds down the Jiva in continuing rebirth. Jainism teaches the way of escape, of losing the weight of Karma, and it points particularly to the example of those who have already achieved this.

They are the Jinas ('the Conquerors'), from whom the name Jain is derived. The main Conquerors (i.e., Jinas) are the twenty-four figures who have shown the way to cross the gulf that separates the world of rebirth, with its karmic entanglements, from the attainment of the highest bliss. These twenty-four figures are therefore known as 'the Makers of the Ford', the Tirthankaras.

Jains believe that time is a continuously turning wheel, and that in each 'turn of the wheel', the twenty-four Tirthankaras appear. In the present 'world age', something is known historically of the twenty-third, Parshva (c.850 BCE), and of the twenty-fourth, Mahavira (Great Hero) who lived at roughly the same time as the Buddha: traditionally his dates are 599–527, but it may have been a century later.

The son of a king, Mahavira followed the shramanas and renounced the world, becoming a wandering beggar. For thirty years he pursued a life of asceticism, going naked for the rest of his life. He attained enlightenment, and founded the Jain community. During the rainy season, he went into retreat with his first followers, and finally he got rid of his Karma and attained Moksha, total release. He died at Parva.

Release (Moksha) means that the soul (Jiva) obtains the highest summit, totally free from this world and in no contact with it. At first sight, this belief seems to be contradicted by the fact that Jains have in their many temples images of the

Tirthankaras whom they revere, addressing prayers to them. But they do not expect the Jinas to answer their prayers or to interact with them. Jain worshippers are expressing gratitude to the Tirthankaras for their example, and expressing also their own hope and commitment to follow the same way and gain the same goal. It is thus a learning experience of the most profound kind.

In general, Jain life rests on three commitments, known as the Three Jewels: right belief, right knowledge, right conduct. But what is also required eventually is a commitment to asceticism. This may be attempted by laypeople, but only as preparation for rebirth as an ascetic. They take the five so-called 'Lesser Vows' (*anuvrata*), which are a less demanding form of the vows taken by the ascetics:

- Ahimsa;
- Satya, truthfulness in all one's dealings, especially in business;
- Asteya, honesty in all one's dealings, especially when one might otherwise 'get away with it';
- Brahmacharya, control in all sexual matters;
- Aparigraha, a moderate lifestyle, giving any surplus to the needy and to religious causes.

The five 'Great Vows' (*mahavrata*) are taken by those who join the ascetic orders:

- Ahimsa, in practice and also in the mind;
- Satya, speaking and being that truth;
- Asteya, not taking what is not given, and thus relying entirely on alms, and not even staying in one place for too long;
- Brahmacharya, renouncing all sexual activity and avoiding any kind of contact with women;

- Aparigraha, detachment from possessions and from all objects of the senses.

The two main ascetic orders are those of the Digambaras ('clothed in air', who wear no clothes) and the Shevetambaras ('white-clothed'). They divided sometime around the fifth century CE, when the Shevetambaras migrated south during a famine and began to wear clothes. The dispute between them became at times bitter and violent. They share many beliefs in common, but are divided over such things as the wearing of clothes, whether women can attain Moksha without first being reborn as men, and which texts count as the sacred writings with authority.

Despite the differences over what counts as 'canonical', both Orders agree on the central importance for Jain belief of the work of the second-century-CE monk Umasvati, *Tattvarthadhigama Sutra, A Manual for Understanding All That Is*. The Sutra emphasizes the characteristic features of Jain life, non-violence, the importance of not hanging onto possessions, and the validity of different understandings of the same subject-matter. This philosophical belief in 'the many-sidedness of reality', known as *anekantavada*, has changed the world for Jains profoundly: it means that different viewpoints can be expressed and defended, and that all are needed in order to build up a true picture of reality. They expressed this belief in the image of the blind men attempting to describe an elephant when each of them can only touch one part of it. Each of their descriptions is valid but limited, and all their viewpoints are needed to build up a more accurate picture.

The validity of different viewpoints has meant that there have been differences of opinion and practice among Jains. For example, some Jains have raised questions about the central importance of temples and rituals. In the fifteenth century, Shah Lonka (perhaps under the influence of Muslims who were destroying many Jain images and temples) attacked image-worship, as did the Sthanakvasis ('hall-dwellers'), who would lodge anywhere rather than in a Jain temple. They emerged in the seventeenth century and continue in small numbers to the present. They take the commitment to Ahimsa with such seriousness that they wear face masks to ensure that they do not accidentally breathe in and kill an insect.

A Sthanakvasi monk, Bhikanji (1726–1803) combined this same commitment with an even more extreme asceticism, and founded the Terapanthis. They believe that they must not only pursue characteristic Jain actions, like buying captive animals in order to set them free, but also enter empathetically into the ensouled nature of all appearance. Thus the eighth leader, Tulsi, believed that to enter into the very nature of the least atom is the only way to counter the use of atoms in a bomb.

The same mistrust of rituals and of sectarian divisions underlay the work of another reformer, Shrimad Rajacandra, who was born as Raichanbhai Mehta (1867–1901). He believed that Jains are right to concentrate on the importance of this life, making the most of its opportunity to achieve Moksha. He emphasized that each individual soul is the agent of its own acts, and is thus entirely responsible for what happens to it. He did not believe that an ascetic withdrawal from the world is necessary, but that progress can be made while remaining in the world. His influence on Gandhi made Gandhi say that in moments of spiritual crisis, Rajacandra was his refuge.

Jains are a small minority in India (about five million), but with an influence far beyond their numbers. Although at times they have been attacked and persecuted, they have remained remarkably tolerant. For Jains, their beliefs in Ahimsa and in the validity of different viewpoints change the world, not least the worlds of violence and of threats to the environment and the planet.

Parsis

Christianity and Islam are Indian religions in the sense that they have been a significant presence in India for many centuries, but they came in origin from outside India. The same is true of the Parsis. Parsis are 'those from Persia', who, when they were persecuted by Muslims, began to settle on the west coast of India from about 937 CE. When Muslims started to expand their rule in India, Parsis fought with Hindus against them – unsuccessfully: but Muslim rule in India was not so harsh as it had been in Persia. Under the British, the Parsis became successful traders, especially in Bombay. They now number under 100,000, but many have moved overseas.

The Parsis were originally the followers of the prophet Zarathustra or Zoroaster, and are therefore known as Zoroastrians. Parsis believe that Zarathustra is the first and oldest of all the prophets, who lived at around 6000 BCE. Historically, a date somewhere between the twelfth century and the sixth is more likely. He seems to have lived in what is now north-east Iran.

His own original teaching is preserved in seventeen hymns known as Gathas, in a text known as *Yasna*, though much more has been passed on in other hymns and traditions. Zarathustra believed that God, the source of creation and of all goodness, had commissioned him personally to proclaim that God is the Father of Order, Ahura Mazda. In that case, the question has to be asked, 'From whom or from what has evil and disorder come?'

Zarathustra taught that evil comes from the Father of Destruction, Angra Mainyu, or in Pahlavi (an early language in Persia) Ahriman. It is a fundamental belief of Parsis that Angra Mainyu is as eternal as Ahura Mazda. In other words, the opponent of God by whatever name he is called – for example, the Devil (in Christianity) or (in Islam) Iblis or (in India) Mara who fought viciously against the Buddha after his Enlightenment – is not a fallen or rebellious part of God's creation who in the course of time will be subdued and defeated: Angra Mainyu is as eternal as Ahura Mazda, and the two are in constant conflict.

This belief in the unending duality between good and evil is known as 'dualism'. All religions recognize the reality of evil and wrong-doing, but beliefs vary greatly about the nature of evil and about what can be done to resist it. Religions vary from dualism to a belief that evil is the absence of good and that good will ultimately prevail. In either case, religions take seriously the ways in which humans experience and are tested by evil as though it is an attack by an agent of some active kind. That belief is expressed in personal and mythological language, as a consequence, for example, of the Devil, of Diabolos (in Greek) or of Iblis (in Arabic), of Mara in India, of the Ten Kings of Hell under Yama in China, and so on. It is a belief that has had extensive consequences because it has enabled people to engage with evil, not as an abstraction, but as an urgent and necessary encounter. Parsis have such a strong sense of the constant presence of evil, and are always engaged in battle and warfare against it, that it has completely changed their understanding of the world. It creates an entirely different sense of individual and personal responsibility.

That comes about because Angra Mainyu is the source, not just of moral evil, but of every kind of corruption and decay, from the pollution of the planet to the decay and rust which erodes all things. Parsis are thus committed by their beliefs to fight against Angra Mainyu in all these areas, and were committed to 'saving the planet' long before others recognized the crisis. As part of the battle, Parsis lay out, on a Daxma or Tower of Silence, dead bodies for vultures to devour, since they believe that the body is possessed by Angra Mainyu's corruption and cannot be disposed of in the good creations of earth or water.

Parsis believe that the fight can be won. Human beings are the focal point of this battle between good and evil. With the help of Ahura Mazda, they have the capacity to overcome evil, and that is why there is such a strong emphasis on personal responsibility.

This is reinforced by the fact that the final judgement will be based on an exact reckoning of the balance between good and evil works. At death, the soul is led to the Bridge of Judgement, the Chinvat Bridge. Those whose good thoughts and deeds predominate are taken over to an abode of bliss, but the predominantly wicked fall off, to be 'guests in the House of the Lie', a place of rotten food and foul smells, of long torment and woe.

It will be clear from this that Parsis have imaginatively pictorial ways of describing the battle between good and evil. Angra Mainyu, for example, does not fight an abstract battle, but recruits agents such as *khrafstras* in the form of snakes, rats and flies (he is the Lord of the Flies) who bring death and disease. Today, some Parsis do not take the pictures literally, but believe that they stand for the evil tendencies in human nature.

This process of seeking the inner or underlying meaning of myths and pictures occurs in all religions and is known as 'demythologization': the myths and pictures are not discarded, since usually they are the only 'language' through which the most important truths about ourselves can be told; instead, each generation has to find its own way of connecting those truths with a changed and changing world.

Zarathustra's teaching was originally opposed by the ruling authorities (an example of the war between good and evil), but when Cyrus the Great overthrew the Babylonians in the sixth century BCE, it was his policy to encourage the many different belief-systems in his new empire, as a way of securing their loyalty. He encouraged the return of the exiled Jews to Jerusalem (536 BCE), and he made Zoroastrianism a state religion because it was itself Persian in origin.

The encouragement given to Zoroastrianism came to an end when Alexander began his eastern conquest (334–330) of lands including Persia. Alexander has gone down in history as 'the Great', but not to Zoroastrians and Parsis, because he destroyed the imposing city of Persepolis and killed many of the Zoroastrian Magi. The Magi were ritual and astrological experts, and it is they who appeared in Bethlehem at the birth of Jesus (the belief that they were three kings is much later in Christian history).

The Greek influence (known as Hellenism, against which the Maccabeans rebelled) lasted until the second century BCE, when the Parthians established a new regime and empire, constantly raiding the eastern edges of the Roman empire, even in 40 BCE capturing and holding Jerusalem until Herod with Roman help drove them out. The Parthians did much to revive Zoroastrianism, gathering oral traditions into Scripture, the *Avesta*, and increasing the number of fire temples. In Parsi belief, fire is one of the good creations of Ahura Mazda, and it plays as prominent a part in their rituals as does Agni and fire for Hindus.

In the third century CE, the Sassanians from the south-west overthrew the Parthians in the north, and created an official version of Zoroastrianism to legitimize their rule. This state-enforced Zoroastrianism is different from the early beliefs, and is known as Zurvan, 'Time'. Zurvan brings all things into being and carries them away, controlling (even predestining) humans in what they do – a far remove from the moral responsibility of Zoroastrianism.

When Muslims invaded Persia in the seventh century CE, more than a thousand years of Zoroastrian history ended. They defeated the Sassanians at Nihavend in 642, and the last Sassanian king, Yazdegird III was killed in 652. At first the Muslims did not attack Zoroastrians, simply imposing taxes and making Arabic the official language. There was even speculation whether Zoroastrians were a 'People of the Book', which would give them, like Jews and Christians, the protected status of *dhimmis*.

Suspicion, however, of Zoroastrian worship increased (were they, in their fire rituals, worshipping idols?), and persecution became severe, especially under the Qajars (1796–1925). Some converted to Islam, a few persisted in Persia against extraordinary odds of persecution, but many moved to India.

During the twentieth century, the position of the Parsis in Persia improved greatly. In 1882, provision had been made for greater access to education and health services. In 1906, a parliament (Majles) was established, with a Zoroastrian being elected, and in 1909 a place was reserved for each minority community. In 1925, the then prime minister was made Shah of Persia, as Reza Shah Pahlavi (he ruled until 1941). The Zoroastrians were seen as the true descendants of the original Iranians and were encouraged to play a central part in the life of the country – and many Parsis actually returned to Persia. Their favoured position continued under the second Shah, Muhammad Reza, but when he was deposed by the Ayatullah Khumayni in

1979, the rights of Zoroastrians were restricted again, and a new exodus began – not only to India, but to many other parts of the world.

Meanwhile, in India, Parsis remained prosperous and influential. They helped in setting up the Indian National Congress, and some were caught up in the moves to show the connections between inherited religious traditions and the modern world. Reformers set up Ilm-i Kshnoom, the Path of Knowledge, which, while gaining much from Theosophy, claimed to have recovered secret teachings of Iranian masters in Iran. They are vegetarian and abstain from intoxicants in order to create a personal aura of wisdom. The divide between traditional and reforming beliefs continues to the present.

Sikhs: Guru Nanak

The word *sikh* means 'learner' or disciple. Sikhs are those who follow the Gurmat, the teaching of the Gurus, and Gurmat is the Sikh name for what in English is called Sikhism.

The word *guru* ('heavy') is a common word in Indian and Asian religions for an inspired and well-trained teacher. Sikhs believe that they have three kinds of Guru: Sat Guru (the one who is truly God); Guru Nanak (who introduced the Sikh religion) and his nine successors; and the Guru Granth Sahib, the holy Scripture in which the teachings of the Gurus and some other inspired teachers are gathered.

Guru Nanak (1469–1539) was born in the Punjab, a large area of India now divided between Pakistan and India. He was married and worked in business, but spent much of his time chanting hymns with Mardana, a Muslim musician, three of whose verses are in the Guru Granth Sahib. In 1499 at Sultanpur, he was bathing in the river Bein when he entered into an intense experience of God. He returned after three days knowing that God had given him a direct commission to go and share with others the love of God.

In Sikh belief, God is far beyond human description or understanding. God can only be approached in worship, above all in reciting the name of God in profound reverence. The Nam (name) is the nearest on earth that humans can approach to God, and this concentration and meditation on the Name (*Nam simaran*) is at the heart of Sikh belief and worship. Sikhs refer to God as Ik Onkar, or Ik Oankar, God is the only One who is and who therefore matters.

That is a belief shared by other religions, but it changed the world of India in which Guru Nanak and his followers lived, because it unites all religions that are devoted to God, and makes them partners of each other. Guru Nanak said, 'There is no Hindu or Muslim, so whose path shall I follow? I shall follow the path of God.'

That is often understood to mean that all religious differences are obliterated for those who truly devote themselves to God. In fact, it may mean that there are no Hindus or Muslims who faithfully practise their religions. But either way around, it expresses the belief, fundamental for all Sikhs, that in relation to God, the divisions between religions are irrelevant: what matters is to be completely devoted to God, not to an institution.

Guru Nanak was not alone in expressing that belief. During the fifteenth and sixteenth centuries in India, movements had come into being whose members are known collectively as the Sants. They had drawn together followers in order to teach them this way of devotion, in which the differences between religions become trivial in comparison with God. One of the greatest of these was Kabir (d. 1518), who found God everywhere he looked. 'Banaras [home of Krishna] is to the east, Mecca [centre of Muslim pilgrimage] is to the west, but go into your own heart and you will find Ram [Rama] there.' God is called by many names: Hari (Krishna) and Ram in India, Allah, Karim and Rahim (the Merciful One) in Islam. What matters is finding God above the names, and that can be done in the simplest way:

> Hari dwells in the east, they say, and Allah resides in the west: search for him in the heart of your heart, for that is where he dwells, Rahim-Ram. All men and women ever born are nothing but forms of God. Kabir is the child of Allah-Ram, he is my Guru and my Pir.

How directly Kabir influenced Nanak cannot now be known. Nanak certainly learned much from the Sant tradition, and stories exist of the two men meeting, but these seem to have been told later in order to show how the much-revered Kabir acknowledged Nanak as greater than himself.

After receiving his commission from God to teach others, Guru Nanak gave away all his possessions and spent the next twenty-four years travelling widely with Mardana. He went as far east as Assam and as far west as Mecca, perhaps even Baghdad. Everywhere he went, he taught hymns, engaged in discussion and set up a place of worship, known as *dharmsala*. Eventually he settled in Kartarpur, where he began to organize his followers into a community.

Guru Nanak believed that concentration on the Name of God in devotion and love brings a person directly into contact with God without the need for rituals or for intermediaries like priests and prophets. The popular stories of Guru Nanak's life, known as *janam-sakhis*, give many examples of his refusal of ritual. When he reached Hardwar on his travels, he saw people throwing water to the east to give sustenance to their dead ancestors. Guru Nanak started to throw water westward, and when the worshippers protested, he replied that if their water could reach their ancestors in the east, his could as easily reach his thirsty crops in the west. When he arrived in Mecca, he lay down with his feet facing the *qibla* (i.e., the direction of prayer for Muslims). When he was rebuked, Guru Nanak asked that his feet should be pulled round until they were facing in a direction where God was not. As he was pulled round, so the *qibla* moved round miraculously with him.

With this belief that religious ritual is unnecessary went the belief that all people are equal in the sight of God, and that the divisions of society, above all in the systems of Varna and caste, should be ignored and in practice abolished (though not all Sikhs subsequently have succeeded in implementing that belief). There is no spiritual or religious elite, as though, for example, those who practise great austerity are superior to those who live in the world. In fact, Guru Nanak realized that the true 'battlefield' is in the world and in everyday life: by meditating on the Nam, people can overcome the Five Evil Passions within them, and this can only be demonstrated by the way in which they live and work.

In Guru Nanak's belief, much that happens in existing religions is thus an impediment standing in the way of people reaching God. On the other hand, Guru Nanak realized that the learning and practice of the way of devotion cannot happen by chance or accident. It requires an organization through which these things can be passed on from one life and from one generation to another. The formal organization of the Sikhs came to be known as the Khalsa, and although the details of that were worked out by the Gurus who succeeded Guru Nanak, Guru Nanak laid the foundations of the later organization while he was alive. In particular, he placed great emphasis on a communal meal during which Sikhs can give encouragement, as well as correction if necessary, to each other, and can offer hospitality.

This meal is held in the Guru-ka-langar, a kind of 'free kitchen'. In every Sikh place of assembly (known as the gurdwara), vegetarian food is cooked and given to all people who want it, irrespective of caste, race or creed, and with no order of precedence. By feeding the needy, Sikhs serve the Guru and worship God. By working in the Guru-ka-langar or by providing money and food, Sikhs demonstrate their belief that life must be lived in the service (Punjabi, *seva*) of others.

Central in all gurdwaras, and accorded the reverence due to God, is the Guru Granth Sahib, since this is the living Guru who continues to instruct and inspire all Sikhs. The Guru Granth Sahib is also known as Adi Granth, the first volume in distinction from Dasam Granth, the tenth or supplementary book. The Adi Granth is 1,430 pages long, with each page being printed identically, so that every copy has a standard length and page numbering. The contents are metrical and intended for singing or chanting, and there are hymns, not only from the Sikh Gurus, but from Muslims and Hindus, such as Kabir, Namdev and Surdas. The Adi Granth therefore contains a variety of languages, and comes from different periods, but the message is consistent: salvation and release from rebirth depends, not on caste or ritual, but on constant meditation on God's Nam or Name, and on complete immersion in God alone.

All this is summed up in the *Mul Mantra*. This is one of Guru Nanak's first compositions, and it stands, not only at the head of the Adi Granth, but at the head of each one of its thirty-one sections, or *rags*. In Sikh belief, the *Mul Mantra* is the foundation of their faith expressed in its briefest possible form. As a result, it is impossible to translate. Roughly it means:

> There is One Being
> whose Name is Truth
> Source and Creator
> without fear, without hostility
> timeless in form
> unborn
> self-existent
> the grace of the Guru.

That God can be known only through the grace of the Guru shows how important the Guru is in Sikh belief. Ultimately the only Guru is God, who is both a goal of the human quest and also the means to reach God in many different ways:

> The Guru is the ladder, the boat, the raft by means of which a person reaches God. The Guru is the lake, the ocean, the boat, the sacred place of pilgrimage, the river. If I please you, I am cleansed by immersion in the Ocean of Truth . . . Without the Guru there can be neither devotion [Bhakti] nor love, without the Guru there is no way to join the company of the holy people [Sants], without the Guru we cast about blindly in futile endeavour.

The Sikh Gurus

As Guru Nanak grew old, he realized that the community of believers would still need a Guru to guide and teach them. He therefore appointed as his successor Angad (1504–52) – and not his eldest son. Guru Angad organized the Guru-ka-langar in a more systematic way, so that there would be few variations in Sikh practice – and to that end he encouraged physical fitness to make sure that the Sikh virtue of service in the community (*seva*) could be undertaken effectively. He also began the collection of Nanak's hymns, the nucleus of what became the Adi Granth.

As third Guru, Angad appointed Amar Das (1479–1574) – and again, not his oldest son, thus establishing the principle that the succession of Gurus is determined by God, not necessarily by descent. This underlies the Sikh belief that all the ten Gurus (Nanak and his nine successors) are equally to be revered because they all manifest the same divine light, just as one lamp is lit from another. Amar Das became Guru in 1552. He made the Sikh community less distinct from the Hindu majority by ordering Sikhs to gather on Hindu days of celebration, such as Vaishaki and Divali, to worship the One God. He strengthened the Guru-ka-langar and made sure that distinctions of caste would not creep in – an important issue, because although in Sikh belief caste should be abolished, that has still not happened in important family matters like marriage.

As fourth Guru, he appointed his son-in-law, Ram Das (1534–81) who became Guru in 1574. In 1577, he founded the spiritual centre of the Sikhs, first known (among other names) as Guru ka Chak, but later as Amritsar ('pool of the water of immortality'). Guru Ram Das cleaned and further excavated the sacred pool there, and also built a brick temple, but that was only the beginning of the buildings which now adorn Amritsar.

As fifth Guru, he chose a son, Arjan Dev (1563–1606) who became Guru in 1581. He continued to excavate the sacred pool at Amritsar, and undertook the building of the Harimandir ('Temple of God'), completed in 1601. It is called the Golden Temple because Ranjit Singh encased the outer walls in gilded copper sheets. Arjan Dev discovered that others were writing hymns to further their own ambitions, and he therefore decided to make an authoritative collection of the hymns of the Gurus and other holy people, the collection that became the Adi Granth. This was completed in 1604 and installed in the Harimandir at Amritsar. The Sikh community under Guru Arjan Dev was becoming increasingly numerous and strong – so much so that Arjan Dev was called by some 'the True Emperor'. The actual emperor, Jahangir, arrested him and charged him with treason and sedition. After prolonged torture he died, though not before he had appointed Hargobind to succeed him.

Guru Hargobind (1595–1644) became the sixth Guru in 1606. Realizing the threat to Sikhs from those who feared or envied their growing strength, he organized Sikhs to defend themselves, particularly against the Mughals. The earlier Gurus had worn a sacred cord, called *seli*, to distinguish them, but Hargobind, when he became Guru, rejected the *seli* and said, 'My *seli* will be my sword belt.' He built a fortress in Amritsar, and established the Akal Takht ('Immortal Throne') where the deeds of the Gurus and of the Sikh martyrs (*shahid*: cf. the word 'witness' in Islam) are celebrated. Between 1628 and 1634 he was victorious in four engagements with Mughal forces, before he died in 1644. He appointed his grandson, Har Rai, as his successor.

Har Rai (1630–61) became seventh Guru in 1644, and backed away from the militant policy of Guru Hargobind. He once said that a broken temple can be repaired, but not a broken heart. He was succeeded by Har Krishan as eighth Guru from 1661 to 1664. As he was dying unexpectedly from smallpox, he indicated that his successor would be an older man from Bakala. Twenty-two local men promptly claimed the succession. Tyag Mal was picked out by a merchant who had vowed in a shipwreck that if he survived he would give 500 gold pieces to the Guru. Brought to all the claimants, he offered them each a few coins until he came to Tyag Mal, who refused them saying that he had promised 500 gold coins.

Tyag Mal (1621–75) earned the name by which he is known as ninth Guru, Tegh Bahadur, 'hero of the sword', but his greatest skill was in making peace, first with the other claimants who refused to accept him, then with the Mughal emperor Aurangzeb and other rival rulers. This did not stop Aurangzeb attacking non-Muslims and seeking their conversion to Islam. Some Hindus begged Tegh Bahadur to go to Aurangzeb and find a peaceful way of coexistence. As he and five companion Sikhs made their way to Delhi, they were arrested and tortured to make them become Muslims. They refused, and on 11 November 1675, Tegh Bahadur was beheaded. During his captivity he composed more than fifty hymns, all included in the Adi Granth, whose main theme is that the praise of God, the only support in trouble, is the way to escape from imprisonment in this fleeting world.

The tenth Guru was Gobind Rai (1666–1708), who became known as Gobind Singh. It was Guru Gobind Singh who said that after him there would be no further human Guru, but that the Adi Granth would in future be the only visible Guru. The fate of Tegh Bahadur made him realize that the Sikhs must be better organized for their own defence, and for support and encouragement of each other. He therefore introduced the teaching that there can be a justified war, known as Dharam Yudh, the war of righteousness. He laid down five conditions that must be met:

- all other means to achieve settlement must have been tried first;
- war should be undertaken without passionate feelings or desire for revenge;

- no territory should be seized, nor should there be any looting;
- the Army must be made up of committed Sikhs;
- minimum force must be used.

To strengthen the community he also brought into being the all-important and central institution in Sikh belief, the Khalsa.

The Khalsa may include any true Sikh, but the term is used more usually of those Sikhs who have been formally initiated and who undertake to keep the rules of discipline known as the Rahit or Rahit Maryada. Khalsa Sikhs take as a second name Singh ('lion') to obliterate any inherited caste or other distinctions – hence Gobind Rai became Gobind Singh. They must be fearless in battle in defence of the community, they must abstain from intoxicants, and they must rise early to recite hymns and meditate on the Name of God.

Khalsa Sikhs are distinguished in particular by the Panj Kakke, more popularly known as 'the Five Ks' because these symbols all start with the letter K. They are:

1. *Kesh*, uncut hair: as a sign of strength, no hair must be removed from the body, but, unlike the matted hair of Hindu ascetics, it must be kept clean.
2. *Kangha*, a small comb to keep the hair tidy, as a sign of controlled spirituality.
3. *Kirpan*, a steel sword, originally full-size, but now often in much smaller form, as a sign of courage in defence of truth.
4. *Kara*, a steel bangle worn on the right wrist, as a sign of the embracing unity of Sikhs and of their loyalty to God and the Gurus.
5. *Kacch*, long shorts, as a sign of continence.

Guru Gobind Singh engaged in long conflict with Aurangzeb, in which two of his sons were killed. When Aurangzeb died in 1707, Guru Gobind Singh turned against the governors, such as Wazir Khan, who had persecuted Sikhs, but he himself was killed by two Pathan assassins in 1708. He instructed the Sikhs not to look for any more human Gurus, but to regard the Adi Granth as their Guru – the reason why the Adi Granth is known as Guru Granth Sahib.

Because of the Muslim destruction of temples and their campaigns to encourage conversion to Islam, Sikhs and Hindus were increasingly thrown together in self-defence in the eighteenth century. As a result, some Sikhs began to accept Hindu beliefs and practices that the ten Gurus had forbidden – *sati*, for example, reverence for the cow (*go*), the caste system. Reformers emerged to call Sikhs back to their origins – for example, Dyal Das (1783–1855) who founded the Nirankaris (regarded by other Sikhs as a separate sect), and Ram Singh (b. 1816) who founded the Namdharis. Namdharis, who were prominent in resisting British rule in India, aim to create a more just society based on Sikh beliefs. Ram Singh was exiled by the British to Rangoon, and Namdharis still await his return to usher in a new age – in other words, they do not believe that he died, although non-Namdhari Sikhs (who regard Namdharis as a separate sect) believe that he died in 1885.

In 1873, the Singh Sabha (Sikh Assembly) was formed to defend Sikhs against further attempts to convert them, either to Christianity or to Hinduism. It did this mainly through extensive programmes of education and publication. During the first half of the twentieth century, the Singh Sabha became aware that the main threat to the Sikhs had become political, with the organization of both Hindus and Muslims into political parties and organizations, increasingly in pursuit of independence. As a result, Sikhs formed the Akali Dal in 1926, which has continued to seek, if not independence, then greater autonomy for a Sikh state in the Punjab.

Buddhism

Overview

Buddhism began historically when Siddhartha Gautama, a prince of the Shakya clan, became Enlightened and thus the Buddha (the Enlightened One). He was born in India in the fifth or sixth century BCE, perhaps about 480 BCE (the date is uncertain). He gathered around him a group of followers, but he emphasized that he was not founding a religion. He looked at the unsatisfactory nature of life, bound up as it is in decay and suffering, and he showed people what makes life unsatisfactory, and how they can find a way out. He therefore compared himself to a doctor or physician, who understands the symptoms, diagnoses the illness, and suggests the cure. But it is then up to the ill person to follow that advice – or not.

When the Buddha died, the informal association with the Buddha of those seeking to follow his way became more formally organized into communities of monks (Pali, *bhikkhus*: because Buddhism began in India, the transliteration of words is often given also in Sanskrit, in this case *bhikshu*). Together these communities are known as the Sangha, in which the teaching of the Buddha (Dhamma/Dharma) is put into effect. Thus the fundamental commitment of Buddhist belief is expressed in the Three

Jewels or Refuges: I take refuge in the Buddha, I take refuge in the Dharma, I take refuge in the Sangha. 'Taking refuge in the Sangha' means in practice that there is a strong connection and interaction between bhikkhus and lay-people, with the lay-people supporting the monks, and the monks bringing teaching, rituals and other benefits to the lay-people.

In the first three centuries after the death of the Buddha, divisions began to grow between those who believed that Buddhists should stick as closely as possible to the original teaching of the Buddha, and those who took seriously his statement that his teaching does not come to an end with the death of his body and will continue. Indeed, some thought that the Buddha had entrusted teaching to his followers which was only to be made public when people were ready to receive it.

A result of this has been that Buddhism has divided between Theravada and Mahayana. There are many differences of belief and practice, as we will see, but there is agreement that all traditions and teachers must be able to trace a direct line of transmission from the Buddha. The lines of transmission are known as Lineages. The two major lineage groups are Theravada and Mahayana, with Vajrayana being reckoned sometimes as a third group, or sometimes as a group within Mahayana.

Early Buddhism traditionally divided into eighteen lineages, although traces of at least thirty-four have been recovered. Of those lineages, the oldest surviving lineage is that of Theravada (the teaching of the Elders). Theravada is strong in Sri Lanka and South East Asia.

The Mahayana (Great Vehicle) lineages share a belief that the Buddha's teaching did not end with the death of his body but still continues when people are ready to hear it. As a result, they regard Theravada not as false but as limited, and they call it

'Hinayana', lesser vehicle. Mahayana is strong in Tibet, China, Korea and Japan (and in surrounding areas, such as Mongolia).

Because in Mahayana the teaching of the Buddha continues and thus extends the ways in which people can reach Enlightenment, Mahayana has developed into many different Schools, and the history of Mahayana is in effect the history of these Schools in many different countries. The differences are sometimes so great that they have become in effect separate systems.

Thus in Tibet, the form of Buddhism is known as Vajrayana, the way of the diamond – or thunderbolt – and it has developed lineages of its own. China has many lineages whose lines of descent are not always clear, since they have interacted with each other. Thus, Chan (in Japan Zen) which claims its descent from the Buddha through Bodhidharma (c.fifth century), and Jingdu, 'Pure Land', were merged during the Song and Ming Dynasties to form the basis of modern Chinese Buddhism. Japan received many of the Chinese lineages through Korea in the sixth century, but it developed them in its own distinctive ways.

Vietnam also received its lineages from China, but it has made repeated efforts to merge the lineages into a distinctive form of Vietnamese Buddhism. For example, the Unified Buddhist Church of Vietnam was founded in 1963. Cao Dai, 'supreme tower' or 'altar', was claimed by its founder Ngo Van Chieu in 1919 to be a new 'third revelation'. The movement took the process of merging even further by including other religions. Its strongly nationalistic commitment enabled it to survive suppression by the Communists, and today it has about two million members throughout the world.

Buddhism has now spread far beyond Asia, and it has taken root in the West. There are now about 400 million Buddhists.

The Life of the Buddha

Siddhartha Gautama (in Pali, Gotama) who became the Buddha lived at about the same time as Mahavira, the twenty-fourth of the Jain Tirthankaras. 'Buddha' means 'the Enlightened One'. He was called *muni*, 'the wise one', a title also given to the Paccekabuddhas, and since he belonged to the Shakya clan, he is also known as Shakyamuni.

Gautama was the son of a king (as was Mahavira) in Kapilavastu. His dates are uncertain: according to the so-called Long Chronology, he lived *c.*566–486, but according to the Short Chronology, he lived *c.*448–368. Others claim that he was born in 480. The first connected biographies are later (first century CE onward), but the outline of his life is clear.

According to one story, his father brought him up in his palace keeping him away from all distressing experiences. But then Gautama was driven through Lumbini Park on successive days. On the first day he saw an old and decrepit man, on the second a diseased man, and on the third a dead man. After his sheltered existence, he was greatly disturbed, because he realized that the same fate awaited him also. On the fourth day he saw a religious ascetic, a shramana, who seemed to be completely at peace. Gautama decided to seek peace in the same way, so he left his wife and son, Rahula, and went to the forest to renounce the world and to practise asceticism.

He went first to two teachers, but their teachings did not lead to escape from the fact of transience, the fact that all things which come into being pass away. He therefore went off on his own to practise such extreme austerities that when he touched his stomach he could feel his backbone. He succeeded in freeing himself from the attractions of this world, but that victory, impressive in itself, did not bring him escape from the common human experience of transience.

He therefore decided to try a 'Middle Way' (a common name for Buddhism) between the pleasures of the palace and the austerities of the forest. He sat down under a large tree (subsequently known as the Bo or Bodhi Tree, the Tree of Enlightenment), and there, after some days in meditation, he broke through to perfect Enlightenment and saw with total clarity what the nature of transience is and how it can be transcended.

His first inclination, after he became the Enlightened One (i.e., the Buddha), was to stay exactly where he was, in a state of perfect insight and peace. Tradition says that it was one of the Indian Deities, Brahma Sahampati, who persuaded him to share with others that insight and the way to Enlightenment.

The Buddha therefore began his ministry of teaching. His first sermon was preached in the Deer Park at Sarnath. In it, the heart and foundation of Buddhist belief is summarized in the Four Noble Truths (*catvari-arya-satyani*) and the Noble Eightfold Path (*astangika-marga*).

The Four Noble Truths are the analysis of transience, which he called Dukkha. Dukkha is often translated as 'suffering', but it is more specifically the suffering involved in the transience of all things. The Four Truths are: (1) the fact of Dukkha; (2) the cause of Dukkha; (3) the cessation of Dukkha; and (4) the way that leads to the cessation of Dukkha.

The First Truth is that all existence is on the move (transient), that nothing is permanent, and that all human experience is in the end unsatisfactory. There are many pleasant experiences in life (*sukha*), but none of them continues for ever, nor can any life escape change and decay: the fact of Dukkha is the suffering that transience brings with it.

The Second Truth is the cause of Dukkha. Transience would not matter if we did not resent it or fight against it, but we do, even at the trivial level of seeking to deny it by trying to look younger than we are. More seriously, the cause of Dukkha is our thirst or craving (*tanha*) for things in this world as though for a moment we might stop the flow of transience. Or it is a thirst for an escape from transience in ways that, in the Buddha's belief, simply do not exist – the thirst at one extreme for eternal life, and at the other for oblivion after death. In Buddhist belief, neither is possible.

The Third Truth is that the cessation of Dukkha is possible: it lies in giving up all thirst or craving for things of this world – all attachment, in other words, to that which cannot endure. But how can that be done?

The Fourth Truth is the path that leads to that goal. It is a path with eight interlocking parts, and that is why it is known as the Eightfold Path. The Eight parts are not meant to be practised one after another, like steps when climbing a ladder. They have to be practised together, and they are in effect the whole of Buddhist life and belief. They are:

- right understanding (or right views about the true nature of reality disclosed in the Four Truths);
- right thought (based on learning to overcome *tanha*);
- right speech (which articulates the first two);
- right action (which came to be summarized in the Five Precepts that all Buddhists undertake to keep: Ahimsa, not taking anything not given, avoiding any conduct that involves sense-desires, avoiding untruth in speech or conduct; avoiding intoxication from drugs or alcohol);

- right living (in terms of work and vocation);
- right effort (doing things for the right reason and avoiding anything that might attract bad Karma);
- right mindfulness (this is at the heart of Buddhist meditation: beyond the yoga in which the mind is stilled, Buddhists in meditation seek to become more truly aware of their nature and of its transience, but also of the opportunity which it offers to move toward Enlightenment);
- right concentration (*samadhi*, the unifying of all aspects of mind and being into a single point of focus, in which all distinctions between subject and object disappear).

Those are the beliefs that changed the Indian world in which the Buddha lived – and which continue to change the world of people and societies down to the present day. At first sight, many of those beliefs seem very close to those of others in India – of the Paccekabuddhas, for example, or of the Jains, or of those seeking escape (Moksha) from rebirth in other ways. Yet in fact the beliefs of the Buddha were radically different from those of the many other ways of being religious in India: even fundamental words like 'rebirth', 'enlightenment', 'God' and 'nirvana' take on a new and utterly different meaning, as we will see. And that is why the Middle Way (or what we call Buddhism) became a separate religion with a varied and different history of its own.

Meanwhile, the Buddha responded to the request of Brahma Sahampati and set out to share his insight and wisdom with others. This teaching was later gathered together and (along with the way of life associated with it) is known as the Dharma (Pali, Dhamma). As the Buddha attracted followers, he began to organize them in communities of monks (bhikkhus/bhikshus) later known collectively as the Sangha. Together these three belong together as 'the triple jewel', the Triratna, more often translated as the Three Jewels. It is the basic commitment of Buddhist belief to say, 'I take refuge in the Buddha, I take refuge in the Dharma, I take refuge in the Sangha.'

During his teaching years, the Buddha reminded his followers that he had not instructed them 'with the closed fist of a teacher' as though they now had a set of doctrines to follow. He had been a physician or doctor: he had diagnosed their illnesses and offered an appropriate cure, but it was up to them whether they would 'take their medicine' – or not.

He moved around from place to place, but during the rainy season he and his followers went into a retreat to deepen their meditation – a pattern followed to this day, even by lay-people who at least occasionally try to go on retreat during this time. It is an example of the way in which Buddhists believe that there is a dynamic and interactive relationship between bhikkhus and lay-people, a belief which has laid down the basic pattern of life in Buddhist communities. Lay-people support and serve the Sangha (particularly with alms and food), and in return the bhikkhus support and serve the community around them with prayers and rituals, especially at times of death.

While he was on one of his teaching journeys the Buddha died, at the age of eighty – or more accurately, his body died, since, in Buddhist belief, 'he' had already gone in the attainment of Enlightenment (*parinirvana*, final Nirvana at the end of the Buddha's earthly existence). His last words were: 'Now, monks, I declare to you: all conditioned things are of a nature to decay – strive on untiringly.'* Just before those last words he said to one of

---

* *Digha Nikaya* 2.154–6, translated by Maurice Walshe, *The Long Discourses of the Buddha: A Translation of the Digha Nikaya* (Somerville, MA: Wisdom Publications, 1996).

his followers: 'Ananda, it may be that you will think: "The Teacher's instruction has ceased, now we have no teacher!" It should not be seen like this, Ananda, for what I have taught and explained to you as Dhamma and discipline will, at my passing, be your teacher.'

Buddhism in India and South East Asia

So what was the teaching of the Buddha? Since the Buddha lived and taught in India, the teaching of the Buddha (known as Buddha-dharma or Buddha-sasana, a common name for what we call 'Buddhism') is an Indian religion. Not surprisingly, there-fore, many concepts and beliefs found in other Indian religions appear, at least superficially, in Buddhism – for example, a belief in Deities (it was one of them, Brahma Sahampati, who per-suaded the Buddha to teach others), a belief in rebirth, with the outcomes in a new life determined by Karma (the moral law in the universe), and a belief that there is a final goal known as Nirvana.

Yet in fact Buddha-dharma is radically different from other Indian religions. Even when its beliefs look the same, they have entirely different meanings and applications. Thus, to take the three examples above, Buddhists certainly believe that there are realities or appearances correctly identified as gods and god-desses. In other words, Buddhism is not, as is often claimed, atheistic; it is not 'a non-theistic religion/philosophy'. But like the Jains, Buddhists believe that the deities are simply one form of appearance doing their best, like others, to advance toward Enlightenment and release. There is certainly no supreme and absolute 'God' who created the universe and remains distinct from it; a deity is simply the form of appearance that is able and willing to interact with humans in answer to their prayers. That is why many Buddhists do in fact pray to God. On the other hand, the Buddha was clear that the deities cannot be manipulated by bribes, and he vehemently opposed the rituals and sacrifices of the brahmans.

To take the second example: Buddhists believe that the flow of rebirth (Samsara) will continue until they gain release, and they may be reborn as humans or as animals, in heaven or in hell. The outcome is determined by what they have said and done, for better or for worse. That sounds like common Indian belief, *except* that the Buddha insisted that there is no soul or self being reborn. In other words, there is no Atman, a belief known as 'no-soul', *anatta/anatman*. There is only the constant flow of moments of appearance, with one moment immediately giving rise to the next, so that the consequences of Karma work themselves out though the sequence of reappearances. It is the privilege and opportunity of the human form of appearance that it can understand this and can direct the flow to a good rather than a bad outcome.

The nature of the final outcome in Nirvana (Pali, *nibbana*) is the third example above. In Hindu belief, Nirvana is a place of serene peace and satisfaction, where, according to *Bhagavadgita*, union with God (*brahmanirvana*) is attained. The Gita also says that Nirvana is like a candle far removed from a draught: it burns with a steady, unflickering flame. In contrast, Buddhists believe that Nirvana is the candle blown out. Nirvana is not a place, it is the condition to which the flow of reappearance can be brought in which all entanglement in thirst and desire (*tanha*) has ceased and there is no longer any interaction with anything at all. Nirvana is not extinction, but neither is it the soul arriving at the gates of heaven, since there is no soul (*anatta*) to arrive anywhere.

These beliefs are a radical separation from Indian beliefs, and they certainly changed the Indian world. From a small group of followers, the Buddhists rapidly spread into India. The informal association of the Buddha and his followers became more formally organized into the communities of monks (Bhikkhus) known collectively as the Sangha. Those who wished to join the Sangha had to make a commitment of belief through the Three Jewels and show their humility by wearing the earth-coloured (i.e., saffron) robe. Community buildings (*viharas*) were built to accommodate the monks, especially during the rainy-season retreat, but many otherwise went out to share the Buddha-dharma in India.

What was the Dharma that they were sharing? The Buddha had not taught, as he put it, with 'the closed fist of a teacher', so it became important to coordinate Buddhist teaching and practice. An assembly (the First Buddhist Council) was held at Rajagriha soon after the Buddha died in order to gather the Buddha's teaching into 'three baskets', or Tripitaka, the name given to the so-called 'Pali Canon', the works that have authority for all Buddhists. The First Council could not make that collection so soon after the Buddha's death, but at least it recognized the importance of the task.

There is nothing in Buddhism equivalent to a text believed to have been revealed by God, such as Tanach or Quran, so there is no 'Buddhist Bible'. There are, however, authoritative texts, and these are gathered into three collections put together into 'the Three Baskets', or Tripitaka/Tipitaka. The three collections are

- the Sutra (or Sutta)-pitaka, gathering originally the discourses of the Buddha;
- the Vinaya-pitaka, containing rules dealing with the life and

behaviour of the Sangha (the individuals and communities of bhikkhus);
- Abhidhamma-pitaka, containing logical and philosophical analysis, and the discussion of doctrinal issues.

As, however, Buddhism developed and divided, more than one Tripitaka was created, and the Tripitakas vary greatly from one another. The eldest of the surviving Tripitakas is the Pali Tripitaka, often known as the Pali Canon. The Chinese Tripitaka is called *San-cang*, 'Triple Treasury' (or also *Da Cang-jing*, 'Great Treasury of Texts'), but despite the word 'triple' it is not actually divided into the three major collections. It contains a vast array of different writings including most of the texts in the Pali Canon. Some of the Chinese Buddhist schools treat San-cang more as a library than a Canon – not surprisingly since the current edition contains more than 2,000 texts in fifty-five volumes. Since Chinese Buddhism is a part of Mahayana, it contains many Mahayana Sutras. Mahayana Buddhists believe that not all the teaching of the Buddha was recorded in the early years, and that much was held back until people have gone through the early stages of belief and are ready for the more advanced teaching. A fundamental division of the material is into the words of the Buddha (*buddhavacana*) and the authorized commentaries.

The development of the Sutra tradition led to four major collections, of which the most widely known is the collection of the Wisdom Schools known as Prajnaparamita, or the Perfection of Wisdom. The Tibetan Tripitaka is less formally organized, although Tibetan Buddhists revere texts greatly. However, in Tibetan Buddhism the mind of any teacher has to be undifferentiated from the mind of the Buddha, so that there is no duality between the teacher and the Buddha. In those circumstances the teacher becomes a living text.

The formation of the different Tripitakas lay in a future far beyond the First Council. The Second Council was held at Vaishali about a hundred years later, in order to settle questions about the behaviour of monks, particularly in the handling of money. The Third Council was held at Pataliputra in 250 BCE, to deal with a tension, familiar in the history of religions, between those who believed that they must stick to the original teaching of the Buddha, and those who believed that the open hand of the Buddha as teacher encouraged the development and application of his teaching to new and changing circumstances. At the Council, the Sthaviras argued for the first position, the Mahasamghikas for the second.

From this dispute began the great divide between the two different kinds of Buddhism, usually known as Theravada and Mahayana Buddhism. Theravada means 'teaching of the elders' and it is the only major surviving school of the many that used to make up the Sthaviras – those who wished to conserve the Buddha's original teaching. Theravadins are in a majority among Buddhists in Sri Lanka and South East Asia.

Mahayana means 'great vehicle' (i.e., of teaching), and they give to Theravada the name Hinayana ('little vehicle'). Mahayana developed into many different forms of Buddhism, in Tibet, China, Korea, and Japan. They all believe, as we have seen, that every tradition of teaching must have its own line of authorized teachers, its own Lineage, which can (at least theoretically) be traced back to the Buddha. It is this which creates in Mahayana Buddhism the formal structure of the many different Lineages, each with its own history. For example, a form of Buddhism in China developed new ways of meditation and is therefore known as Chan ('meditation') Buddhism. When this went to Japan it became known as Zen Buddhism. But like streams flowing from a single spring, different teachers in Chan and Zen created Schools of their own, some saying that it will take many re-appearances to reach Enlightenment, others saying that Enlightenment can be sudden and may happen in the next second. The history of Mahayana Buddhism is the history of the ways in which the many different Lineages extended the teaching of the Buddha.

In doing this, they were not losing touch with the original teaching (at least in their own perception), because they believed that the Buddha had entrusted much more teaching to his fol-lowers than appears in the Pali Canon, but he had asked that some of it should only become public when people were ready for it – when, in other words, they had grown up in the long sequences of reappearance to the point when they were ready to receive the advanced teaching. The Buddha taught according to the capacity of those who were listening to him, so that this way of 'skill-in-teaching' (*upaya-kaushalya*) is in itself an act of compassion.

The further teaching is contained in the many Sutras which Mahayana Buddhists revere. The same word 'sutra' is used for the collections of teaching that the Buddha delivered during his life-time, and it does emphasize this – that there is a seamless continuity from the early to the later. In Mahayana belief, the Sutras of the real and continuing presence of the Buddha who continues to teach more advanced understanding and practice for those who are now ready to receive it. The Mahayana Sutras are held in such reverence that in some Mahayana schools it is believed that a particular Sutra (for example, the *Lotus Sutra*) is all that is necessary for Enlightenment.

The validity of this 'delayed teaching' rests on the belief that the Buddha (and all Buddhists) must teach according to the capacity of those who are being taught. That is why, in the whole canon of Buddhist teaching, there will be development and even contradictions. This belief, 'skill-in-means', *upaya-kaushalya*, is so vital in explaining why Mahayana differs from Theravada. It is the crucial perception of 'two truths' summarized by Nagarjuna in his classic work *Mulamadhyamakakarika* (*The Fundamental Wisdom of the Middle Way*):

> The Buddha's teaching of the Dharma
> Is based on two truths:
> A truth of worldly convention
> And an ultimate truth.
>
> Those who do not understand
> The distinction drawn between these two truths
> Do not understand
> The Buddha's profound truth.
>
> Without a foundation in the conventional truth,
> The significance of the ultimate cannot be taught.
> Without understanding the significance of the ultimate,
> Liberation is not achieved.*

For about two centuries after the passing of the Buddha, his Dharma spread throughout India. In 272 BCE, Ashoka became

---

* *Mulamadhyamakakarika: The Fundamental Wisdom of the Middle Way*, translated by Jay L. Garfield (New York: Oxford University Press, 1995), 24.8–10.

ruler of the Mauryan empire which covered most of north India. He became a Buddhist and replaced conquest by force (*digvijaya*) with conquest by righteousness (*dharmvijaya*). He proclaimed ethical principles throughout the empire through his Edicts, implementing the Buddhist commitment to compassion and Ahimsa (non-violence):

Here no animal is to be killed for sacrifice, and no festivals (*samaja*) are to be held, for the king finds much evil in festivals except for some which he considers good. Formerly in the kitchen of the Beloved of God, several hundred thousand animals would be killed daily for food, but now at the time of writing only three are killed – two peacocks and a deer, though the deer not regularly. Even these three animals will not be killed in future.

I have in many ways given the gift of clear vision. On people and animals, birds and fish I have conferred many boons, even to saving their lives; and I have done many other good deeds.

All people are my children. Just as I desire that my own children shall have every kind of welfare and happiness in this world and in the next, I desire the same for all people. (Rock Edicts 1, 2, 15)[*]

After his death in 232, the Mauryan empire lasted only another forty years. There were still many Buddhists in India, but after the Muslim invasions, Buddhism virtually disappeared from India, making up today only about 1 per cent of the population. However, Ashoka had sent four monks to Sri Lanka, where Theravada Buddhism has remained the major religion.

---

[*] Translated in William Theodore de Bary, *Sources of Indian Tradition* (New York: Columbia University Press, 1958).

He also sent monks to South East Asia, to the Land of Gold, probably Indonesia. Theravada Buddhism took root in Burma, Cambodia, Laos and Thailand. In Thailand, Buddhism was supported by the Chakri dynasty (end of the eighteenth century to the present day) and in return received support from the Buddhist monasteries and monks. As a result, Thailand has kept its independence through the vicissitudes of European colonialism and Japanese expansion. There have been tensions between traditionalists (Maha Nikai) and reformers (especially Buddhadasa, 1905–83), but Thailand has remained an example of Buddhist belief uniting and characterizing a whole society.

Mahayana Buddhism

Meanwhile, the many forms of Mahayana were coming into being and spreading beyond India. The original differences between Mahayana and Theravada were relatively small matters of monastic discipline, but they raised the issue of whether such matters should be resolved by sticking as closely as possible to the beliefs and teachings of the Buddha, or whether further guidance and interpretation were needed.

Before long, however, the differences became far more serious. For example, Theravadins believe that there is only one wholly Enlightened One in each world cycle. Since the Buddha has already appeared in this world cycle, it follows that the furthest anyone can advance in this world cycle is to the stage just before Parinirvana, when he becomes, not a Buddha but an Arhat (Pali, Arahant). An Arhat is one who is free from any basis for reappearance, 'whose track is as difficult to know as that of a bird in the sky', and who has in effect reached the goal.

Mahayana Buddhists, in contrast, regard the aim of the Arhats as selfish: they attain the goal but leave others behind them. How can that be an exercise in the fundamental Buddhist virtue of compassion? They therefore developed the belief that those on the last step of the way turn back to help any in the world who are still in ignorance, pain or suffering. These figures (and in Mahayana belief there are millions of them) are known as Bodhisattvas (Pali, Bodhisattas), 'Enlightenment Beings' who make a vow that they will not enter into Nirvana while they know of any who need their help.

From this it can be seen that in Mahayana belief it is possible for anyone to become a Bodhisattva or even a Buddha, and many do. The world of Mahayana is filled with countless Buddhas and Bodhisattvas, and those seeking Enlightenment are encouraged to seek their help in worship, meditation and prayer.

The quest is greatly encouraged for Mahayana Buddhists by the further belief that the Buddha is not far off, like the distant end of a marathon race. In fact, the Buddha is extremely close at hand. The Buddha-nature, the essence of the Buddha, can be found in all sentient beings, if you know how to look. It was the great achievement of Nagarjuna to explain how this can be.

Nagarjuna (who lived at some time between 150 CE and 250) was the founder of the school of philosophy and analysis known as Madhyamaka. He was a brahman who lived in south India and converted to Buddhism. His teaching became fundamental for subsequent Mahayana Buddhists, and for that reason they regard him as 'the second Buddha'.

Buddhists before his time had accepted the Buddha's teaching that there is 'no self' (Anatta), and that there is nothing in existence except the continuous flow of appearance, with one moment giving immediate rise to the next. But then surely there must be a moment when there *is* something – some 'thing' that only lasts for the briefest possible time before it gives rise to the next moment.

Against that, Nagarjuna developed the teaching of the Buddha that nothing has independent and enduring existence. Everything that exists arises in an interconnected web of conditions that give rise to particular appearances. The origin of any appearance is dependent on an interlinked network of conditions, none of which has any real or independent existence. This belief is fundamental to the Buddha's understanding of what appears in the world. 'Dependent origination' or 'causal genesis' (*paticca-sam-uppada*) explains the sequence that begins in ignorance and ends in Dukkha:

> On ignorance depends Karma; on Karma depends consciousness; on consciousness depend name and form; on name and form depend the six organs of sense; on the six organs of sense depend contact; on contact depends sensation; on sensation depends desire; on desire depends attachment; on existence depends birth; on birth depend old age and death, sorrow, lamentation, misery, grief, and despair. (*Mahavagga* 1.1)*

There is, therefore, no entity that exists even for a moment. On the other hand, there clearly is an underlying connection between the moments of appearance. What connects the moments of appearance is essentially the Buddha, the Buddha-nature, Buddhata. The Buddha-nature sustains appearances, but they themselves do not really exist. The Buddha-nature is all that is. The fleeting appearances that constitute the world, the universe

* Translated by Henry Clarke Warren, *Buddhism in Translations* (New York: Atheneum, 1896).

and everything in it are completely empty of any enduring characteristics of their own. Seen properly, they are only the Buddha-nature appearing in different forms.

Nagarjuna did not deny that it is right to talk in everyday language about appearances as though their characteristics are real. It is sensible, therefore, to say such things as 'the sun is hot' or 'the car is at the door'. But suns, cars and doors all have the same underlying nature: there is no fundamental difference between them. Nagarjuna even went so far as to say that there is no difference between Samsara (the world of continuing reappearance) and Nirvana because there are no independent characteristics which might enable one to differentiate between them.

That is what Nagarjuna meant by a word and concept that is fundamental to all Mahayana life and belief. The word is Shunyata (śunyata). It is often translated as 'emptiness' or 'the void', but that might be misleading – and Nagarjuna warned how dangerous it is to misunderstand Shunyata (*Mulamadhyamakakarika* 24.11):

> By a misperception of Shunyata
> A person of little intelligence is destroyed
> Like a snake incorrectly seized
> Or like a spell incorrectly cast.

In Nagarjuna's understanding, Shunyata really means 'not having any differentiating characteristics': all things seem real and look very different from each other, but those differences are an illusion. In truth, they are floating on the surface of the Buddha-nature that underlies and sustains them. All things are thus essentially the same ('not having any differentiating characteristics') because they are all dependent on the Buddha-nature. This means that all who have the trained and inner eyes to see can discern the Buddha-nature in all sentient beings – and the word 'sentient' is extensively inclusive. The many Schools and Lineages of Mahayana Buddhism are different ways of helping people to acquire those 'eyes' and to open them.

The simple key is to realize that since all sentient beings are dependent on the Buddha-nature, this must necessarily include myself. The purpose, therefore, of my life, if I am wise, is not to strive after some distant goal, like heaven or even Enlightenment: it is to uncover and find what is already true about myself (and everybody), that I am already the Buddha-nature. I do not need to take off into distant space in order to find the Buddha-nature. I am already that (cf. the Great Sayings of the Indians).

In Mahayana belief, all have the potential to become Buddhas, and many realize their potential. From this it follows that the Buddha Gotama is not alone, but is one among many Buddhas. Nevertheless, he is recognized as being one of the Perfectly Awakened Buddhas (*sammasambuddha*), at first seven in number, to whom the shrines known as stupas were originally built. Stupas were originally built as burial mounds, but now they are the centre of Buddhist devotion and pilgrimage because they contain relics of the Buddha and his associates. A *sammasambuddha* can be known because he bears the marks on his body of a supreme monarch, and is usually shown in art or sculpture setting the wheel of teaching, or Dharma, in motion.

Other Buddhas often have their own domains (Buddha-worlds) over which they preside. Some (for example, Amitabha, known in Japan as Amida) invite the faithful into a paradise of bliss and light – long-lasting, but not as a final resting place, only as a staging-post on the way to Nirvana. Devotion to these

Buddhas is widespread and important in Mahayana Buddhist life.

The belief in many Buddhas was eventually summed up in the Trikaya (Three Bodies) understanding of the Buddha and the many forms of the Buddha. In the first 'body' or form, the Buddha is identical with all that is, in its ultimate and absolute truth (*dharmakaya*); in the second, Buddhas are manifest in sublime and celestial forms (*sambhogakaya*); in the third, they are manifest in earthly or physical form (*nirmanakaya*). In *sambhogakaya* they create splendid paradises where they teach would-be Bodhisattvas (enlightenment beings) the perfections they need in order to make progress – especially the Perfection of Wisdom, which, in Mahayana Buddhism, became a major School of teaching, producing many important Sutras.

The Wisdom School is only one among many Schools or Lineages in Mahayana Buddhism. In Tibet there are four major Lineages, though these have sub-divided many times. In China there were many more, of which four were particularly important: Tiantai, Huayan, Jingtu (Pure Land) and Chan (Meditation) Buddhism, which became Son in Korea and Zen in Japan.

In Korea, the first Lineages were simply extensions of the Chinese. But Wonhyo (617–86) attempted to draw the most important of those into a new system, called Dharma Nature, or Popsong, as well as adapting Huayan. Chan or Son was introduced by Pomnang in about 630, but was opposed by the Lineages (known as Kyo) who believe that discipline and learning are more important than the pursuit of sudden Enlightenment. The dispute between Son and Kyo continued intermittently throughout the history of Korea. Son itself divided into nine Lineages until the highly respected Chinul (1158–1210) attempted to unite them with each other and with Kyo. The disputes were eventually 'settled' by the Japanese when they unified all the Lineages in 1935, under the name Chogye.

The many splits and divisions within the Lineages are a consequence of the Buddha's refusal to use 'the closed fist of a teacher', and of his encouragement to his followers to 'seek your own Enlightenment with diligence'. There is thus no single 'orthodoxy', nor any authority (outside each of the Lineages) to impose a single and uniform belief and practice – though within some Lineages there is extremely strong authority over its members. This openness about belief took luxuriant root in Japan, where many hundreds of Lineages or subdivisions of Lineages appeared, about 200 of which are still in being. Where attempts were made in Korea to bring the proliferation of Lineages under control, Japan has allowed them to flourish.

Just as there are many forms of Mahayana Buddhism, so there are many texts that have authority. They are not Scripture in the sense that they have been revealed by God, and there is no single collection of texts that might be called 'the Buddhist Bible'. Nevertheless, collections (in threefold 'baskets', Tripitaka) have been made, in various areas of Buddhism, of texts that have authority, divided between the words of the Buddha (*buddhavacana*) and commentaries. The major forms of those collections have already been described.

Tibet

When Buddhists moved north from India to Tibet, they met an existing and ancient religion. This religion is usually called Bön, but the form of Bön that survived and has persisted in Tibet has been heavily influenced by Mahayana Buddhism. The history of early Bön cannot be recovered, beyond the fact that initially it opposed the coming of Buddhism with sufficient strength to make the settlement of Buddhism in Tibet a process with two stages, known as 'the First' and 'the Second' Diffusions.

Buddhism was introduced into Tibet by the king, Songsten Gampo (c.609–49/50), when, in the course of extending his empire, he acquired two wives from China and Nepal, who were devout Buddhists. He built for them two temples to house two Buddha images that they had brought with them as dowries. One of these, the image of Jowo Rinpoche ('The Precious Lord'), now in the Jokhang, remains especially holy for Tibetans. Songsten Gampo also created a Tibetan alphabet suitable for the translation of Sanskrit texts, with the result that Tibetan translations are often the only form in which early Buddhist texts have survived.

The First Diffusion of Buddhism in Tibet began when the king, Trisong Detsen (c.750–97), became a Buddhist. Despite the commitment to Ahimsa (non-violence), he extended the empire from Samarkand to Xian in China (in fact all Buddhists have ways of justifying warfare in particular circumstances, a reason why Buddhists are involved in some of the conflicts listed at the beginning of the Introduction). Trisong Detsen built the first Tibetan monastery at Samyé in c.787, and invited teachers from India, including Shantarakshita (c.705–88) and the famous Padmasambhava, often regarded as 'the second Buddha'. This meant that Tibetan Buddhism followed the Indian Mahayana Buddhism rather than the Chinese.

In 836, Langdarma seized the throne from his brother. He and his successors were strong supporters of Bön, and for two centuries Buddhists were persecuted and driven to the margins of Tibet. The return of Buddhism, the Second Diffusion, began with the arrival from India in 1042 of Atisha, the effect of whose work has lasted to the present.

When he arrived Atisha found a large accumulation of texts, but little understanding. He therefore reformed monasticism, and emphasized that progress can be made toward Enlightenment only under the guidance of a trained teacher. In Tibetan Buddhism, therefore, the structure of teacher and pupil is fundamental: it is called 'the Fourth Jewel' in addition to the Three which are the foundation of all Buddhist belief. Teachers are known as *bla.ma* ('the higher one'), or lamas. That is why Tibetan Buddhism is sometimes called Lamaism: that is misleading since not all Tibetans are lamas, but the name rightly emphasizes the lama–pupil relationship in Tibetan belief.

Atisha also implemented the belief that people must be taught according to the level of understanding they have reached (*upaya-kaushalya*, 'skill-in-means', as we have already encountered it). Brilliant forms of Tantra were developed in Tibet, but Atisha insisted that these could not be attempted until the foundations had been laid in the disciplines of Buddhist life and philosophy.

From that belief emerged the great schools of training and teaching which make up Tibetan Buddhism. The four major schools are: Nyingma, Sakya, Kagyu and (the largest) Geluk.

The Nyingma trace their School back to Padmasambhava (above), retaining elements of Bön in their tradition, but they were formed into a distinct Order only after 'the Second Diffusion'. They give high value to the canonical scriptures. They value equally 'the spiritual treasures' (*terma/gter-ma*), teachings entrusted to chosen disciples, then hidden by Padmasambhava, to be found by reincarnations of those disciples when the times are ready for the teachings involved. The disciples are known as Tertons (*gter.ston*, treasure-finders), and among the texts discovered in this way is *The Tibetan Book of the Dead*. They believe also that the Tertons remain in direct communication with Padmasambhava through 'the pure visions'.

The Sakya came into being when a Nyingma, Konchok Gyalpo, learnt new tantric traditions from a wandering Indian teacher and founded the Grey Earth (Sa.skya) monastery in 1073. Under the Gongma Nga (the Five Exalted Ones), many sutras and tantric texts were brought into Tibet (including *Hevajra Tantra*) – but the foundations still have to be laid in study and meditation.

The Kagyu goes back to Tilopa (988–1069), also known as Prajnabhadra. He received special teaching which he passed on to Naropa (1016–1100), who passed it on to Marpa (1012–96) who included among his disciples the famous Milarepa (*c*.1050–1135), thought by some to be the only Tibetan who became a perfect Buddha in one lifetime. Milarepa passed it on to Gampopa (1079–1153), who had many disciples from whom have come, as streams from a single spring, the many different schools that make up Kagyu.

The Kadam (Oral Tradition) was established by Dromdon, a pupil of Atisha, when he built the monastery of Radeng in 1056. It emphasized the Mahayana teachings of universal compassion and altruism as the necessary foundation of life. Kadam gave rise to the Geluk/Gelug Order (originally called New Kadam) when Tsong Kha pa (1357–1419) achieved complete enlightenment in 1398, and began his 'major works' in order to renew Buddhism in Tibet, including the rebuilding of the Temple of Maitreya (the Buddha of the future) in Dzingji, the renewal of monastic discipline, and the establishing of the long New Year prayer festival at the Jokhang (national shrine) in Lhasa (where he established the Ganden monastery in 1409). It is to this School that the Dalai Lama belongs. Dalai is a Western form of the Mongolian *Ta Le*,

'Ocean of Wisdom'. The title was bestowed in 1578, by a Mongolian ruler, on Sonam Gyatso (1543–88). In Tibetan belief, the Dalai Lama is their spiritual (and, where allowed, temporal) leader whose succession by reincarnation is determined by finding a child with clear traces and memories of his previous birth. The Panchen Lama is the spiritual head of the monastic tradition, whose succession, again by discerning reincarnation, has been pulled into politics by recent Chinese attempts to control the process.

Buddhism in Tibet has developed its own form of Tantric belief and practice, known as Vajrayana (the Way of the Thunderbolt) or Mantrayana (the Way of the Mantra: mantras in Indian religion are formulae of words and chants of immense and different kinds of power). The word *vajra* also points to the hidden treasure to be found within: the enlightened mind lies like a *vajra*, or 'diamond', hidden in the clutter of human delusion: it is there simply waiting to be found.

Vajrayana is an esoteric and tantric form of Buddhism, in which the aim is to bring an immediate liberation to all beings by ending the ordinary experience of time (of being bound to the Wheel of Time). The word 'Tantra' (Tibetan *rgyud*) means in this context a continuous extension, an unbroken way leading from ignorance to enlightenment. Tantra texts (and experts, or yogis) teach the often complex and sophisticated ways through which that unbroken way can be found, from the gross and material world to the Buddha-nature. The Buddha-nature is the only true reality which underlies the false and superficial appearance that all things are different and real.

The teachers of Tantra are the trained yogis. To help them find and realize their Buddha-nature they choose a *yi dam* to be a kind of guardian deity. There are four kinds of *yi dams*, corresponding to the variations among human beings: they may be male or female, peaceful or wrathful. The male peaceful *yi dams* have their female counterparts who bring Wisdom to the male energy, so that together they form a perfect union. This is often represented (in art and practice) in the sexual union of Yab (father) and Yum (mother). The male wrathful *yi dams* are called Herukas and their female counterparts are Dakinis. All of them can help people deal with their emotions and pass beyond them.

These guardian or meditation deities do not have any independent being or substance, although they are often talked about and addressed as though they do. They are forms or resonances of the fully enlightened mind. They take the form of whatever needs most to be engaged with and dissolved in any particular person. But whether *yi dams* are wrathful, erotic, or peaceful, their purpose is compassionate. It is to help the yogis, through the visualization of them, to break out of the bondage of the everyday world of delusion, and to transform the energies involved from their destructive to their constructive form.

Thus the wrath of the wrathful deities is far removed from the angers and hatreds of human life. The wrathful deities transform those destructive energies of our ordinary states of delusion into the energies of enlightenment. This is done through tantric disciplines and practices, including visualization through which the yogi moves into complete insight, and forms with the *yi dam* a perfect union of wisdom and compassion.

Those who achieve this are known as Mahasiddhas (Great Practitioners). The immediacy of this enlightenment is achieved in the interior or subtle body, even while the exterior and material body remains visible in the world. Thus much tantric practice is designed to move from the gross to the subtle reality, and the forms of tantra are analysed in immense detail in the many tantric texts.

China

In the outward spread of Mahayana from India, Tibet was among the earliest, but China was not long behind, and Tibet and China remained closely linked. Buddhism began to reach China at about the time of the Eastern Han dynasty (25–220 CE) or a little earlier. It did not have a large following until the fall of the Han dynasty which was followed by a long period of conflict in China. In those circumstances, the Buddhist belief in Dukkha made sense, but even more to the point, the Buddhas and Bodhisattvas offered help to those in crisis or pain, in a way that Confucius did not.

So it was that toward the end of this period, the four great Schools of Chinese Buddhism were founded: Huayan (founded by Dushan, 557–640), Tiantai (derived from Zhiyi, 538–97), Chan (Meditation, derived from Bodhidharma, c.470–520) and Jingtu (Pure Land, popularized by Tanluan, 476–c.560). The Four Schools each have long and complicated histories in which they were developed into well-worked and comprehensive systems.

Huayan (taken to Japan as Kegon) believes that Buddhism is a structure in which the other forms of Buddhism are progressive steps leading up to the full teaching of Huayan as the Buddha intended it for the far-advanced. Fa Zang (643–712) argued in *The Essay on the Golden Lion* that the whole of appearance is, like a gold lion, made up of two aspects: *shi* is the materiality which looks like a lion, but underlying the appearance is *li*, the essence of gold which is brought into different forms of appearance. So all appearance is different in *shi*, but identical in *li*, the underlying Buddha-nature. Thus all appearances are identical, illustrated in Indra's Net: this was a network of linked jewels illuminated by a candle, so that every jewel is reflected in every other jewel. In Huayan belief, 'Every living being and every minute thing is significant, because even the tiniest atom contains the whole mystery.'

Tiantai (taken to Japan by Saicho, 767–822, as Tendai) also believed that the different forms of Buddhism are progressive stages to the ultimate truth – to be found in *Nirvana Sutra* and *Lotus Sutra*. Mahayana Sutras are teachings of the Buddha which were held back until at least some people were ready for them, and the *Lotus Sutra* is one of the most revered. It develops Mahayana belief in dramatic ways, particularly in its understanding of the Three Bodies (Trikaya) of the Buddha, since it claims that the *Lotus Sutra* was revealed in his Heavenly (Sambhoga) form: Shakyamuni Buddha is simply the Buddha manifested in human form, teaching according to the limits of human comprehension. The Sutra emphasizes the fundamental importance of compassion and of the Bodhisattva's vow to help all sentient beings in need.

The second two Schools, Chan and Jingtu, were also highly organized, but they were more accessible to ordinary people in their daily life.

Chan, or Meditation, Buddhism (the word Chan comes from the Sanskrit *dhyana* and the Pali *jhana*, meaning 'meditation') goes back to a moment when the Buddha was asked by a disciple, Mahakasyapa, to summarize his teaching. The Buddha lifted up a golden flower. Mahakasyapa was silent for a while, then he raised his head and responded by smiling. From this direct transmission of teaching and understanding developed a Buddhist way of seeking Enlightenment known as 'mind-to-mind transmission' or as 'special transmission outside the written texts'. Bodhidharma, the twenty-eighth leader (or Patriarch) of this school, is said to have taken this teaching from India to China in 520 CE. To him is attributed a four-line poem that summarizes Chan (in Japanese, Zen):

> A special transmission outside the Scriptures,
> not founded upon words and letters
> by pointing directly into the mind
> it allows us to see [our true] nature and thus to attain the
>   Buddha-nature.

Chan and Zen offer people training and practice to do exactly that, in meditation and in many other ways – for example, in gardens, in Chado (the tea ceremony), in Kado (the way of flowers) and in calligraphy. At the heart of this training to discern and enter into the Buddha-nature (in Japan, *bussho*) are: 'sitting in meditation' with the mind held in the present moment in identity with the Buddha-nature; and 'challenging question' (*gong-an*, better known in its Japanese form as *koan*), in which the mind of the pupil is challenged to break out of the ordinary thinking of the everyday world.

Chan Buddhism in China developed into many Schools, all with the same early Lineage. A major division came in a dispute over the sixth successor of Bodhidharma, leading in 732 to the Southern Schools in which it is believed that Enlightenment can be sudden, and the Northern in which it is believed that Enlightenment has to be gradual, based on learning and practice.

Pure Land or Jingtu (taken to Japan as Jodo) is even more accessible to ordinary people, because it is based on the belief that the Buddhas establish realms (Pure Lands, Foyu, Jap., Butsudo) over which they preside, and into which they invite those who long for them and for Enlightenment. There are many of these, but the one most loved by Chinese and Japanese is that of the Buddha Amitabha or Amida/Amita. Amitabha's realm is in the West and is therefore known as 'the Western Paradise', Sukhavati (Jap., Gokuraku) meaning 'utmost bliss'. Sukhavati is not the final goal, which remains Nirvana, but it is the penultimate step: those who reach Sukhavati cannot fall back into the bondage of Karma and reappearance. To reach Sukhavati all that is required is total devotion to Amitabha and trust in his saving power. This is expressed in the Nianfo, or, in the Japanese form, Nembutsu: Nan-mo A-mi-tuo-Fo, or Namu Amida Butsu, 'homage to Amida Butsu'. In effect, this means that 'I take refuge in the Buddha Amida' (cf., the 'Three Refuges'). This commitment, if said with belief and trust, even by the worst sinners on their death-beds, will take them to Amitabha.

With the unification of China and the advent of the Tang dynasty (618–906), Buddhism gained a widespread following. It was criticized by those Chinese who thought that it subverted some key Chinese beliefs: in particular, it did not give adequate value to the family, because it held out celibacy as a higher way, and it did not support the building up of a prosperous society, because it thought that monks should beg and not work. Even worse, the Chinese, before the coming of Buddhism, had revered the ancestors and had, through various ceremonies and offerings, kept them as a part of the family. The Buddhists introduced the belief that the ancestors, if they had acquired bad Karma, might now, in their new form of reappearance, be burning in the fires of hell.

Chinese Buddhists met those criticisms by adapting Buddhism

to Chinese thought and belief, and the Four Schools (above) did this extensively. Thus they linked Buddhist rituals to the reverence for the ancestors, and showed how the monks can help the dead through the transference of good Karma – sometimes an actual transference, by offering to the dead in symbolic form the things they will need, like money and food – or today, DVDs, mobile phones and TVs.

This creative interaction with Chinese thought and belief was particularly strong with Daoism. By the time of the Northern Song dynasty (960–1126), Buddhism was accepted as an equal of Daoism and Confucianism, and it was said that 'the three traditions are harmoniously one' (*sanjiao heyi*). Even so, Buddhism remained suspect as a foreign innovation, and anti-Buddhist feeling could flare into violence when China (or some part of China) was under threat.

The growth of Buddhism under the Tang dynasty was much assisted by the increasing ease of travel between China and India. Along the trade routes, splendid shrines were built in cave-complexes, as at Yungang and Longmen, in which the beauty of devotion to Buddhas and Bodhisattvas was made manifest to those who came on pilgrimage. Equally the trade routes made the exchange of monks straightforward and common. With this exchange came from India a huge number of Sanskrit Buddhist texts, with the result that the Chinese Buddhist canon is immense: when a modern edition was published in Japan between 1922 and 1935, it came to fifty-five volumes, each one about 1,000 pages long.

By the end of the eighth century, Buddhism began to decline, partly because the creative exchange with India became more difficult: the Muslim expansion meant that the western end of the trade routes was now blocked. After a major persecution in

845, Buddhism was no longer central in Chinese life. Attempts were made in the nineteenth century to make a synthesis between Daoism and Buddhism, and Taixu (1890–1947) initiated a reform movement which gained ground until from 1949 onward the Communist regime of Mao Zedong suppressed and regulated all religions.

Korea and Japan

Buddhism arrived in Korea in the fourth century CE, during the period (when Korea was divided) known as the Three Kingdoms (Koguryo, 37 BCE–668 CE; Paekche, 18 BCE–660 CE; and Silla, 57 BCE–668 CE). It brought to Korea a civilization and learning that had not previously been experienced, and for that reason laid the foundations for the achievements of Korea down to the present day.

In 372 CE, two monks from China, Sundao and Adao, brought to Koguryo Buddhist images and sutras, and began to build monasteries. In 384, an Indian monk, Marananta, brought Buddhism to Paekche, and in 527, the Silla kingdom accepted Buddhism. In contrast to China, there was no conflict with already existing beliefs, and Buddhism rapidly became the court and state religion – or more precisely, the court-protecting religion, *hoguk pulgyo*.

When the kingdoms came together in the Unified Silla period, Buddhism played an important part in making the unified kingdom work. People from all parts and all levels of society became Buddhists and monks, and a creative interchange began, not just with China, but also with India. As a result, the Chinese Schools were introduced and given a Korean form. Two prominent monks, Uisang (625–702) and Wonhyo (617–86) established a

Korean version of Huayan known as Haedong Hwaom. This set out to achieve 'harmony of disputes' (*hwajeng*) while at the same time making the practice of Buddhism popular through dance and song.

Under the Koryo dynasty (918–1392), Buddhists continued this quest for reconciliation and unity. Uichon (1055–1101) introduced Tiantai and created a synthesis of the two main, and often opposing, Buddhist ways, that of teaching (Kyo) and that of meditation (Son, the Korean for Chan). He also began the work of collecting and translating the texts that were eventually published in the thirteenth century as the Korean Canon or Tripitaka.

That work of harmonizing was continued by Chinul (1158–1210) who founded the Chogye School to bring together the many different Schools of Son Buddhism: his teaching of 'sudden enlightenment and gradual practice' (*tono-chomsu*) was another way of giving equal weight to two otherwise divided forms of Buddhism.

In the early years of the Choson dynasty (1392–1910), political power was held by neo-Confucianists (described in the chapter on China), and the status and privileges of Buddhism were cut down, often severely. In the fifteenth century, the different Schools were reduced to two, Kyo and Son. The royal family, however, continued to support Buddhism, and were sometimes Buddhists themselves.

Even that support came to an end with the Japanese invasion in 1910, when the two Schools, in order to simplify administration, were forced to become one, under the name Chogye. Buddhist monks had been the centre of resistance to the Japanese in two earlier invasions, in 1592 and 1597, and they were so again. They were, for example, prominent in the March 1st Movement against Japanese colonial rule in 1919.

Since Korea's independence in 1945, the deep Korean desire for reconciliation has been frustrated by the division into north and south. It remains alive, however, in the transformation of Chogye from a bureaucratic convenience to a powerful Buddhist commitment to the building of a compassionate society.

Buddhism arrived in Japan from Korea in 538, when Song, the king of Paekche, sent to Kinmei, the Japanese emperor, tribute which included an image of the Buddha and Chinese Buddhist texts. For the next six centuries, Buddhism was the means through which Chinese culture and civilization were imported into Japan.

Buddhism did not meet a highly organized system of Japanese beliefs, but it was nevertheless opposed by those who saw it as foreign and as subverting the social system based on family and on reverence for the spirits (Kami) who sustain Japanese life. The history of Buddhism in Japan is the history of this contest, now with one side prevailing, now with the other. The history of Japan is usually referred to by periods listed in the Japan overview.

Initially, Buddhism was welcomed by Prince Shotoku (574–622), who saw religion as the basis on which the people could be united in loyalty to the imperial house. He was an enthusiast for Chinese science and learning, and for Confucianism and Daoism, and he sent monks to China to bring back all they could, and especially texts. Everything was adapted to Japanese needs, thus beginning the distinctive forms of Buddhism found in Japan.

During the Nara period, Buddhism became the state religion. Six Schools were brought from China, including Jojitsu and Kegon (Huayan). The emphasis was on philosophy and the construction of temples and monasteries, with Buddhism being regarded by the rulers as a source of power and control.

In 789, the capital of Japan was moved from Nara to Heian-kyo (present-day Kyoto). Some Buddhists took the opportunity to escape from state control, in particular two monks, Saicho and Kukai, who founded Schools based on the Chinese, but distinctively different in Japanese form.

Saicho, also known as Dengyo Daishi (767–822), went to China in 804 to study Tiantai, and came back in 805 to establish Tendai as 'the treasure of the nation'. The emperor Kammu welcomed the Tendai training of leaders whose lives were based on the Five Precepts and on discipline undertaken for the sake of others.

Kukai, also known as Kobo Daishi (774–835) introduced Shingon, a form of esoteric Buddhism. 'Esoteric' means that there are teachings and practices which are never written down or made available to people in general: they are transmitted from teacher to pupil. Shingon teaches the Three Secrets of body, speech and mind, which lead to the goal of 'becoming a Buddha in this body' (*sokushin jobutsu*).

In 1185, a successful family of military leaders took power and moved the capital to Kamakura. As leaders, they were called Shoguns. They kept the emperors in place as the centre of Japanese unity and loyalty, but the emperors had little actual power. Not that unity was easy to achieve: the period of the Kamakura shogunate was one of internal conflict and the threat of war. The Kamakura Shoguns continued the process of eliminating Buddhists from political and military power, although the Tokugawas supported Buddhism as a way of uniting the country and resisting Christian missionaries.

The conflicts and rivalries of the Kamakura period illustrated the Buddhist belief that we are living in the age of *mappo*, the point of deepest decline in the unending world cycles, when no one can achieve Enlightenment in the ordinary way. Extraordinary forms of Buddhism were offered to help in the crisis, and they achieved considerable success.

In Zen Buddhism, two major Schools emerged. The first is Soto founded by Dogen (1200–53), in which Buddhist techniques and devotion to Buddhas are concentrated in the practice of Zazen (sitting in focused meditation). His School became known as 'Zazen alone' (*shikan taza*), and calls itself Mokusho Zen, silent illumination Zen.

> If you wish to attain enlightenment, begin at one practice: zazen. For this meditation you need a quiet room; food and drink should be taken in moderation. Free yourself from all attachments and bring to rest the ten thousand things [everything that exists]. Do not think of good or evil, do not judge what is right or wrong; follow the flow of mind, will and consciousness; bring to an end all desire, all concepts and all judgements . . . Once your bodily position is in order, regulate your breathing. If a desire arises, make a note of it and then put it on one side. If you practice in this way for a long time, you will forget all attachments, and concentration will come naturally. That is the art of zazen. Zazen is the Dharma gate of great rest and joy.

The second major School is Rinzai founded by Eisai (1141–1215) which emphasizes the 'sudden shock' or 'great shaking' ways of attaining sudden enlightenment (with shouts and beatings, or with the challenging sayings known as koans). Koans are challenging problems or questions which cannot be answered in any conventional way – 'What is the sound of one hand clapping?'; 'If you meet a man on the way, greet him with neither words nor silence: so how will you greet him?' Koans are not unanswerable puzzles: all of them have answers, and the pupil, in order to break through to sudden Enlightenment, must seek the answer 'like a thirsty rat seeking water, like a child longing for its mother'.

Even more dramatic was the School introduced by Nichiren (1222–82). Nicheren tried out all the main forms of Buddhism current in Japan before he discovered the *Lotus Sutra*. Here, he believed, was the whole truth, and Enlightenment becomes possible for everyone who makes a simple act of trust and faith, known as the Daimoku: 'namo myoho renge kyo': 'I take refuge in the Sutra of the Lotus of the Wondrous Dharma.' Nichiren began radical and outspoken attacks on the government. He was condemned to death and miraculously saved, and was then exiled twice. The School of Nichiren has continued this tradition of opposition to inept or unfaithful governments.

Pure Land Schools were developed by Honen (1133–1212), Shinran (1173–1262), and Ippen (1239–89), in which nothing is required except complete trust in Amida. Shinran believed that even one thought alone of Amida would be enough to reach the goal.

In all these movements, monastic Buddhism, with its discipline and formal practices, became far less important than personal salvation achieved by simple means. Each of them maintained its own boundaries, emphasizing its own way to the exclusion of all others. For the first time, Buddhism became sectarian in character, and this has been encouraged by the Japanese inclination in the nineteenth and twentieth centuries to produce, as we will see, a proliferation of new religions.

China

Overview

There is no single religion that is dominant in China. There is not even a word for 'religion'. The nearest equivalents are *men* (meaning 'door' or 'gateway'), *dao* (meaning 'way'), and, more commonly, *chiao*, now spelt *jiao* (meaning 'teaching'). But clearly these words do not define what the teaching is or to what the open door leads. They are therefore attached to the particular teaching involved, as in Daojiao (the teaching of Daoism) or Fojiao (the teaching of the Buddha). Rujiao is the School of scholars commited to the teaching of Kong Fuzi or, in earlier transliteration, Confucius. They may also be described as -*jia*. *Jia* meant originally the cohesion of a family home, so it came to mean the bonding of those who belong to a common tradition.

There are four major traditions in China, all of which have their own histories, and all of which constantly interact with each other. It is not expected that people will belong to one only. They enter into each of the traditions according to the circumstances and their own needs.

The four major strands which make up religion in China are Rujia+Rujiao (old spelling Jujia+Jujiao, Confucianism); Daojia+Daojiao (Daoism, or as it used to be spelt, Taoism);

Fojia+Fojiao (Buddhism); and folk or popular beliefs and practices. In addition, Christianity and Islam have a considerable
following in China. Exact numbers are impossible to tell because
of the Communist state control and sometimes suppression of
religion, which has created the phenomenon of Christian 'under-
ground churches' in contrast to state-recognized Christianity.

The history of religion in China has traditionally been divided
into four periods named after the seasons of the year, Spring,
Summer, Autumn and Winter. The early part of the Spring period
is known mainly from archaeological remains, including the
oracle bones of the Shang Dynasty. Within the later part there is
a specific period, 771–484, known as the Spring and Autumn
Period (from the title *Spring and Autumn Annals*, records of the
state of Lu). This was a time that produced the great teachers who
established the major traditions in China: Kong Fuzi (Confucius,
*c.*551–479); Laozi (possibly not a person but the name of a text)
and Zhuangzi (*c.*399–*c.*295), founders of Daoism; Mo Di (fifth
century BCE), founder of the relatively short-lived but influential Moism; and Zou Yan (third century BCE) who organized the
School of Yin-Yang and the Five Agents, again short-lived, but
adapted into later Chinese systems.

At the end of this period, the first major attempt to create a
unified empire was made by Qin Shihuangdi (ruled 221–210
BCE), the first emperor of the Qin. Strictly speaking, therefore,
he was not emperor of 'China' except in the sense that that was
the name of his home state (Qin is pronounced *chin*). The name
China was first used by outsiders.

The Summer period (206BCE–900CE) began with the
Western and Eastern Han dynasties (also known as 'former' and
'later'), during which time renewed attempts were made to create
a unified empire, but they were constantly challenged by

warlords and rebellions. That kind of disorder and instability continued to the end of the Summer period, but recruitment of military strength from the North and the involvement of Buddhism in a Confucian society (see 'Buddhism in China') led to a 'golden age' under the Sui and Tang dynasties. When Wendi founded the Sui dynasty in 581, he endorsed 'the practice of Buddhist virtues' and the pursuit of peace. Confucianism, Daoism and Buddhism played such a dominant part in Chinese history that they are known as San-jiao, the Three Religions. They might be in rivalry or conflict, but attempts might also be made to draw them into a formal alliance. In any case, each has its own history, with Confucianism applying itself particularly to government, administration and society, and Daoism to the needs of popular religion.

The Autumn period (900–1912) began with a period of conflict under the Five Dynasties, followed by three relatively peaceful centuries under the Song,,which was achieved through skilful diplomacy. Even so, the Jin invasion in 1127 drove the Song into the south until they and the rest of China were overwhelmed by the Mongol invasions from 1234 onwards. During the ensuing Yuan dynasty, the Mongols, far from adapting to Chinese ways, treated the Chinese as inferior.

The Yuan rule was ended in 1368 by a popular uprising led by Zhu Yuanzhang. As a result, the traditional ways of the Chinese were restored under the Ming dynasty who made a deliberate attempt to renew the imperial tradition. This was achieved by autocratic and centralized government, with a strong belief in the emperor as the link with Tian (Heaven) securing the unique status of the Chinese people. The belief in China's supremacy was reinforced by the completion of the Great Wall excluding outsiders, so that "he who treads the Wall of China, on the one hand sees cities and their civilities, and, on the other – lions." It was further reinforced by the building of the Forbidden City, begun by Yongle (1403–24).

The Forbidden City places and protects the Emperor at the centre of the world, surrounded by the administrators of the Empire and by brilliant consequences in art and learning of all kinds. It is built on the principles of *feng-shui* ('wind-water'), a belief, now widespread outside China, that habitations of the living and the dead must be aligned to harness the positive vitality of the Qi (literally 'breath' or 'air', roughly, 'pervasive spirit') that energizes the universe. The Forbidden City translated into architecture and geography the belief in the authority and supremacy of the Emperors.

In 1644, the non-Chinese Manchus, the Qing, invaded and overthrew the Ming dynasty. Because they were anxious to be accepted, not as foreigners, but as legitimate holders of the Mandate of Heaven, they made strenuous efforts to adopt and renew Chinese tradition. This was a time of many attempts to recover the original nature of Chinese religion, with new Schools and systems derived from San-jiao. Not all of these were public reformations. Some claimed that the goals of the San-jiao could only be reached by those initiated into secret or esoteric teaching, and the end of this period became a time of secret societies. The Chinese Triads are a well-known example.

In contrast to Meiji in Japan, the Qing emperors resisted the incursions of the Western powers as far as they could. It was, though, with increasingly little success as those powers established trading centres, often protected by treaties. In, for example, the Opium Wars (1839–42), the Chinese, having attempted to stop the import of opium, were eventually overwhelmed by the British. In the Treaty of Nanking (1842), ports were opened to

British trade, and Hong Kong was ceded to the British. The ensuing 'gunboat diplomacy' left China open to foreign trade and annexation.

The Winter period began after a rebellion in 1911 against the Manchus under Sun Yatsen. In 1912, Sun Yatsen, in a formal ceremony, gave the land of China back to the imperial ancestors. The new Republic of China, however, discontinued the association of Confucianism with state education, and attacks, based on scientific views of the world, were launched on so-called 'superstitions'. The rise of Japan was a constant threat until after the Second World War, when the Communists took power. In 1949, Mao Zedong stood in the gate of Tiananmen Square and proclaimed that China at last was standing on its own feet. In the classical analysis, the Winter period is one of decline and of persecution under the Communists. However, it is not regarded as an end or conclusion, but as the final moment before rebirth and renewal returns. Indeed, from early in the 1980s all traditional religions were reported to be on the increase again throughout mainland China.

The Major Dynasties and the Emergence of China

In addition to the division of Chinese history into 'the four seasons', periods in the history of China are usually referred to by the names of their dynasties. In the early centuries there was no single dynasty ruling over the area now known as China. Qin Shihuangdi called himself the First Emperor, intending that his successors would be second, third, fourth, etc., though in fact his dynasty was short-lived.

Qin Shihuangdi was, therefore, not 'emperor of China'. China was a word first used by outsiders who took it from 'the First

Emperor's' home state, Qin (pronounced Chin). The Chinese use names like 'the Middle Kingdom', 'the Central Land', or Tian Xian, 'All under Heaven'. The borders were eventually defined by seas to east and south, and by Tibet and the Himalayas to the west, and Qin sought to secure and defend the borders. Tibet, while it was independent, was a possible threat, but only after it was united in the sixth century. The Mongols ruled Tibet from the thirteenth century through Buddhist leaders whom they called the Dalai Lamas. Alliances were sought though marriages, and Tibetan Buddhism became a major influence in China. After the fall of the Mongol dynasty in China (1368), China ruled Tibet increasingly through its own agents. Tibet was independent from 1913–50, when it was declared a part of China as the Tibet Autonomous Region. The north, however, was open to invaders, and Qin Shihuangdi built the connected forts that became eventually the Great Wall of China. He also left the amazing Terracotta Army of Xian to guard his tomb. But he was ruthless in his methods: in 213, for example, he ordered all books to be burned that might describe or advocate other forms of government. One of his advisers said of him, 'His chest resembles that of a bird of prey, and his voice is like that of a jackal: he is merciless, with the heart of a tiger or a wolf.' His cruelty created a reaction after his death leading to the break-up of the empire.

In the early centuries after Qin Shihuangdi, the Han dynasties consolidated the *ideal* of a unified empire, but *in practice* there was much conflict. When Guang Wudi founded the East Han dynasty in 25 CE he faced eleven rival claimants. He prevailed after such bitter conflict that he forbade the word 'war' to be uttered in his hearing.

When Wendi founded the Sui dynasty in 581, he issued an edict stating that he intended 'to spread the ideals of the Buddha and the practice of the Ten [Buddhist] Virtues, and to regard the weapons of war as offerings of flowers to the Buddha.' The resulting integration of Buddhism and Confucianism led to a 'golden age' under the Sui and Tang dynasties.

The fall of the Tang dynasty (907) was followed by further conflict and invasions from the north, driving the Song dynasty into the south until they too were defeated by the Mongols in 1279. Khubilai (related to the Kubla Khan of Coleridge's poem) began a century of the Yuan dynasty in which the Mongols, far from adapting to Chinese ways, treated the Chinese as inferior.

In 1368, a popular rebellion led by Zhu Yuanzhang resulted in the Ming dynasty and three centuries of expansion and comparative peace. Emphasis was placed on the emperor's absolute authority as he implemented and enforced 'the Mandate of Heaven' (Tian).

This belief in the authority of the Emperors enabled the non-Chinese Manchus to secure the support of the Chinese people when they overthrew the Ming dynasty in 1644, particularly when, as the Qing dynasty, they continued the well-established customs and procedures of the Chinese. In contrast to the Meiji in Japan, they resisted the incursions of the Western powers as far as they could – though with increasingly little success. The increasing failure of China led to a rebellion under Sun Yatsen that ended the Qing dynasty and the imperial system in 1912.

Since periods of history are usually referred to by the names of the emperors and their dynasties, the names of the dynasties are important. There are too many to be listed here, particularly during the period of division, or of the Warring States, when China was not united and there were rival dynasties in different areas. The early dates are approximate and are not agreed: some

are traditional, and variants to these are given after //. The names
are given according to the Pinyin system of transliteration (introduced in the middle of the 20th century), but since older books
use the Wade-Giles system, that is given, where it differs, after /.

China Dynasties

Xin (*c.*2205–*c.*1600)

Shang (*c.*1766–1122//*c.*1523–1027)

Zhou/Chou: **Western Zhou** (1122–722//1027–771)

            Eastern Zhou (700–255//770–256)

Warring States (475–221)

Qin/Ch'in (221–207//6)

Western Former Han (206–8 CE)

Eastern Later Han (25–220 CE)

The Three Kingdoms (220–280), **Wei, Wu, Shuhan**

followed by 800 years of division (including the **Six Dynasties**,
222–581), during which competing rulers claimed the
Mandate of Heaven, but were unable to control all the regions.

Important among the many dynasties were:

Western Jin/Chin (263–316)

Eastern Jin/Chin (317–420)

Northern Wei (386–535)

Sui (581–617)

Tang/T'ang (618–906)

Five Dynasties (907–60)

Northern Song/Sung (960–1126)

Southern Song/Sung (1127–1279)

After the Mongol conquest, **Yuan** (1279–1368)

Ming (1368–1644)

Qing/Ch'ing (1644–1911): the emperors were Manchus from

south-east Manchuria who took the dynastic name of Qing (meaning 'Pure').

From Oracle Bones to Confucius

Anyang was the capital of the Shang dynasty. It was here (at the end of the nineteenth century) that the bones of oxen and the shells of tortoises and turtles were discovered on which were scratched writing in the form of small pictures (pictographs).

The bones seem to have been used in making oracle predictions. About half the surviving pictographs have connections with later Chinese writing (also based on pictographs). Among them are pictographs representing Di, the Lord, and Shang Di, the Supreme Lord.

These are the earliest signs of a belief that formed the Chinese world for nearly three thousand years. Shang Di is the source of goodness and blessing, in association with Tian. Tian is usually translated as 'Heaven', less helpfully as God, and was believed to be the source of moral order. Together they create the way in which humans should behave, rewarding them if they do, punishing them if they do not. Above all, they create the way in which the emperors should live, since the emperors carry with them the fortunes of the entire people. If emperors want their people and country to prosper, they must live according to the Mandate of Heaven (Tian-ming); and if people wish to prosper, they must treat the emperors with the respect due to the representatives on earth of Tian. An emperor is the living embodiment of Tian, and he became known as Tian-zi, the Son of Heaven.

Tian took on many extended meanings in later Chinese history, particularly when it was adopted in Daoism and Buddhism, but the fundamental meaning of authority derived from Heaven did not disappear. During the time of the Zhou dynasty, the emperor or ruler became the vital channel of communication between the people and Tian. Only he could offer prayers and sacrifices to Tian. This meant that he had to take great care to maintain all the many rituals that preserve the union between Tian and the people.

During the Han dynasties, this belief was developed even further. Tian, earth and humans were thought of as a single reality, although in threefold form. This means that Tian is not like the God of the Abrahamic religions who creates and remains separate from his creation. Tian is the source of order *within* creation. In Chinese belief, maintaining the harmony of this threefold reality is the foundation of life: 'In all things, one must not violate the way of Tian, nor disrupt the principles of earth, nor confuse the laws governing humans.' A major consequence of this belief is that all people are related to each other and to Tian, so that the family is (or should be) the reality of Heaven on earth. From this comes the strong emphasis in China on respect for elders and on 'filial piety' (*xiao*), the obligation of children to respect and care for their parents.

The link between Tian and the ruler made sense while the kingdom prospered, and it made sense also if the ruler was evil and was struck down by disaster. But what if disaster struck a ruler who was evidently attempting to rule justly and in accordance with the Mandate of Heaven? And what if Tian seemed to make no response to sacrifice, prayer and ritual? Where then was the Mandate of Heaven?

These questions were raised sharply toward the end of the Zhou dynasty (the period of the Warring States) at a time of conflict, natural disasters and oppressive government. New thinkers emerged to grapple with these questions, among whom was

Kong Fuzi, or (in a Latin version) Confucius (c.551–479). Confucius sought an understanding of society and authority that would be of practical use, and it took him half his life to find it. He said of himself, 'At fifteen, I took to learning, at thirty to standing firm, at forty I ceased to doubt, at fifty I knew the will of Heaven, at sixty my ear understood, at eighty I did what I desired – and broke no rule.' He worked for the ruler of Lu (a province in China), but his ideas were not being put into practice, so he spent thirteen years (497–484) travelling, looking for some ruler who would implement what he was advising. He found no takers, and returned to his home, teaching his followers and writing poetry and music.

The teaching of Confucius is found mainly in *Lunyu*, the *Analects*. The 'analects' are roughly 500 remarks and conversations with his followers or with rulers whom he met, of which the following section is an example:

Zigong said: 'Poor without servility, rich without arrogance.
    How is that?' The Master said: 'Not bad, but better still: poor
    and yet cheerful, rich yet considerate.'
The Master said: 'To study without thinking is futile. To think
    without studying is dangerous.'
Lord Meng Wu asked about filial piety (*xiao*). The Master said:
    'The only time a dutiful son ever makes his parents worry is
    when he is sick.'
Ziyou asked about filial piety. The Master said: 'Nowadays
    people think they are dutiful sons when they feed their
    parents. Yet they also feed their dogs and horses. Unless there
    is respect, where is the difference?'
Zilu asked how to serve the spirits and gods. The Master said:
    'You are not yet able to serve men, how could you serve the

spirits?' Zilu said: 'May I ask you about death?' The Master
said: 'You do not yet know life, how could you know death?'
(*Analects* 11.12)*

The aim of Confucius was to bring into effect the will of Tian in
the creation of a well-ordered society. Confucians believe in the
Three Guiding Principles (*san gang*) and the Five Enduring
Regulations (*wu chang*) as the non-negotiable foundation of
every life and society, and the first of the Principles is the
obedience of the subject to the ruler – at whatever level. This
commitment to the importance of a stable society can only be
achieved by a serious knowledge of the past and its ways, in order
to create people who learn how to live lives of humane goodness
in relation to others.

This quality of humane goodness is the supreme virtue in
Chinese belief, and is called Ren (in older spelling, Jen). Before
the time of Confucius, only the nobility were thought capable of
possessing great virtue of this kind, but Confucius believed that
all are capable of leading a generously moral and benevolent life.
They are the true nobility, and Confucius called those who live in
this way Junzi, the highest aristocracy in Confucian belief. They
are people who do their best for others and who are completely
serene and at ease even when they themselves are overtaken by
misfortune.

Not only did Confucius think that all people are capable of
Ren: he also thought that they could learn it, partly by education,
partly by practice in the world. This belief became the foundation of Chinese education until the end of the nineteenth century.

---

* Translated by Simon Leys, *The Analects of Confucius* (New York: W. W.
Norton & Co., 1997).

It involved a great respect for the experience of the past, and that is why Confucius regarded the rituals that sustain society as so important. It requires an attitude summed up in the word Li. Confucius taught that there are two levels of Li, the outer and the inner. The outer Li is made up of the rites, ceremonies, manners and customs that bind humans to each other in a single community. The inner Li consists of the disposition to enter into all this with determination and goodwill.

The teaching of Confucius was certainly a belief, or system of beliefs, that changed the world, because it became the foundation of education, philosophy and government in China for 2,000 years. Of course it changed greatly itself in that time, mainly because Confucius did not leave behind him an organized system. What were left were texts which are known as 'the Confucian Classics', and it was these that became the foundation of Chinese society. They were memorized by students, tested in the imperial examinations that led to civil office and appointments, as well as quoted extensively in Chinese literature and correspondence.

The Six Classics (*Liu Jing*) show how wide is the foundation of Confucian life. The first four preceded Confucius: they are The Books of Rites, Poetry, History, and Changes (*I Ching* or *Yi Jing*, a book of divination now popular outside China). *The Book of Music* was lost early on, but much of its contents can be recovered from other works. *The Book of Spring and Autumn Annals* may have come from Confucius himself, with the other texts having been edited by him – but the exact relationship of Confucius to these texts (author or editor or transmitter?) is disputed.

The Five Classics (as they had become with the loss of *Music*) were engraved in stone in 175 CE, and made widely available in block-printed books between 922 and 953. Other texts were added later, including *The Analects* and the *Book of Mengzi* (older spelling Mencius, 372–289 BCE). The book *Mengzi* is an edited version of his teaching. *Mengzi* became enormously important in Chinese belief, because it taught that Tian produces in humans four potentials which, if they are pursued and cultivated through education and practice, lead to lives in which the four great virtues are expressed. They are Ren and Li (above), Yi (right disposition and action) and Zhi (insight or wisdom). These help to establish a just and compassionate society, and they also bring profound satisfaction to those who acquire and practise them. During the Song dynasty, Mengzi came to be regarded as 'a second Confucius'.

From Confucius to the Neo-Confucianists

Not all people agreed with Confucius. The Warring States period had produced those like Xunzi (*c*.313–238) who were pessimistic about human nature, believing it to be innately corrupt and in-educable: goodness must be instilled by discipline, with the wayward kept in strict control. That view was taken further by the so-called Legalists (Fa Jia). They were not a School following a founder, but simply 'a family' (*jia*) of people who shared the same point of view. They believed that the Confucian idea of ed-ucating people in the ways of the ancients, in the hope that they would become virtuous, was unrealistic: 'When the people are taught like that, it is certain that the country will fall apart.'

What is needed, they insisted, is a body of clear and well-known laws, exercised by a strong central government, with severe punishment for those who disobey. Fa Jia reached the height of its influence during the period of the Warring States and under the Qin dynasty, when, with these strong policies, China was united for the first time. Subsequently, they were less obviously important, but in times of war or rebellion the beliefs of the Legalists have been adopted by governments down to the present day.

Mediating between early Confucianism and the Legalists was Mo Di (or, as a title, Mozi, older spelling Mo Tzu, *c*.470–*c*.380). He agreed with the Legalists that Confucians spent too much time in ritual (Li) and poetry from the past. Furthermore, the Confucians spoke about following 'the will of Heaven [Tian]' but did little in practice about it. Mo Di emphasized the importance of the recognition of Tian through offerings. In contrast, however, to the Legalists, Mo Di believed that love is in the nature of human beings, as well as desire to help others, and that the task of governments is to create the opportunities for this 'universal love' (as he called it) to be exercised: in their laws they must endorse and reward it:

> Those who object to universal love point out that universal love may be humane and righteous, but is it meant to be put into practice? They say that universal love is as possible as picking up Mount T'ai and leaping over rivers with it. So, then, universal love is but a pious wish, and how can anyone expect it to be materialised? Mo Di replied: to pick up Mount T'ai and leap over the rivers is a feat that has never been accomplished since humans first existed. But universal love and mutual aid have been personally practised by the great sage-kings of old ... Now, as to universal love and mutual aid, they are incalculably more beneficial and less difficult. It seems to me that the only trouble is that there is no ruler who will encourage them. If there were a ruler who would encourage them, bringing to bear the lure of reward

and the threat of punishment, I believe that people would tend toward universal love and mutual aid like fire attending upward and water downwards – nothing in the world could stop them. (*Mozi* 28.3)*

Under the Qin dynasty, the Confucians suffered greatly, but under the Han, they recovered. Confucian beliefs made the emperors central to the well-being of the state, and offered an educated 'civil service' to assist and support the government. Emperor Wu, who ruled from 140–87 BCE, established, with the help of the brilliant Dong Zhongshu (179–104), the Confucian Classics as the foundation of education and of the state, and made reverence for Confucius the state cult.

By the end of the Han dynasty, it was increasingly obvious that the imposition of Confucian beliefs was becoming academic and sterile. By now, Daoist beliefs had become important in China, and scholars emerged, including the Seven Worthies of the Bamboo Grove (*zulin qixian*), who gave to the Confucian Classics an interpretation which linked Daoism to the Confucian tradition. They produced a system of belief known as the Mysterious Learning (*xuan xue*).

The Mysterious Learning has been interpreted by some as a Daoist movement which they call neo-Daoism. But in fact it was an attempt to revitalize Confucianism by showing how its emphasis on moral order is linked to the Daoist belief that order and morality lie in the natural order. The Mysterious Learning then argued that moral order cannot be taught or imposed in a traditional way: it must arise first and

* Translated in William Theodor de Bary, *Sources of Chinese Tradition* (New York: Columbia University Press, 1960).

fundamentally in discerning what belongs to the natural order – or, as they called it, the Dao. Some of the scholars of the Mysterious Learning went further and said that people should then follow their nature, including their physical desires, rather than submit themselves to moral codes that suppress those desires. Beliefs of this kind are known as 'antinomianism', from the Greek 'against the laws'.

This challenged the Confucians to rethink, on the basis of the Confucian tradition, 'the nature of human nature', and they did this under the stimulus of the arrival and popularity of Buddhism in China. Confucians respected the sharp way in which Buddhists analysed human (and indeed all) nature, but they argued vigorously against what Buddhism had become in practice, with its quest for escape from this world and its worship of Buddhas and Bodhisattvas.

The founding of the Song dynasty began a period of greater stability in which an attempt was made to shift the focus in Confucianism from the exegesis of the ancient texts to the creation of an understanding based on body-mind and nature-destiny (*shenxin xingming*) – Buddhist questions but with a Chinese answer. In contrast to Buddhists, the new understanding of Confucianism, usually called neo-Confucianism or Li Xue ('the learning of principle'), extended Confucius' emphasis on personal responsibility for developing a virtuous character and applying it to the good of society. Neo-Confucianism dominated China for the next 800 years, and, as it was taken overseas, it also changed the worlds of Korea and Japan.

The beginning of this new development is sometimes known as the School of Song Learning (*song xue*), founded by the Five Masters.

Zhou Dunyi (1017–73) developed the Confucian belief that humans are the highest creatures in the universe because they can understand themselves and the world around them, and then on the basis of that understanding, can embody in themselves the characteristics of the ideal human being. They must live these out in complete consistency and sincerity, in a quality known as *cheng*. The ideal person lives in stability and peace, and does not race around seeking something new to do.

Shao Yong (1011–77) put this into practice, refusing all official posts and calling himself Mr Happy. He believed (as do Daoists) that all things come from the same ultimate source, and that consequently all things contain the same principles: wisdom lies in discerning and respecting these principles which he believed were linked to each other by the pattern of numbers to be found fundamentally in *The Book of Changes* (*I Ching* or *Yi Jing*). It is through mathematical analysis that the universe can be understood.

Zhang Zai (1020–77) borrowed from both Daoists and Buddhists. Daoists believe that life and well-being depend on understanding the energies that sustain the vigour of life. These are known as Qi (older spelling, *ch'i*). Zhang Zai integrated Qi into the Confucian tradition. Qi is the ultimate source from which all things come. Qi itself is beyond all possibility of description (devoid of characteristics: cf. Buddhist beliefs about Shunyata). Qi divides with the light part (Yang) becoming Heaven and the heavy part (Yin) becoming earth: from their interaction all things come into being. For Zhang Zai, the purpose of life is to achieve a harmonious balance between Heaven and Earth.

Cheng Hao (1032–85) and **ChengYi** (1033–1107) were nephews of Zhang Zai, but they went in a different direction by insisting on the distinctions between the Confucians on the one hand and Daoists and Buddhists on the other. For them, only the Confucian tradition could resolve the tensions, or even conflicts, between the principles derived from Heaven, present in Nature (Tian Li, something like 'natural law'), and human desires and passions. They laid out a practical way in which this can be achieved.

Cheng Hao thus addressed a petition to the Emperor asking him in effect to move back to the foundations of Chinese life:

> Your servant considers that the laws laid down by the kings of old were based on human feelings and were in accord with the natural order . . . If you take the underlying basis of government – the teachings by which the people may be safely guided, the principles which remain unalterable forever in the natural order, and on which the people depend for their very existence – on these matters there has never been divergences, but rather agreement among the wise men of all times, whether early or late. Only if life established in that way begins to fail cannot think of those laws ever being changed . . . This is the clear and evident lesson of history.

On these foundations, Zhu Xi (1130–1200) created a systematic synthesis of neo-Confucian beliefs. He took these back to the Classics and their necessity for the endorsement of present-day practices. At the same time, there must be an equally rigorous understanding of the principles that underlie the universe and are manifest in everything within it. The insistence of the Chengs on the unique truth of the Confucian tradition was combined with Zhu's teaching to create the Cheng-Zhu Harmony or School.

This synthesis did not sweep the board. There were some (like Lu Jiuyuan, 1139–93, founder of the Idealistic School) who believed that the practice of the good life must be a great deal simpler, since otherwise it is out of reach of all but scholars. The School is 'idealistic' because it believes that the goodness of all things, including humans, is innate, and simply has to be brought to the surface of awareness and recognized. Nevertheless, the Cheng-Zhu Harmony prevailed, even though in the Yuan and Ming dynasties it was made slightly more accessible by combining with it the teachings of Lu Jiuyuan.

Confucianism and neo-Confucianism have a different history in Korea and Japan, where they were both, at different times, the foundation of philosophy and government. In Japan, for example, under the Tokugawa Shoguns, neo-Confucianism became the official code of conduct. Under the Communists in China, Confucianism was rejected for having supported ancient feudalism and oppression of the people. Even so, the moral values endorsed by Confucianism have survived, and, outside China, have continued to be important in the morality of the modern world.

The Dao

Dao-jiao and Dao-jia, religion and philosophy, make up what is usually otherwise known as Daoism (old spelling Taoism). Daoism is one of the three major traditions of China (along with Confucianism and Buddhism) known as San-jiao. Daoism has an immensely complicated history in China, because its two parts (popular religion and philosophical reflection) have separate histories and yet they are completely entangled in each other, and Daoism also interacts with the other religions of China.

Daoism began with Laozi and Zhuangzi, and from the two texts bearing those names. It is not known whether Laozi was a historical person (though many stories are told about him) or is simply the name of the text attributed to him, *Laozi*. *Zhuangzi* was compiled by pupils of Zhuangzi from his teaching, but again, virtually nothing is known of Zhuangzi except that he lived during the fourth century BCE, in the period of the Warring States. That perhaps explains why *Zhuangzi* draws on many different elements of Chinese belief, almost as though it is trying to reconcile them in a unifying vision. It has even been questioned whether it is a Daoist work at all, although certainly it mentions and develops Daoist themes in important ways.

The stories told about Laozi place him in the sixth century BCE, because they tell of Confucius coming to him and acknowledging his superior wisdom. They tell also of Laozi going to India and instructing the Buddha. But these read like strategic arguments in the later contests between the religions of the San-jiao. The text itself is short (just over 5,000 words), and yet (outside the Christian Bible) it is among the most translated works in the world. The work is divided into two parts: one explores the nature of the Dao, the other explores how the Dao becomes manifest in effect and consequence, in what it calls De. The two belong so inextricably together that a more common name for *Laozi* is *Daode jing* (older spelling Tao-te Ching), 'The Classic Text of the Dao and its Power to be Manifest'. The text is now printed with the Dao in the first half and the De in the second, but the earliest surviving text has them the other way round. This was discovered by archaeologists in 1973, hand-written on silk and dating from about the second century BCE. So we know that the Dao and the De are a part of one another. But what are they?

The opening words of *Daode jing* make it clear, not only that we cannot know, but also that it is foolish to ask the question expecting an answer:

> The Dao that can be described as Dao is not the eternal Dao. The name that can be named is not the eternal name. Nameless, it is the origin of earth and heaven; able to be named, it is the mother of all things. Always non-existent, that we may apprehend its inner secret, always existent, that we may discern its outer manifestations: these two are the same; only as they manifest themselves do they receive different names.

Much of the history of Daoism is the working out of the meaning and implication of these profound words. The Dao is the source of all appearance, the unproduced Producer, of all that is – the reason why anything exists at all. The Dao is far beyond human comprehension and description (cf. in other religions *neti, neti,* Ein Sof, the *via negativa*). Nevertheless, *something* can be said because the Dao is manifest through its effects, through De (which is an inextricable part of itself, not an agent doing its work). Through De, the potency in all things to become something rather than nothing, all appearances are brought into being, so that the Dao can be discerned in the effects. All that exists is a consequence of Dao, almost, as we might say, of primordial energy, of particles and atoms hurtling into new architectures of appearance – plants and planets, stars and suns. The Dao, the Source, cannot be found as one object among other objects in the universe; rather, it supplies the possibility of all nature and of all individual appearances; and those are the Dao as it becomes nameable.

To explain how this happens, the *Daode jing* drew on ideas already existing in Chinese belief about the Yin and the Yang. These are the contrasting energies out of whose interaction particular things come into being. The Yin represents whatever is receptive and calm, such things as the feminine, the moon, water and clouds, while the Yang represents whatever is aggressive and hard, such as the masculine, the sun, stones and storms. The Yin and the Yang are often spoken of as opposites in conflict with each other, but in fact each contains the seed of the other: the black and white spots in the famous Yin-Yang symbol represent the way in which each lies at the heart of the other. Thus winter may seem like the absence and defeat of summer, but the seed of summer lies at the heart of winter in spring. These beliefs were first organized into a coherent system by Zou Yan (*c*.third century BCE) who argued that the Yin-Yang, in quest for harmony through contest, work through the Five Agents (water, fire, earth, wood and metal) to produce the world and human history. Zou-Yan's School of Yin-Yang did not endure, but the importance of Yin and Yang and the Five Agents remained paramount in Chinese belief.

For Daoists, the secret of life, whether of individuals, societies or governments, becomes clear: it is to understand the Dao-De and the Yin-Yang, and to work with its principles which bring the universe into being and sustain it – and not to ignore them and seek to live 'against the grain of the universe'. Living in this way is known as *wu-wei*, another Daoist term that is impossible to translate. Roughly it means 'being active but in a non-active way': allowing the Dao to unfold through one's life without resisting or rebelling against it.

For that reason, the *Daode jing* contains much practical advice to rulers, some of which, inevitably, expects that force will have to be used. At the same time, the counterbalancing consequences of force have to be remembered in the creation of political strategy: 'Any victory should be treated like a funeral.'

The second foundational text in Daoism, *Zhuangzi*, is even less systematic than *Daode jing*. It is full of stories, anecdotes and paradoxical sayings taken from Chinese beliefs of the time. It does explore the nature of the Dao, but whereas *Laozi* teaches how to live with Dao in the world in a non-striving acceptance, *Zhuangzi* teaches how to rise above the world into a kind of spiritual freedom. The way to achieve this lies in seeking the transcendent Dao beyond the confused and confusing life that humans otherwise experience. Then the true distinctions can begin to be made which transform our understanding of that experience. 'The dream and the butterfly' is often quoted, but usually leaving out the final sentence:

> Once Zhuangzi dreamt that he was a butterfly, fluttering about and enjoying itself, not knowing that it was Zhuangzi. Suddenly it woke up and there he was, Zhuangzi. But he did not know whether he was Zhuangzi who had dreamed he was a butterfly, or a butterfly dreaming he was Zhuangzi. Between Zhuangzi and the butterfly there must be some distinction, and this is what is called the transformation of things.

On those foundations, it is not surprising that philosophical Daoism developed in many different ways, since the texts are short and often enigmatic. Of later philosophers, He-shang Gong (date and identity uncertain, perhaps late Han) is important because his commentary on *Laozi* offered a way of unifying Dao-jia and Dao-jiao, and it was regarded almost as a second *Laozi*. He adopted the

Chinese belief that the universe and all things in it are pervaded by Qi. For He-shang Gong, Qi is the means through which Dao-De pervades all things and sustains them in being. The body is a microcosm which, like all else, is pervaded by Qi. To find and develop the Qi within oneself is to find the Dao and thus (as an aware part of the Dao) to overcome disorder and death.

These basic beliefs of Daoism have changed the world, not just of China, but also of Korea and Japan, and now far beyond. The Dao as the underlying principle unfolding in the coherent manifestation of life and the universe has led to books with titles like *The Tao of Physics* and *The Tao of Pooh*. Since Daoists have always applied their beliefs to the practical tasks of government, this has led to management seminars on the Tao of business. But in China, the main consequence has been in the many forms of religious Daoism, for these offered practical ways in which the dreams of philosophy could become real.

The Development of Daoism

Laozi and *Zhuangzi* are not the origins of Daoism, since they incorporate much that had preceded them (for example, Yin and Yang). It is more historically accurate to see philosophical Daoism as one of many strands brought together in the forming of practical or religious Daoism. That process of binding other beliefs into Daoism continued long after *Laozi* and *Zhuangzi*. It can be seen in two important early examples, the Way of the Heavenly/Celestial Master and Mao Shan.

The Way of the Heavenly Master is also known as the Way of the Five Pecks of Rice from the tribute expected from its followers. It began in 142 CE when Laozi appeared to Zhang Daoling (Zhao Ling, the Heavenly Master) and commissioned him to establish the true Dao. He therefore abolished the popular quest for healing and happiness through sacrifices to demons by offering more effective healing. He drew on the many healing religions of the time, especially shamanism, and wove them into Daoism. The line of the Heavenly Masters continues to the present day in Taiwan.

Mao Shan began with Wei Huacun (251–334), who received in visions the first section of the writings known as *Shang-qing*: they became the scripture of the new movement. When she died, she was succeeded by her son. He employed an official called Yang Xi who, in 364, was commanded to go to Mount Mao where Wei Huacun dictated the rest of the *Shang-qing*. Rituals have always been of great importance in Daoism because they are a formal and practical way of uniting oneself with the Dao. But they are also a way of generating ecstatic chants and visions, and early Mao Shan developed these by using and adapting Buddhist rituals and ways of chanting. These chants were known as 'sacred treasures', *lingbao*. In Mao Shan, however, ecstasy was never an end in itself, and under Tao Hong-jing (456–536), the emphasis moved to the kind of profound meditation that he took from Buddhism, but which in his case led to union with the Dao and thus to immortality.

Mao Shan is also important in the history of Daoism for the emphasis it placed on sacred texts and scripture. It thus contributed to the immense collection or Canon of sacred texts in Daoism, known as the Dao-Zang which, by the time of the early Ming, contained 8,000 texts.

These two movements show how deeply Daoism was embedded in popular religion. In China, this is the religion which worships Deities and looks to them for help, and which seeks immortality. Both these were supremely important in the history of Daoism and in the forming of life-changing beliefs among the Chinese.

For Daoists, the world is alive with the sound of Deities who are their constant companions and who help them in everything from fertility and birth to marriage and death, from passing exams to keeping well and growing healthy crops. The Deities of Daoism are a vast internet into which people can 'log on' in prayers, rituals, sacrifices and offerings. There are many temples where particular Deities can be worshipped, and these are the visible face of religious Daoism, but the home is equally important as the place where the Deities are met.

There are in fact so many Deities that they cannot possibly be listed. Various attempts were made (notably in the work *Feng-shen Yan-yi* of the sixteenth century) to organize them into a coherent system, based on the hierarchy of the Chinese imperial order – which means, in reverse, that the Emperor and his court reflect on earth the order of the Deities in Heaven.

On that basis, the head of the hierarchy is the Jade Emperor Lord on High, Yu Huang Shang-Di. The worship of Yu Huang became widespread in the eleventh century after a Sung emperor justified an unpopular treaty he had signed by claiming that he had received orders from Yu Huang in a dream. Yu Huang is widely revered, supreme above all other Deities. He is so far above human thought and imagination that often no image of him is made. Instead, a tablet bearing his name and titles is placed on the altar – if that: in Fukien, he is believed to reside in the ash of the incense fire, and not even a tablet is allowed. He is believed to be the final judge of human conduct, and is approached in worship with great care lest he be offended. He runs the universe with the help of a kind of 'civil service' of Deities, each with his or her own department. There are Deities looking after virtually everything from war and wealth to weather and the various Chinese arts.

Beneath the hierarchy of the Heavens is a lower level of Deities who are the executive agents. These are the Deities who, for example, control the seas in the form of Dragon Kings and the Empress of Heaven (not the consort of the Jade Emperor, but the Goddess who protects the navies and fishermen of China). At the opposite extreme are the Ten Kings of Hell, ruled over by King Yama. Each of the Hells has its own king. Over the first reigns Qin-guang who judges each soul as it arrives: those without fault are returned to earth; the others are punished in the appropriate hell where the punishment exactly fits the crime.

Between the two extremes are the Deities who help in all the 'changes and chances of this mortal life', especially in the form of the Three Gods of Happiness: their figures are as common in Chinese homes and workplaces as figures of St Christopher on the dashboard of cars. They can help in immediate necessities, but the ultimate necessity is to find an escape into immortality.

Qin Shihuangdi sought protection in his tomb with his Terracotta Army, but what if he could avoid the tomb altogether? The Chinese had long been telling legends and stories about the Isles of the Immortals. He threw himself (or rather he threw parties of explorers) into the quest to find them. None came back, and so the quest went on.

The quest for immortality is a basic part of Daoism and takes many different forms. Partly this remained a quest for the Isles of the Immortals, and for the Eight Immortals, the Ba Xian, to whom countless Daoists still pray to help them in their quest. The Eight Immortals are now surrounded by legend and story, but at least some of them are connected with historical people. They show how the eight conditions of life (youth, age, poverty, wealth, high rank, low or no rank, feminine, masculine) can all equally be transcended, and how, therefore, from any condition, immortality can be attained. Thus Li Dong Bin, the most popular of the Immortals, is associated with medicine and healing; Di Guai Li, also popular, is often found as a beggar assisting the poor; Zhang Guo Lau helps those who want children; Cao Guo Lao is a reformed murderer; Han Xiang Zi is a dweller in mountains encouraging the love of solitude; Han Zhang Li was an imperial official during the Han dynasty; Lan Cai He is found as both male and female; He Xian Gu is a woman who gained immortality through her asceticism.

In China itself, the Golden Mother, Jin-mu, the Queen Mother of the West, presides over those who have actually attained immortality, and she grows the peaches of immortality which ripen only every 3,000 years. But at least this holds out hope that immortality is possible.

There are, however, two other routes. One is by finding the secret medicine or elixir of immortality. This quest is known as the Outer Alchemy, and it involved attempts to 'steal the secret of heaven and earth', the secret of Life – often with fatal results.

The other is the Inner Alchemy, in which an attempt is made to harness the energies within the body and direct them to the prolongation of life. The body is pervaded by Qi, known more usually in the West in its old spelling as Ch'i. Daoists developed many exercises to promote Qi, to balance the Yin and the Yang, and to eliminate the destructive spirits. To help the Qi circulate and to achieve balance, practitioners stand leaning forward with knees slightly bent – familiar now with those seeking, not immortality, but relief from stress.

It was this pose that led Europeans to call them 'boxers', as in the Boxer rebellion in 1899–1900 in northern China to expel all foreigners. Its failure led to radical demands for the abolition of the imperial line and a republican China.

The Boxer rebellion was led by the Righteous and Harmonious Fists Society (I-ho Chuan), one of many Societies in China with secret teachings and therefore suspect to the government. Thus the Taiping Rebellion (1850–64) was led by the Heavenly Kingdom of Great Peace, a mixture of Confucianism and Protestant Christianity; the White Lotus mixed Daoism and Buddhism and rebelled from 1796–1805. Since some of these Societies also became criminal (e.g., the Triads), governments have usually kept a wary eye on them – a pattern repeated at present with Falun Gong (Fa-long Gong, 'Practice of the Wheel of Dharma'). Falun Gong was founded by Li Hongzhi in 1992, and it promotes meditation and exercises with claims to health and medical benefits. It is being opposed and persecuted by the Chinese government on the grounds that its claims are spurious and subversive, and that it is an anti-government cult.

Japan

Overview

The history of religions in Japan is sometimes divided between the major religions (particularly Shinto, Buddhism, neo-Confucianism), because each of them has its own history in Japan, but that makes the *interaction* between all religions in Japan difficult to follow. The history, therefore, is often followed through the major periods known from the political capital cities or from a ruling dynasty. That can be equally difficult because it fails to bring out the important continuities in religions for which the political changes may make little difference. Nevertheless, in this book the division into periods is followed because it makes the story easier to follow, and it allows cross-reference to the section on Buddhism in China in the previous chapter – but the point about continuities from one period to another should be borne in mind. The major periods and people are:

Pre-Nara up to 710 CE
Nara 710–787/794
Heian 794–1160
Taira 1160–1185
Kamakura Shogunate 1185–1333

Ashikaga Shogunate 1336–1537 (also known as Warring States
    Period)
Oda Nobunaga 1534–82
Toyotomi Hideyoshi 1536–98
Tokugawa Ieyasu 1537–1616
Tokugawa Shogunate 1603–1868
Meiji 1868–1912
Taisho 1912–25
Showa 1925–89

The early history of religion in Japan was made up of several
strands that were not brought together in any unity. The arrival
of Buddhism offered an opportunity of unity, and Buddhism
was endorsed by Prince Shotoku (574–622) who established a
central government and drew up the first Constitution. But
local native religion was also important to him, with its strong
belief in the spirits who sustain life in the natural and human
world, and on the rituals that bind families and the spirits
together. These spirits are the Kami. The Kami are so fundamental in Japanese life and religion that the native religion of
Japan came to be known as 'the way of the Kami', Kami no
Michi, or, from the Chinese *shen-tao* ('the way of the divine
beings'), as Shinto.

As one family gained increasing power, they established themselves as emperors, and began to create the sense of Japan's
ancient history by collecting myths and legends to tell how Japan
and the emperors were the creation and the gift of the sun-
goddess or Kami Amaterasu. They established their capital at
Nara, basing it and their government on Chinese models. They
continued to endorse Buddhism (strictly under their control),
and much of the subsequent history of Japan and religion in

Japan is of the interaction, sometimes hostile, sometimes cooperative, between Buddhism and Shinto.

During the Heian period, Buddhists began to assert independence from imperial control with the founding of two Schools, Tendai and Shingon. They came from China but were adapted to Japanese ways and beliefs. Shinto was also developed in more structured ways, and attempts were made to find a form of religion, *shinbutsu shugo*, in which Buddhism and Shinto could be combined. One result of this was the development of Shugendo, a Japanese religion that drew on all available religions to gain magical powers and to achieve Enlightenment during this life.

The same wide-ranging religious explorations and innovations continued under the Kamakura shoguns (military rulers). In Buddhism, the emphasis was on making the way to enlightenment much simpler. Shinto began to reassert itself against a common Buddhist belief that the Kami were local manifestations of Buddhist Buddhas and Bodhisattvas. In a Buddhist perspective, the Kami were some way down the ladder of manifestations on their way to Enlightenment. In reaction, the Watarai family established a renewal of Shinto based on the shrines at Ise, devoted to Amaterasu and emphasizing the role of the imperial family in protecting the nation. In 1484, Yoshida Kanetomo neatly reversed the Buddhist subordination of the Kami by insisting that the Buddhas and Bodhisattvas are simply particular Kami with specific but limited work to do in Japan. This was the beginning of Yoshida Shinto.

Christianity entered Japan with Francis Xavier in 1549. It was drawn into the fluctuating way in which the central authorities used the support or the suppression of particular religions to implement political strategies. After initial success, Christianity aroused suspicion that it was introducing European conflicts into Japan, and it was banned in 1612 and again in 1638. The persecution continued until 1873: it did not eradicate Christianity, but produced 'hidden Christians', Kakure Kirishitan.

Under the Tokugawa shoguns, Japan was reunified after more than a hundred years of civil war. The Samurai, originally noble warriors with good ancestry, became prominent as a distinct class of warriors with their own code of conduct (Bushido, 'the way of the warrior'), emphasizing loyalty and overcoming fear of death. There was a renewal of Shinto in which it was seen as the foundation of Japan. Even so, Buddhism was still supported as a useful instrument of government and local good order, and many new temples were built.

In 1868, the young emperor, Meiji, became the focus of a new attempt to renew Japan under the slogan, 'Enrich the nation, strengthen its arms.' Appeal was made to a golden age of the emperors before feudalism and military government took over, and Buddhism lost its state support and patronage. Shinto in a form known as State Shinto (Kokka Shinto) became the foundation of Japanese life, in contrast to individual traditions which were known as Sect Shinto (Kyoha Shinto). Provided that commitment to Japan was expressed through allegiance to State Shinto, other religious commitments were allowed, and this was a period when many new religious sects or movements were introduced. The New Religions, which have to be formally registered, are known as Shinko Shukyo.

After the Second World War, Shinto was separated from the State, but the Imperial family retained its position in unifying and bringing well-being to Japan. It is difficult to say how many followers of Shinto there are because Shinto does not have formal membership, but about 80 per cent of Japanese are associated with some kind of Shinto practices and beliefs.

The Emperors and the Kami

Little is known of the earliest religion in Japan. It was local and not united into any single system of belief. The Ainu people, who lived on the main island of Honshu until they were driven north in about 300 BCE, believed in Deities whom they called *kamui*. It is possible that these are the forerunners of the Kami, the sacred powers who play such an important part in Japanese life and religion – so important, in fact, that the religion of Japan is called Kami no Michi (the Way of the Kami) or in Chinese *shen-tao*, hence Shinto.

The Kami are the spiritual powers that exist in all things and sustain them in life. They are not Deities in the sense that an Indian, for example, might recognize. They have their own histories, and they live and die. Yet in terms of reverence and ritual, they were treated as Deities, at least in the early history of Japan.

Later, they were regarded as the spirituality that gives character and form to all things, the vitality and energy which makes them what they are. But whereas words like 'spirituality' and 'energy' are abstract, the Kami are the individual embodiment of these abstractions, in such a way that people can interact with them.

This interaction is fundamental in Japanese life and religion. It takes place in shrines and temples, and also in the home and family, and since the Kami are in all things, they can be met anywhere. The hills are alive with the presence of the Kami: there are therefore countless billions of them. In a traditional saying, there are *yaoyorozu no kami*, 'vast myriads of *kami*', and that is why streams and meadows, mountains and rivers are all holy ground. They are 'places of the *kami*'; and must be treated with reverence for that reason.

In the same way, Kami are the sacred powers in people, dead as well as alive: humans as well as nature are 'children of the Kami', and it is the Kami Amaterasu who bestows sacred powers and authority on the emperors. In the eighteenth century, when attempts were being made to renew ancient Japanese beliefs, Motoori Norinaga (one of the leaders in that attempt, as we will see) made an attempt to define the Kami:

> I do not yet well understand the meaning of the word *kami* (and all the old explanations are wrong), but in general, the word *kami* refers to, first of all, the various Kami of heaven and earth spoken of in the classics, and the spirits [*mitama*] enshrined in their shrines, and it goes without saying that it also refers to people, and even birds and beasts and grass and trees, ocean and mountains – and anything else which has superior and extraordinary power, provoking awe. Here, 'superb' means not only superior in nobility and goodness, but also awe-inspiring things of great evil and weirdness, anything which provokes a high degree of wonder. Of people, those called Kami of course include the most exalted lineage of emperors, who are called 'distant Kami' since they are so far removed from the ordinary person, and worthy of reverence. Then there are the human Kami, who existed long ago and also at present; a certain number of human Kami exist in each province, village, and house, each in accord with his or her station . . . In this way, Kami are of manifold varieties, some noble and some base, some strong and some weak, some good and some evil, each being immediately in accord with its own mind and behaviour.*

---

* Translated by Norman Havens, in Inoue Nobutaka (ed.), *Kami* (Tokyo: Kokugakuin University, 1998).

This is a belief which changed the world of Japan. The sense of the Kami pervading all life and nature, and sustaining the emperor and other authorities, created a sense of reverence and respect as much for Nature as for authority. *Shi-zen* was originally a Chinese word to refer to the whole of the natural order and to the way in which humans must consciously participate in it. It is a belief that underlies important Zen practices, as we have already seen. Furthermore, it made Japan central and special, because it is the home of the Kami. More specifically, the Kami of warriors gives them great strength, and if they die in battle overseas, their Kami will find their way back to Japan.

The dramatic consequence of this belief became obvious in the Second World War, when Kamikaze pilots flew their planes to certain destruction as 'flying bombs' in the Pacific war. The word 'Kamikaze' means 'Divine Wind', so-called from the strong winds that dispersed two Mongol invasions in 1274 and 1281. Kamikaze pilots were first used at Leyte Gulf in October 1944, and extensively at Okinawa. They wore white scarves and a white cloth, taken from the *hachimaki*, the cloths worn by samurai warriors.

In Japanese belief, the spirits of warriors who die in obedience to the emperor return to Japan, and in particular to the Yasukuni (Country of Peace) shrine in Tokyo (hence the ironic words of soldiers before battle, 'See you in Yasukuni'), where remembrance of them is made. This shrine was founded in 1879 as the Tokyo Shokon Jinja (shrine). Originally the spirits of all who died in battle returned to Yasukuni, since all who died for the emperor were reckoned to be followers of Shinto. Since 1945, only those who had themselves adhered to Shinto have been included, since those of other religions (especially Buddhists and Christians) resist the *post mortem* conversion of their ancestors.

Those of other countries (e.g., Korea and China) have objected to the enshrinement of those who were subsequently convicted as war criminals. Feelings can still run high about formal state ceremonies in relation to the war dead being held at the shrine, and about less formal visits to the Shrine by prominent figures. Thus there were protests from China and South Korea in 2014 when prominent lawmakers visited the Shrine and the Prime Minister, Shinzo Abe, sent a masakaku tree in tribute.

When Buddhism arrived in Japan, it was welcomed by Prince Shotoku (574–622) to such an extent that he became known as 'the father of Buddhism'. But he also saw the potential strength of the native Japanese beliefs, and issued a decree in 607 requiring the veneration of Shinto Deities. This was taken further as the imperial family, extending its power, looked for ways in which it could justify its claims. Temmu (emperor 672–86) initiated the collection of ancient stories and traditions which was issued in 712 as *Kojiki* ('Records of Ancient Matters'), followed in 720 by *Nihongi*, the Chronicle of Japan.

Beginning with the creation of Japan, these works together tell how the supreme Kami, Amaterasu Omikami, sent her grandson, Ninigi, to establish divine rule on earth. In Japanese mythology, the origins of Japan are taken back to Izanagi and Izanami. In the beginning everything was an ocean of chaos out of which grew Kunitokotachi as a reed that gave rise to Izanagi and Izanami. Crossing the Floating Bridge of Heaven, they stirred the waters with a sacred spear: a drop from this created the first island and its people. Izanami died giving birth to fire, and when Izanagi sought her in the underworld and discovered the corruption of the grave, a tear fell from his eye which gave birth to Amaterasu. She, having defeated disorder and evil in the heavenly realms, became the 'heavenly shining Kami' (Amaterasu-o-Mikami) and sent her grandson, Ninigi, to drive out disorder from Japan (or Nippon, 'origin of the sun', or 'land of the rising sun'). In that way the earthly Kami became subordinate to the heavenly Kami, and the imperial family was brought into being to continue to represent the heavenly Kami on earth.

Beliefs of this kind about origins appear in all religions and have profoundly changed the ways in which people live and behave. Thus a Tokugawa scholar, Hirata Atsutane (1776–1843), used this Shinto belief about origins in order to argue that Japan and the Japanese are superior to all others because the Kamis brought them into being, whereas other peoples and nations were formed out of the froth and foam of the sea.

Ninigi is thus the legendary first emperor, and from him the imperial line is descended so that the emperors of Japan came to be regarded as 'Manifest Kami' (*akitsu kami*). From this belief comes the extreme Japanese reverence for the Emperor. He is the incarnation of the supreme Kami, but not of God (because of the distinction in Japanese belief between Kamis and God). When the Emperor was required, at the end of the Second World War, to make a formal denial of his divinity, he could do so with equanimity, because he had never claimed to be God in the first place. However, even on a slightly lower level, the Emperor has been revered (and still is by most Japanese) as the Manifest Kami.

When the capital was established at Nara in 710, Buddhist and Chinese influence was strong. Nara itself was modelled on the Tang Chinese capital, Chang-an. Six Schools of Buddhism were brought in from China, three of which (Sanron, Kegon and Ritsu) continue to the present day. Shomu (emperor 724–49) organized a network of state-supported Buddhist temples, monasteries and nunneries whose task was to protect the nation through ritual and spiritual exercises. At the centre was Todaiji, from where the State controlled the monks through the system known as *ritsuryo*.

In 794, Kammu (emperor 781–806) moved the capital to Heian-kyo, now known as Kyoto. There was an attempt by Buddhists to break free of State control, and new forms of Buddhism came into being. Their emphasis on individuality was helped by the Japanese belief in 'innate enlightenment', *hongaku*. This is the ability of all people to encounter the Kami and to achieve their spiritual goals (although these goals would be differently described in Shinto and Buddhism). This belief became important in the Japanese creation of many New Religions, since they too could be ways to meet the spirituality innate in all humans. It also helped in this period in the creation of the Shugendo, a religion drawing on many different traditions and Schools. The aim of its practitioners was to achieve Enlightenment in this life.

For Shinto, all this was on the edges. Between 905 and 927, *Engishiki* ('Procedures of the Engi Era') was produced to systematize the practice of Shinto. Its first half (*Jingikan*) deals with religious Shinto, the second half (*Dajokan*) with its application in government. Forms of prayer (Norito) were compiled to unify the worship and rituals offered to the Kami. Worshippers address their prayers to the Kami and are led to participate in the reality of the Kami who are already a real presence in the words when appropriately spoken. At this time also the first attempts were made formally to unite Shinto and Buddhism in Shinbutso-shugo. Underlying this is the belief that the unity of Japan is a gift and an obligation from the Kami.

From Kamakura to Tokugawa

In 1185, a newly emerging warrior class, the Samurai, led by feudal landowners called *daimyo*, won power and moved the political capital to Kamakura, leaving the now impotent emperors in Heian-kyo. The successful *daimyo*, Yoritomo Minamoto, compelled the emperor to make him Shogun (conquering general). The Shoguns, hereditary military rulers, held military and political authority until 1868.

The Samurai were originally retainers of local warlords and provincial governors, at a time when the central government could not control outlying provinces and districts. The bond between the lord and his retainers led to heroic stories which in turn led to the Bushido ('Way of the Warrior') code of honour and duty. This was made systematic in the seventeenth century, after which the Samurai following this code cultivated total loyalty and fearlessness in the face of death. To avoid the disgrace of being captured in battle the Samurai were taught the ritual of self-disembowelment known as *seppuku*, or more popularly as *hara-kiri*.

Conflicts and disasters in the Kamakura period produced sects and religions in which people could find strength and support. In addition to those of Buddhism, the Shugendo gained a wide following. The Shugendo ('the way of developing ascetic powers'; members are called Yamabushi, 'mountain sleepers') are groups of ascetics who seek renewal in the mountains through pilgrimage and meditation.

Mountains are believed by the Japanese (and not only by the Japanese) to be sacred and awe-inspiring places. They reach from earth to heaven, and while they can be places of danger, they are also places of isolation and retreat. As active volcanoes they can be terrifying, but when they are quiet or extinct, the craters are a gateway to the Kami. In Japan, there are more than 350 sacred mountains, the home of the Kami of the mountains. Of all sacred mountains, Mount Fuji, sixty miles from Tokyo, is supreme. Followers of Fuji-ko believe that Fuji is the home of the immortals, so that pilgrimage to the top, and then into the heart, of Fuji leads to immortality.

Chinese beliefs had been dominant in the Nara and Heian periods: neo-Confucianism formed the foundation of government and education, with Buddhism as the dominant religion and philosophy. Shinto shrines remained important in local areas, but Shinto as such was regarded as a kind of preparation for the coming of Buddhism.

That belief was expressed in words that became prominent in the history of religions in Japan, *honji suijaku*, 'original substance manifests traces'. Buddhists took this to mean that the Kami were incarnations of the original Buddha-nature, or more often of particular Buddhas or Bodhisattvas. They may be helpful in many ways, and that is why the rituals and offerings to them are important. But they are not the fundamental truth which can only be found in Buddhism. Two attempts were made during this period to unite Shinto with two forms of Buddhism Tendai and Shingon. The union with Tendai was called Sanno Ichijitsu ('Mountain-king, one-truth'), that with Shingon was called Ryobu ('Dual') Shinto.

This senior-junior way of understanding the relationship between Buddhism and Shinto began to be questioned in the Kamakura period, especially after two attempts by the Mongols to invade Japan, in 1274 and 1281, were driven off by the Kami – by the Kamikaze. Kitabatake Chikafusa (1293–1354) began to write *The Records of the Legitimate Succession of the Divine*

Sovereign. This, when it appeared about fifty years after the defeat of the Mongols, argued that Japan is far superior to China and even India, because Japan alone can trace for its emperors a single and direct line of succession from the Gods. Kitabatake Chikafusa wrote:

> Japan is the Divine country. The heavenly ancestor it was who first laid its foundations, and the Sun Goddess left her descendants to reign over it for ever and ever. This is true only of our country, and nothing similar may be found in foreign lands. That is why it is called the Divine country . . . Only in our country has the succession remained inviolate, from the beginning of Heaven and Earth to the present. It has been maintained with a single lineage, and even when, as inevitably has happened, the succession has been transmitted collaterally, it has returned to the true line. This is due to the ever-renewed Divine Oath, and makes Japan unlike all other countries.

At about the same time, the Five Classics of Shinto (Shinto Gobusho) were produced – purportedly from ancient times, but probably more literally 'produced' for the occasion. The Five Classics are made up of the history of an important Shinto shrine, the Ise Shrine, together with an exposition of Shinto ethics and philosophy.

The Ise Shrine is in two parts, the Inner Shrine where originally only the imperial family could worship (until it was made into a Shrine for the whole nation), and the Outer Shrine, run by the Watarai family. Watarai Shinto had originally allowed the superiority of Buddhism, but now it began to reverse the order, and to teach that the Buddhas and Bodhisattvas were simply manifestations of Kami.

All these beliefs were pulled together in a form of Shinto which insisted that Shinto is the oldest religion, and that consequently it, and not Buddhism, should be the foundation of Japanese life. This form of Shinto is known as Primal Shinto, Yuiitso Shinto. Instrumental in bringing it into being was Yoshida Kanetomo (1435–1511), whose family had served as custodians of the Yoshida and Hirano shrines in Kyoto, and had produced some of the great scholars of early Shinto. The family had originally been known by the name Urabe, so that Yoshida or Primal Shinto is also known as Urabe Shinto. Yoshida expressed his belief about Japan in the simple analogy of a tree:

> Japan is the roots and trunk, China its branches and leaves, India its flowers and fruit. Of all laws, Buddhism is the flower and the fruit, Confucianism the branches and the leaves, and Shinto the roots and trunk. So all foreign teachings are offshoots of Shinto.

It was a belief that completely changed the attitude of the Japanese to the world outside Japan. An immediate effect was the persecution of Buddhists. In 1571, for example, Oda Nobunaga (1534–82), destroyed the Buddhist temple-complex of Enryakuji on Mount Hiei, the Tendai Buddhist centre, and suppressed all Buddhist resistance. Initially, he gave some support to Christianity, seeing them as allies, but later they too were persecuted because they were another example of alien religions subverting the unique superiority of Japan.

Christianity had arrived in Japan with Francis Xavier in 1549. He and Alessandro Valignano (1539–1606) followed the policy (also pursued by Matteo Ricci, 1552–1610) of adopting the language and the ways of the country to which they had come. But as other Christians arrived, particularly Franciscans and Dominicans, they rejected the 'making native' of Christianity: as happened also in South America, they insisted on a European statement of the meaning of God, above all in ritual. These conflicting beliefs led to an appeal to Rome, and the Rites controversy was resolved by the Pope who ruled against the Jesuits in 1742 (in the bull *Ex quo singulari*). It was a fatal error, because it confirmed for the Chinese and the Japanese that Christianity was seeking to displace their own religions and customs. In Japan, Christians went into long periods of persecution, and in China, the emperors expelled all Christians unless they followed the Ricci way. Christians in Japan went 'under ground' and became Kakure Kirishitan, hidden Christians: they retained their beliefs and practices but disguised them under Shinto and Buddhist forms. The authorities produced tablets called *fumie*, bearing on them the image of the crucifix, and suspected Christians were required to step on them. Those who refused were tortured and killed.

Under the Tokugawa Shoguns, the revival of Shinto continued with renewed efforts to establish its antiquity. To put those efforts into a more organized and systematic form, Kada Azumamaro (1669–1736) of the Inari Shrine in Kyoto initiated a movement called 'The National Learning', Kokugaku. One of its first scholars was Kamo Mabuchi (1697–1769) who claimed that an anthology of the earliest poetry in Japan, *Manyoshu*, displayed the power of Japanese belief before it was contaminated by foreign religions. This was taken even further by Motoori Norinaga (1730–1801) who made the same claim for other works, especially *Kojiki* and *Nihongi* and *The Tales of the Genji*. Together they produced Fukko ('Restoration') Shinto based on their reconstruction of early beliefs.

The revival of Shinto did not mean that either neo-Confucianism or Buddhism was discarded. Buddhism became an instrument of government control in the provinces so that nearly 500,000 new Buddhist temples were constructed in the Tokugawa period. And neo-Confucianism was made into the official ethical philosophy of the state. Tokugawa Ieyasu employed a Confucian adviser, Hayashi Razan (1583–1657), who worked for him and his successors for fifty years drawing up legal codes, organizing the official histories and establishing a state shrine to Confucius. But this, like Buddhism, was in the service of a Shinto State: the advantage of neo-Confucianism was that it made the family the basic unit of society and demanded from the family upward absolute loyalty and obedience to superiors. A slogan of the time was, '*Chukko ippon*', affirming that loyalty to ruler and loyalty to parents are exactly the same in essence. The centrality of Shinto belief was given expression by the making of the Ise Shrine into the State Shrine – to which in moments of crisis immense national pilgrimages were made in 1650, 1705, 1771 and 1830.

The attempt to isolate Japan from the outside world began to fail in the nineteenth century. In 1846, US warships appeared at Uraga under Biddle demanding that Japan be opened up to trade, a mission repeated under Perry in 1853. The first commercial treaty was signed in 1858. In 1863, the British bombarded Kagoshima in retaliation for anti-foreign riots. The Japanese were split between those who wanted to end the increasingly chaotic rule of the Shoguns, to bring back the Emperors, and to keep foreigners out. Others, including the Shoguns, felt that Japan must be opened up to Western science. The disputes and the split were ended with the restoration of the Emperors under Meiji in 1868.

Meiji and the New Religions

In 1868, the dispute between those wanting to bring back the Emperors and keep foreigners out, and those believing that Japan must welcome foreigners who came with Western technology and science, was resolved by restoring the Emperors in the person of the young Meiji, and at the same time welcoming the new technology and learning of the West. Meiji ruled from 1868–1912, and under him Japan moved from feudalism, Chinese domination (even in a Shinto state) and two centuries of isolation, to a complete renewal of Japan.

Under the slogan 'Enrich the nation, strengthen its arms', the Meiji authorities recognized the importance of the ancient beliefs and traditions of Japan. The efforts of the School of New Learning to recover the earliest Shinto, which they called Fukko Shinto, were taken even further, and Shinto was organized into a coherent system:

Koshitsu Shinto (The Shinto of the Imperial Household) became the focal point for unity and pride in Japan's ancient traditions and achievements.

Kokka Shinto (State Shinto) was created by the Meiji government and continued through the Second World War, to organize national ceremonies and control the different forms of Shinto.

Jinja Shinto (Shrine Shinto) is the Shinto practised in the thousands of Shinto shrines: the practices are not identical, but they are still classified together. In 1946, the Association of Shinto Shrines (Jinja Honcho) was formed to replace Government control, and almost all Shinto sects belong to it. In 1956, it published a summary of Shrine Shinto beliefs under the title *Keishin seikatsu no koryo*, 'Life lived in Reverence of the Kami'. Its main points are to express gratitude for the blessings of the Kami through reverence for the ancestors and observance of Shinto rituals; to mediate the will of the Kami into the world through helping others without thought of reward; to join with others in acknowledging the will of the emperor in seeking the prosperity of the country and of the world. Shrine Shinto has supported national observations of Shinto, including memorial ceremonies at the Yasukuni Shrine.

Kyoha Shinto (Sect Shinto). The Meiji government respected the independence of thirteen Sects, giving each of them official recognition at different dates between 1876 and 1908. Their forms of Shinto are very varied, ranging from mountain-worship to faith-healing, from pure Shinto to Confucianist Shinto. Most of them still have large followings, although repeated sub-divisions mean that there are now many more than the original thirteen.

Shin Kyoha Shinto (New Sect Shinto) is made up of the many movements that have grown up since the Second World War. Initially forty-seven, they have continued to grow in number.

Minkan Shinto (Folk Shinto) is the popular Shinto practised alongside other forms of Shinto. It includes an immense range of family and daily life beliefs.

The Meiji grouped Shinto sects in this way in order to unify the nation with pride in its past. This was reinforced by those who sought to restore the old ways but in a reformed style. Notable among these was Saigo Takamori (1827–77) who led the overthrow of the Tokugawa in order to restore the old Samurai values. This pride in the past was increasingly valuable as some Japanese went abroad to seek education, and others sought to incorporate the ideas and beliefs of nineteenth-century Europe and America into Japanese life. Japan rapidly became a modern nation, the envy of others, while striving at the same time to return to an idealized past.

A consequence of the Meiji restoration is that the definition of Shinto once again changed. Shinto is unusual in that it is not a continuous system of religious beliefs; and that means in effect that it is not a religion with a continuous history. Of course Shinto has often been interpreted as a continuous religion, not least by Motoori Norinaga in his attempt to establish the antiquity of the Japanese tradition. Shinto is made up of many threads, each of which has its own history, but they were only gradually woven together into a single tapestry. The meaning of the word 'Shinto' has changed through time, and it did not emerge as Japan's indigenous religion until the rise of modern nationalism.

The success of the Meiji restoration was seen in a series of notable victories – against China in 1895, against Russia in 1905, and in the annexation of Korea in 1910. On the other hand, Japanese nationalists resented the unequal treaties imposed on them by the West, culminating in the refusal of Germany, France and Russia to allow Japan to occupy the Kwantung peninsula in Manchuria after the defeat of China. The resentment fuelled national pride.

During the Showa period (1925–89, so-called from the reign name of the emperor Hirohito), the argument from Shinto beliefs about the origins of Japan was revived. It had powerful consequences, as Skya has shown in his analysis of the ultranationalists who moved Japan so decisively toward total war in Asia and the Pacific in the 1930s and 1940s:

All of them were highly religious people – Shinto fundamentalists – and as such they believed in the core doctrines of Shinto
ultranationalism: the divine descent and divinity of the living
emperor; the divine origins of the Japanese ethnic group as
against the divine natural evolutionary origins of man; and the
divine source of political authority stemming from the ancestral
deity Amaterasu Omikami. These doctrines were common to all
Shinto ultranationalists as much as the crucifixion or resurrection of Jesus Christ is to Christians. Accordingly, for all these
radical Shinto ultranationalist theorists, sovereignty resided in
the emperor, and no human law was capable of restraining the
sovereign emperor.*

Those beliefs supplied a warrant for the claim that Shinto is older
and therefore superior to other religions, just as Japan (or
Nippon, 'origin of the Sun') is superior to other nations. At its
worst extreme, this belief led to Manchurian prisoners being
classified, not as human beings, but as *maruta*, 'blocks of wood',
so that they could be used for medical experiments. It led more
generally to the ambition that Japan could be 'the light of Asia'.
When Japan entered the Second World War in 1941, it drew up
a 'Basic plan for the establishment of the Greater Asia co-
prosperity sphere', in which 'the ultimate aim in East Asia is to
make East Asiatic peoples revere the imperial influence by propa-
gating the Imperial Way.'

After the War, a new Constitution guaranteed religious
freedom. New religions increased in number – although, as we
have seen, the forming of new religions is much older in Japan.

---

* Walter A. Skya, *Japan's Holy War: The Ideology of Radical Shinto
Ultranationalism* (Durham, NC: Duke University Press, 2009), p. 324.

The Meiji organization of Shinto summarized above ensured respect for Japan, the Emperor, and its ancient religion. But there was no bar on joining (or for that matter creating) different individual religions. The only requirement was that new religions, Shinko Shukyo, must receive official recognition – otherwise they were known as Ruiji Shukyo, pseudo-religions.

The new religions of Japan are so numerous and different in kind that it is impossible to summarize them. In 1951, the Union of New Religious Organizations of Japan (Shin Nihon Shukyo Dantai Re Kai) was set up with eighty-seven members, but since one of its purposes was to put forward agreed candidates for elections, by no means all new religions joined.

The new religions have had a large following, with in some cases important political influence. From the nineteenth century, Tenrikyo ('Religion of Heavenly Truth') illustrates how religions in Japan can change in their relationship to State Shinto. Tenrikyo began with the visions of Nakayama Miki (1798–1887) in 1838, revealing to her the plot of land on which the first man had been created. The Temple of Tenrikyo is built on and around this plot, which is the spiritual centre of the universe. From here, the followers of Tenrikyo receive special help to live lives in the pattern of Nakayama in bodies that have been lent to them by the Creator. In 1908, Tenrikyo was recognized as the thirteenth of the sects of Kyoha Shinto (above). In 1946, it was transferred into the Association of Shinto Sects (Jinja Honcho, above), but in 1970 it withdrew from membership and three months later was transferred to the category of 'other religions', since it claimed to be an independent world religion, and not a part of Shinto.

In addition to new religions and Shinto sects, there has been a large number of Buddhist sects – approaching two hundred. Some of these, even if they are recent developments, go back to the introduction of Buddhism into Japan, to Tendai, Shingon, Pure Land and Zen. Nichiren lived later (1222–82), but many sects are derived from his teaching. Among the most influential are Reiyukai Kyodan ('Association of Friends of the Spirits') which, along with the centrality of the *Lotus Sutra*, advocates great reverence for the spirits of the ancestors; and Soka Gakkai ('Association for Creating Value').

Soka Gakkai was founded in 1930 by Makiguchi Tsunesaburo (1871–1944) and Toda Josei (1900–58) as Soka Kyoku Gakkai ('Creative Education Society'): it became Soka Gakkai in 1937. In 1943, the Government tried to unify all the Nichiren sects under its own control. Makiguchi, Toda and others were imprisoned, ostensibly because they refused to purchase government amulets which were being distributed, as a sign of loyalty, from the Ise Shrine. Makiguchi died in prison, but Toda, who saw his stand against the government as a true imitation of Nichiren, emerged from prison at the end of the war with his faith much strengthened. He reformed the movement, and in 1952 it was incorporated as an independent religious institution, no longer as a Buddhist sect. It has attempted to become, under the leadership of Ikeda Daisaku, a world movement, Soka Gakkai International, and it has entered into Japanese politics through the forming of a political party, Komeito, the Clean Government Party.

It ran into controversy because it followed Nichiren's example in regarding other religions, and other Buddhist (including Nichiren) sects, as false. It was also accused of coercive techniques of conversion, through its technique of 'breaking and subduing', *shakabuku*. It is often accused of having abandoned the fundamental Buddhist belief that all is Dukkha (unsatisfactory transience) and of saying instead that satisfaction can be found in this life. In fact, this is an application of the belief expressed in Shunyata that all is the Buddha-nature and there are no differentiating characteristics, however different things seem on the surface. This means that there is no difference between nirvana and this world – *properly understood*. The purpose of Soka Gakkai is to help people live in the world as, so to speak, all there is.

Conclusion and Further Reading

If information could do its work by floating around the universe like those gossamer threads that drifted as thistledown onto the head and into the memory of Gilbert White, there would be no need for religions. But for information to be informative – that is, to be communicated and shared with others – it has to be coded, protected, transmitted and received. None of that can happen by accident. As we saw in the Introduction in the case of religions, the coding, protection and transmission of information from one life or from one generation to another requires the organization of systems, and systems require boundaries, and boundaries carry with them a necessary degree of isolation, which may, on occasion, require defence.

That is why religions emerged as organized systems to code, protect and transmit information that successive generations of people have come to regard as particularly important. That information is not confined to words. Much of it is expressed non-verbally in actions, gestures, signs, symbols, music, dance, rituals and the like.

The result has been that religions are organized systems in which some particular beliefs and behaviours are endorsed and encouraged, while others are discouraged and forbidden. Religions are protected circles in which people are likely to hold and share beliefs and practices. It is not that everyone necessarily does so, nor is it the case that those who do so agree with each other in every detail. In fact, sometimes they disagree so profoundly that some people will form a smaller group insisting on its own interpretations and practices. They form a kind of inner circle within the larger circle of shared assumptions. Thus within Islam there may be Sunni and Shia Muslims, within Christianity there may be Catholic and Orthodox Christians; and we have seen in this book comparable examples in every religion.

Religions are a consequence of extremely long histories in which beliefs have been tried and tested. Many have changed and some have been abandoned. But the long process of winnowing has led to the many beliefs that have changed the world and which are treasured and protected so that they can be passed on from one generation to another. The achievements and consequences can be seen and heard all around us.

Each religion therefore creates a kind of boundary within which behaviours and beliefs can be monitored, and its tradition can be protected. As a result, beliefs and behaviours can be checked for *coherence* within the circle, and 'the true' and 'the false' can be sorted out. False teachers can be condemned and heretics burned, while those living appropriately within the circle can be rewarded as saints or gurus.

Religions thus established the limits of a life that can evoke approval and the predication of 'good'. They established the codes of behaviour, as well as the sanctions and endorsements to enforce them. And they have worked. For millennia religions have been the social context in which individuals have lived their lives successfully, where success is measured basically in terms of survival and replication, and socially in terms of approval. Success, in this context, is certainly not being measured in terms of individual freedom. It does not need a feminist to recognize that the strategies adopted by religions to protect birth, families and the nurture of children have usually involved the protection of women and the control of their lives by men.

The protected circles of religion thus set limits to belief and behaviour, and can, at least in theory, define what is or is not acceptable. To translate theory into practice requires people to internalize the resources on offer and to make them their own. Whether or not they do so is a matter of individual conscience, but that cannot be left to chance. Conscience itself needs to be informed, and that is why many of the protected circles of religion find ways to instruct the faithful and monitor behaviours. Not surprisingly, therefore, protected systems often have a strong central authority, ranging from a village headman to a king as a 'defender of the faith'. It is a reason why, as we have seen, the Inquisition was set up in Catholic Christianity. Where there is no central authority of that kind, the limits can still be defined, but they are not so easily enforced.

Both possibilities can be seen in the case of Islamic State. It so happens that the word 'limits' translates an Arabic word *hudud* (or in the singular, *hadd*, a word that has passed into legal terminology to refer to offences and punishments as defined in the Quran). In the Quran itself, *hudud* is used to describe the limits set by God on particular human behaviours. So, for example, it describes the laws laid down by God on sex and fasting during the fast of Ramadan (2.183):

Permitted to you on the night of the fasts is the approach to your wives. They are your garments and you are their garments . . . So now lie with them and seek what God has prescribed for you, and eat and drink until the white thread [at first light] appears to you distinct from the black thread; then complete the fast till the night appears, and do not lie with them while you are in retreat in the mosques. Those are the limits of God [*tilka hududu 'Llahi*].

Or to give another example on divorce (2.229):

A divorce is allowed twice; after that, it is a matter of either holding together on equitable terms, or separating with kindness. It is not lawful to take back any of your gifts, except when both parties fear that they would be unable to keep the limits [*hudud*] of God. If you fear that they would be unable to keep the limits of God, there is no blame on either of them if she gives something for her freedom. Those are the limits of God, so do not transgress them. If any do transgress the limits of God, those are the wrong-doers.

We have seen (in the Introduction) that Islamic State claims to be the authentic voice and practice of Islam. In its own 'inner circle', it enforces its authority in unremitting ways. But the question raised by Islamic State for other Muslims is whether at least some of the actions of its adherents have transgressed 'the limits of God'. Of those other Muslims, many believe (given the rules summarized earlier governing Jihad) that these limits have been transgressed, but there is no central authority in Islam to enforce that judgement. On the other hand, it remains a responsibility for individuals (like imams) and institutions (like the revered al-Azhar mosque in Cairo) to articulate that judgement, as indeed they do.

So the protected circles of religion may have either centralized or diffused authority, but in either case they maintain and monitor boundaries. Those boundaries may be of many different kinds. They may be literal: for example, the Indian law code, *Manusmriti*, defines India as the boundary within which alone the proper observance of Dharma is possible (2.17–24):

> The land between the two sacred rivers Sarasvati and Drishadvati, this land created by divine powers is the Brahmavarta. The customs prevailing in this country, passed on from generation to generation, amount to what is called 'right behaviour' (*sadacara*). From a brahmin born and raised in this country, all people should learn their ways. The country where the black antelope naturally moves about is the one that is fit for sacrifice – beyond is that of the *mlecchas* [outsiders and the unclean]. A twiceborn [i.e., Brahmins, Kshatriyas, Vaishyas] should resort to this country and dwell in it; a sudra, however, may for the sake of gaining his livelihood live anywhere.

We have seen in this book other examples of literal boundaries (as in the case of China or of Japan or, for at least some Jews, of Israel). Boundaries, however, do not have to be literal: they may be metaphorical. They are the conditions of continuing community and of adherence to it.

Metaphorical boundaries can be established and maintained in many different ways – for example, by ritual, creed, birth, behaviours, subscription, law, compulsion, consent. The resulting boundaries can be extremely strong and so highly defined that it is clear who belongs and who does not. On the other hand, they may be loosely defined and far more inclusive of inputs from the outside. Both systems of boundary maintenance are viable, and they produce very different and contrasting styles of belief and behaviour. In an earlier book, *Is God a Virus?*, I gave two examples in order to illustrate the contrast, with, at one extreme, the Amish, and, at the other, the Bauls.

The Amish are derived from a strict group of Mennonites who migrated to North America in the eighteenth century. The boundary definition in their case is literally obvious: the Old Order Amish separate themselves from the society around them by retaining the dress and customs of that early period of their origin – beards and broad-brimmed hats for men, bonnets and aprons for women. There are no cars, nor electricity in their homes. They separate themselves, as far as possible, from surrounding society, having their own schools, refusing military service, and not accepting Social Security benefits from the State. Their discipline includes the avoidance of those who are under the ban of excommunication, even if they are within the family, and, as there is no missionary activity and marriage is always within the Amish community, the growth or maintenance of their numbers depends on the large size of their families.

Contrast that kind of strong boundary maintenance with the Bauls of Bengal. Here, again, we are dealing with an inner circle in a larger protected circle. The Bauls are derived, in part, from the Sahajiya, who, in turn, were derived from the Buddhist Siddhas who emphasized the central importance of *sahaja* (hence the name, Sahajiya). Sahaja is the absolute truth, which can be found within the body. It is the essence of everything, the unmoving and ineffable state which makes it Maha Sukha, the great bliss. It is therefore a synonym for Nirvana. When the tide of Buddhism went out of India, the Sahajiyas (i.e., those whose lives are devoted to realizing Sahaja within) did not go with them. They merged with Hindus, but they did not become identical with them. In other words, they maintained the boundaries of their own identity, adherence, and continuity, and they did so in part by identifying the bhakti and tantric exegesis of sexual union with the manifestation of Sahaja. In making this the central religious act they were recapitulating in their own way the divine union of Radha and Krishna which we encountered earlier in this book.

Out of this tradition emerged the Bauls. 'Baul' is Bengali for 'mad', so these people were, as Novalis called Spinoza, 'god-intoxicated men'. They have their metaphorical boundaries of adherence and continuity, but, in contrast to the Amish, the boundaries are extremely weak. They draw on any resource which reinforces their central preoccupation with God discovered within (lending themselves to behaviours that lie far beyond the ordinary conventions), including not just the Buddhist and Hindu traditions of their origins, but also the Sant tradition of North India and the Sufis of Islam. They have no creed, no code of practice, no doctrinal scheme – they simply share a common belief that God is most truly and accessibly to be found within a person as 'the caged bird', known also as 'the Man of my heart'. How do you find and release the caged bird? By following 'the contrary path' (*ulta sadhana*) which leads away from the world and its conventions to the divine within the body. They wear tattered clothes, indicating their rejection of worldly values; they ignore distinctions of caste; and although they may be found in Vaishnava temples and attending festivals, they are not there to find God outside themselves: 'What need do we have of temples when our bodies are temples where the Spirit abides?' The boundaries are so loose that they pay little attention to the history or tradition of their 'Order' as they mistrust reliance on precedents and traditions.

The Amish and the Bauls are two contrasting examples of

what protective circles and metaphorical boundaries can entail. Within those circles, people can internalize the beliefs and practices that give structure and meaning to their lives and that lead, so they believe, to the ultimate goals of God or of Enlightenment.

In that way of internalization, beliefs that change the world change people who change the worlds in which they live. Do they change them 'for better or for worse'? In this book it seems obvious that they do both – harm, yes; but also immense good. But the answer that people give to that question is not straightforward: it depends on their own point of view, and that in turn is rooted in their own beliefs. Some attack religious beliefs because they are, so it seems, not open to criticism, reason or argument, least of all when they lead to prejudice and violence. Others defend religious beliefs because they are inspiring, healing and redemptive, most of all when they are found in experience to be trustworthy.

Both those points of view are looking at the consequences of religious beliefs, and clearly both can be exemplified in the history of religions. Even more fundamental, therefore, is the question of truth: are religious beliefs, or at least some religious beliefs, true? That also turns out to be a far more complicated question than some suppose. In fact, the appeal to 'truth' in the case of beliefs, whether they are religious or scientific or of any other kind, is really an appeal to justification: how can these beliefs be *justified*? To what warrants or evidence can we appeal to justify our beliefs?

In general, appeal is made to correspondence (particularly important for scientific beliefs), coherence (particularly important for religious beliefs), consequence (particularly important in many religions on the Day of Judgement or its equivalent) and participation (inescapably important for all beliefs). That brief list may well be incomprehensible to any who are not already familiar with it, and its meanings and implications are discussed more fully in my recent book, *Why Religions Matter*. The important point here is that none of these so-called 'theories of truth' (though they are more accurately theories about the nature of truth) is sufficient on its own. In this context, there is no conflict between sciences and religions.

Where conflict can arise, however, is when beliefs and their claims to truth in any particular protected circle rest on incontrovertible definition. If the Pope is defined as infallible when speaking in a particular way (*ex cathedra*) on matters of faith and morals, then he is incapable of error (cf., e.g., the Imam in Shia Islam 'who will always distinguish the true from the false'); if the Quran is defined as 'the Speech of God, uncreated, revealed and sent down by God' (abu Hanifa, *Wasiyya* 8; cf., e.g., the Veda defined as 'eternal, divine in origin, and without error, not written by a fallible human hand'), then it cannot be contradicted by human opinion. There can be competing interpretations, but no alteration or denial of what it says. Conflict will arise when claims of that kind from different protected circles are incompatible, and even more when such claims cannot be reconciled with beliefs established on other grounds, as, for example, in the sciences or in the work of historians.

In those circumstances, protected circles can become in effect closed circles because they are not open to argument or negotiation. If that happens, it seems inevitable to those on the outside that the closed circle leads to the closed mind. Even so, it is important to remember that there can still be arguments and negotiations within the logic and vocabularies of the religion involved. The beliefs and practices of Islamic State cannot be challenged by trying to divide Muslims into 'moderates' and 'extremists', not least because Muslim opponents of Islamic State may well resent being classified as less committed. But there are arguments within Islam itself that distinguish between warranted and unwarranted beliefs and behaviours. Those arguments can be articulated as much by non-Muslims as they can by Muslims, and they interlock with the more general arguments that arise from the observation of what belongs to the goodness and well-being of human beings and of the societies in which they live.

But what counts as 'good' or, to go to the opposite extreme, as 'evil'? The answers to that question are given within each of the protected circles of religion, and their definitions of good and evil differ. Even more different may be the answers given outside the boundaries of any religion in terms, for example, of common sense or, to go again to an opposite extreme, of human rights. So the urgent and immensely challenging question is whether ways can be found in which religions can engage more dispassionately, or at least with greater detachment, with each other and with a non-religious world.

But how? How can the religious circles of coherence live alongside each other given that there are beliefs that can only be justified within each circle? How closed must the circles of coherence remain for the beliefs within them to be protected from dilution by the beliefs of others outside? Although some open the boundaries of their circle, others believe that questions of truth (i.e., of coherence) can only be decided within the closed circle, so how then do we approach the non-negotiable certainties of fundamentalism? And does it matter? It clearly does when those certainties are tied to beliefs that 'the end of the world' is a prospect fully justified within its own circle of coherence. When the available means to bring that prospect closer extend to chemical, biological and nuclear weapons of mass destruction, we have reason to be apprehensive.

We do, however, have reason to be less apprehensive when we remember that religions are also a major source of peace and reconciliation. As we began to see in the Introduction, religions (or at least some religious believers) do harmful and destructive things, but they are also the source and inspiration of much that is creative, good and true. In particular, in each of the protected circles of religion believers are required as a matter of *obligation*, not as a matter of goodwill or private inclination, 'to seek peace and ensue it' as it is put in the New Testament (*I Peter* 3.13).

What those resources are and why they are a matter of obligation and not of choice can be seen in the work of a Gresham College seminar published as *Conflict and Reconciliation: The Contribution of Religions*. If we wish to gain insight into the conflicts listed at the start of the Introduction, we have to begin with that kind of analysis and understanding of the beliefs that are involved in them.

How do we make a start in doing that? In a book of this kind, covering so many religious beliefs and so much history, it is not possible to provide a bibliography, but many of my own books, listed below, contain bibliographies. It may be helpful to know that some of them were written to provide a first step in understanding religions.

Mention has already been made of *The Oxford Dictionary of World Religions*, which contains many entries on beliefs together with a Topic Index. All those entries appear in *The Concise Dictionary of World Religions*, but in a shorter form.

A next step would be *The Cambridge Illustrated History of Religions* (Cambridge University Press, 2002), with contributions from experts and including additional religions.

World Religions: The Great Faiths Explored and Explained (Dorling Kindersley, 2001) is an introduction with extensive illustrations.

Why Religions Matter (Cambridge University Press, 2015) offers an introduction to what religions are and why it is so important to understand them.

The Message and the Book: Sacred Texts of the World's Religions (Atlantic Books, 2011) contains a description of the Texts mentioned in this book together with a summary of the beliefs contained in them; *The Complete Bible Handbook* is another Dorling Kindersley book (1998) with an extensive bibliography.

Themes in Religious Studies, (edited with Jean Holm) is a series of 10 volumes on different beliefs in the major religions – for example, *Women in Religion*, *Attitudes to Nature*.

Two books that began as different BBC series are based on interviews with people expressing their beliefs in their own words: *Worlds of Faith: Religious Belief and Practice in Britain Today* (Ariel Books, 1983) and *What Muslims Believe* (One World, 2009).

Among 'the beliefs that changed the world', belief in God has been paramount. *God, A Brief History* is another Dorling Kindersley book (2002) with its usual extensive illustrations.

God: A Very Short Introduction (2014) is one of the series of short introductions published by Oxford University Press.

Finally, on particular beliefs the following may be helpful:

Problems of Suffering in Religions of the World (Cambridge University Press, 1970).

The Meanings of Death (Cambridge University Press, 1991).

Is God a Virus? Genes, Culture and Religion (SPCK, 1995).

An Alphabet of Animals (Key Publishing, 2010).

Books written or edited by John Bowker

The Targums and Rabbinic Literature: An Introduction to Jewish Interpretations of Scripture (1969 and 1979).

Problems of Suffering in Religions of the World (1970, 3 edn 1990).

Jesus and the Pharisees (1973).

The Sense of God: Sociological: Anthropological and Psychological Approaches to the Origin of the Sense of God (1973, 2 edn 1995).

The Religious Imagination and the Sense of God (1978).

Worlds of Faith: Religious Belief and Practice in Britain Today (1983).

The Origins, Functions and Management of Aggression in Biocultural Evolution (1983).

Licensed Insanities: Religions and Belief in God in the Contemporary World (1987).

The Meanings of Death (1991, HarperCollins Prize 1993).

A Year to Live (1991).

Hallowed Ground: The Religious Poetry of Place (1993).

Themes in Religious Studies ed. with J.Holm, (10 volumes on different issues, e.g., *Making Moral Decisions*, 1994).

Voices of Islam (1995; now published as *What Muslims Believe*, 2000).

The Oxford Dictionary of World Religions (ed. 1997).

World Religions (ed. 1997).

The Complete Bible Handbook (ed 1998, Benjamin Franklin Award 1999).

The Concise Dictionary of World Religions (ed. 2000).

God: A Brief History (2002).

The Cambridge Illustrated History of Religions (ed. 2002).

The Sacred Neuron (2005).

Beliefs That Changed the World (2007).

The Aerial Atlas of the Holy Land (2008).

Knowing the Unknowable: Science and Religions on God and the Universe (ed. 2008).

Conflict and Reconciliation: The Contribution of World Religions (ed 2008).

An Alphabet of Animals (2010).

Before the Ending of the Day: Life and Love, Death and Redemption (2010).

The Message and the Book: Sacred Texts of the World's Religions (2011).

God: A Very Short Introduction (2014).

Why Religions Matter (2015).

For children: *Uncle Bolpenny Tries Things Out* (1973).

Index